Strategic management for the public services

MANAGING THE PUBLIC SERVICES

Series editor: Dr Alan Lawton, Open University
Business School

Current and forthcoming titles in the series include:

Paul Joyce: *Strategic Management for the Public Services*
Alan Lawton: *Ethical Management for the Public Services*
John Wilson (ed.): *Financial Management for the Public Services*
Diana Winstanley: *Stakeholder Management for the Public Services*

Strategic management for the public services

Paul Joyce

Open University Press
Buckingham · Philadelphia

Open University Press
Celtic Court
22 Ballmoor
Buckingham
MK18 1XW

email: enquiries@openup.co.uk
world wide web: http://www.openup.co.uk

and

325 Chestnut Street
Philadelphia, PA 19106, USA

First Published 1999

A catalogue record of this book is available from the British Library

ISBN 0 335 20047 8(pb)   0 335 20048 6(hb)

Library of Congress Cataloging-in-Publication Data
Joyce, Paul, 1952–
    Strategic management for the public services / Paul Joyce.
        p.   cm. – (Managing the public services)
    Includes bibliographical references and index.
    ISBN 0-335-20048-6 (hardbound).   ISBN 0-335-20047-8 (pbk.)
    1. Strategic planning.   2. Public administration.   I. Title.
II. Series.
HD30.28.J693   1999
658.4′012–dc21   98-36957
                                                                        CIP

Typeset by Graphicraft Limited, Hong Kong
Printed in Great Britain by Biddles Limited, Guildford and Kings Lynn

Contents

Series editor's preface

Managing the public services is, increasingly, a complex activity where a range of different types of organization are involved in the delivery of public services. Public services managers have had to develop new skills and adopt new perspectives as the boundaries between public, private and voluntary sector organizations become blurred. The management task becomes one of managing ambiguity in an ever-changing world. At the same time, however, there is a certain timeliness to any debate concerning the management of public policies and managers will need to acknowledge the continuing relevance of traditions and the enduring nature of the themes of accountability, responsibility, acting in the public interest, integrity, probity and responding to citizens, clients and customers.

This series addresses key issues in managing public services and contributes to the debates concerning the appropriate role for managers in the public services located within a contested governance arena. Through the use of original research, case studies and commentaries on theoretical models, the books in the series will be of relevance to practitioners and to academics and their students. An underlying theme of the series is the inescapable intertwining of theory and practice such that theory will be tested out in practice and practice will be grounded in theory. Theoretical concepts and models need to be made relevant for the practitioner but at the same time good practice will need to be analysed, tested against theoretical models and disseminated. In this way the series will fulfil its commitments to both an academic and a practitioner audience.

Alan Lawton

Preface

This book came to be written for one main reason: there are many public services managers engaged in strategic management and yet they have few written sources of guidance and insight relating to the practical problems of public services strategic management. This stands in stark contrast to the situation of the practitioner in private sector strategic management.

I responded positively to an invitation to write this book for several reasons. First, I thought there was now enough material appearing in journals for there to be a reasonably thorough attempt to discuss public services strategic management on the basis of sound empirical evidence. And I thought this would establish strategic management in the public services as different from that in the private sector. I believe that this is borne out in the pages of this book. Second, I wanted to provide a book which would be useful to managers of public services, and would not merely offer a detached scholarly account of strategic management in the public services. This is why I hope the book will provide the public services manager with some useful ideas to experiment with in the context of their own situation. Finally, it was my intention to contribute to the democracy agenda through this work on strategic management. In the end this may well be the best justification for describing this book as strategic management *for* the public services, rather than merely strategic management *in* the public services.

At the core of this book are the ideas that democracy means that the public should be influential in setting the strategic framework for public services, and that the users of public services should be consulted about their needs and wishes. In a sense, this concern takes up the pragmatic viewpoint which argues for a view of democracy based on improved conditions of debate, discussion and persuasion, and points out the need for government as a genuine instrument of an inclusive and fraternally associated public.

I believe that strategic management can help new public services emerge. It can do this by helping to decide what should be done and how it should be done, and by creating the dialogue and consensus needed to make the changes. In the absence of effective strategic management, the new public services will still emerge, but in a more haphazard way. Strategic management, done well, can help the called-for transformation to occur more efficiently and creatively.

This is not to say that strategic management is a magic wand, or that it can be counted on to work perfectly every time. It is certainly not a simple method of bringing about fundamental change. At this still early stage in the emergence of the theory of strategic management for public services, it is not even a coherent framework, and it is certainly not one thing. There are still many different views of what are the important things to do strategically. This has created a lot of confusion. Many managers in the public services on hearing the phrase 'strategic management' think that it is some fixed thing and that it is something which is ready for them to use. In fact, strategic management in the public services is unfinished and continues to evolve. This book cannot provide all the answers but it will seek to clarify the different strands of strategic development and point to the ways they are starting to come together. It will help managers to think and act strategically, and even to develop their own strategic plans.

Two strategic developments are especially important in the currently evolving practice of strategic management in the public services, and therefore needed to be considered at length in this book. First, in recent years, there has been a growing interest in, and some experimentation with, strategy which is interorganizational or even community based. The idea has spread that public services managers can no longer be internally focused on service delivery and organizational performance in the narrow sense. Increasingly managers have been expected to work in partnership, with other public services agencies, with third sector organizations and the private sector. There have been attempts to focus on addressing the needs and problems of communities by working with others to mobilize action and resources from a number of different sources.

The second important strategic development picked out for special consideration is the way in which strategic leaders and managers in the public services have used strategic management to address both performance and innovation. Very often, the improvement of performance has been uppermost. Less often, innovation – even transformation – has been the main target. Perhaps it is difficult to pursue both performance and innovation simultaneously. Surely, one of the key challenges for public services management in the years ahead is to find ways in which strategic management may be developed and applied to ensure that both performance and innovation are achieved in the interests of better public services.

Outline of the book

Chapter 1 provides an initial understanding of strategic management for the public services, and suggests why it is important to the future of public services. In Chapters 2 and 3 the basics of the strategic planning process are presented. These should be helpful for anyone trying to do strategic planning in a formal way for the first time. They can be read in conjunction with the appendix to the book which provides a set of worksheets that can be used to document a strategic planning process.

Chapters 4, 5 and 6 build on the understanding of the basics of strategic planning. They, together, deal with the difference between strategic planning and strategic management. In these three chapters the book concentrates on providing insights into how a strategic planning process is embedded organizationally, how strategic plans can be implemented, and how strategic planning takes place on an interorganizational basis with strategic partners.

Chapter 7 focuses on a relatively neglected topic: how organizations handle incipient crisis and its full-blown arrival. Given the general crisis-torn atmosphere that has pervaded so much of the public services sector since the 1970s it is strange that it has not been given more attention in the strategic management and planning literature. In this chapter, different theories and research are assembled and ideas and insights are clarified which show how strategic management can help under crisis, or near-crisis, conditions.

The last two chapters turn to key challenges facing the public services. First, in Chapter 8, we look at how public-friendly strategic management can be introduced. In my view, unless this challenge is accepted and met, the democratic claims of the public services will ring increasingly hollow. This chapter looks at how strategic leaders, managers and professional experts need to evolve their role; the use of community planning; how service users can be involved in reviewing services; and how the public and other stakeholders can become active participants in the process of strategy formulation.

Finally, in Chapter 9, the underlying concern of this whole book with the transformation of public services into a modern and publicly accountable sector is addressed. This matter is approached with a specific question in mind: what kind of strategic management is needed for the modern transformation of the public services? It provides an interim answer to how the current forms of strategic planning can be developed to provide not only a results-oriented but also an innovative and democratic form of strategic management.

Following the chapters, and the appendix containing strategic planning worksheets, is a bibliography which not only lists references in the book but also includes books and articles for the reader who wishes to read more widely on strategic management in the public services.

Acknowledgments

My thanks to Theresa Joyce, Paul Corrigan, Aidan Rose, Alan Lawton, Stephen Osborne, Colin Talbot, Breeda Kennedy, and Aiden McDonnell for ideas, material and feedback on drafts of the book. I would like to also thank Derek Smith at Kings Healthcare in London, Penny Willis and Mr Bootes at Mayday Hopital in London, Anne Eden at the NHS Executive, and Leisha Fullick at the London Borough of Islington. My special thanks to Theresa, Thomas, Caitlin and Patrick.

one

Introducing strategic management in the public services

Key learning objectives

After reading this chapter you should be able to:

1 Understand some of the main approaches to strategic management practice in the public services.
2 Understand the conditions which have motivated the use of stratgic management.
3 Identify the key elements which make up the processes of strategic management.

The importance of strategic management

Many leaders and top managers in large public services organizations now believe that strategic management is indispensable. Their organizations are too large and too complex, and the circumstances too chaotic, to do without strategic management. They are expected to lead their organizations in particular directions, and strategic management is the instrument that helps them do that. They are expected to improve the performance of their organizations, and strategic management provides the necessary means for achieving improvements. They are expected to motivate employees and cooperate with other organizations; again, strategic management is helping leaders and top managers to do that. Strategic management has emerged as a multi-purpose tool which public services management must have to ensure that their organizations survive in the short and medium term and build for a long-term future.

So, strategic management is a versatile and powerful tool. Yet, there are a multitude of definitions of what it is, and how it is used. There are also many examples of the failure of strategic management. This makes the subject a very complex one. In response, this chapter provides an initial definition of strategic management and outlines four different concepts of strategic management. This provides an overall sense of the totality of strategic management, and its constituent processes, which should help to place in context the techniques and issues which are examined in more depth later in the book.

Defining strategic management

Strategic management in the public services is an unfinished and evolving phenomenon. Strategies are normally very fluid things. Chief executives of public services organizations, even those regarded by their peers as very successful, cannot always say definitively what strategy is, or indeed what their own organization's strategy is. Strategies are certainly not to be simply equated with statements included in written business plans and strategic documents.

The fluidity of strategy in the public services partly arises because strategy is about ideas. Leaders and top managers use strategies as ideas to engage their own managers and staff, and to engage other organizations. Leadership in public services organizations rests crucially on engaging managers and staff because, by their very nature, these organizations comprise people who have to be persuaded and convinced. Strategy, therefore, provides a rationale by means of which leaders engage managers and staff in change, and win their consent. Many public services organizations – for example, those in health services and local government – employ large numbers of highly educated professionals who have stong expectations of being consulted and having the chance to debate and argue about how their organization is changing. They will consent to change only if they think it is a good idea.

Ideas also matter as individual public service organizations find themselves discussing and negotiating change with other organizations. For various reasons, the leaders of public services are finding that they are having to position their organizations in relation to other organizations with whom they cooperate, form partnerships and even form cooperative ventures. As the public services seek to cope with major change and bring about new alignments strategic visions are providing the ideas for discussion and agendas to work on. In the absence of an ability to rely on old habits of organizational isolation, strategic ideas are proving extremely influential in the formation of partnerships and alliances in the public services.

Strategic ideas are bound to be fluid under these circumstances. Leaders who engage their managers' and staffs' intellect and emotions using strategic ideas must debate, persuade and negotiate understandings. Public services organizations which attempt to coalign their strategies for the future through discussing strategic ideas have to negotiate and arrive at an acceptable synthesis. Ideas of leaders may be influential, but they are also influenced and changed in the processes of engagement with managers, professionals, front line employees, partners, and even communities.

If ideas are the soft side of strategy, there is also a hard side. Strategy is about positioning an organization and it is about performance. This means that strategy is an instrument for directing and shaping behaviour. It means that strategy becomes real when an organization ensures that strategy is implemented. Internally, this means strategy is used to plan and control behaviour. Operational goals and performance targets are set on the basis of strategy. Performance management systems ensure that units, sub-units and individuals strive to achieve these performance goals. Managers are recruited, promoted, made redundant, encouraged to leave, and so on, in order to create a management organization capable and willing of implementing the strategy. Bids are made to win contracts or get funding to create or add services to the existing service portfolio; services are cut back or lost to other provider organizations. Strategy's hard side is about action, performance and change. And because it is hard, it is also about risk. Wrong strategies bring bad consequences for the public, for public services providers, and for politicians.

Strategic management is also hard to define because it changes as circumstances change and because different types of strategic action can coexist in a single organization. At one point in time, strategic management may seem to be largely something an organization does because it is a political requirement or even a statutory requirement. At another point in time, strategic management is about putting an organization back on its feet after it has become unfocused and crisis-prone. Then again, strategic management can produce a visionary plan to tackle the next 10 or even 20 years. Or it may be all these things simultaneously within a particular organization.

Theoretically speaking, managing strategic issues may be combined with moving in a preselected strategic direction to bring about a strategic vision. All that this requires, on paper anyway, is a search for actions which not only address strategic issues but are also instrumental in realizing the vision. In practice, issue management and strategic change towards a vision of the future may occur separately. The lesson of the experience of King's Healthcare (see Box 1.1) seems to be that the successful practice of strategic management involves both issue management and visionary or foresighted strategic planning, but not at the same time. External events may create issues which have to be dealt with as soon as possible. Issue

---

Box 1.1 Evolution in strategic planning systems at King's Healthcare

When chief executive Derek Smith arrived at King's Healthcare (a university teaching hospital with a medical and dental school in London's Denmark Hill area), he did not feel he had the right conditions for bringing in comprehensive strategic planning and the emphasis was primarily on strategic issue management. There were issues on a number of different fronts: survival, finances, services and a need for more coherence and direction at the top level of management. This was an issue agenda which felt as though it had been largely set by external events.

His first 18 months were spent managing these issues. The trust hospital won out against some of these strategic problems. Morale lifted, and he was able to to set about bringing in quite a different approach to strategic management. This was less driven by external events, and more based on thinking about the future.

---

management is good for solving problems in the short and medium term. Visionary strategic planning enables the management to build a better organization over the long term. At King's Healthcare issue management was a platform for the visionary or foresighted strategic planning which followed. One advantage of this sequence – managing strategic issues before moving on to strategic planning based on foresight – is that the victories in managing issues creates the trust and confidence in the abilities of management to tackle ambitious long-term strategic changes. This is consistent with Eadie's (1983: 448) suggestion: 'narrower applications of strategic planning may for many public organizations be the most utilitarian. While overall blueprints are certainly desirable, if not essential, it is through the narrower approach that near-term pay-off is possible. Such immediate benefits may be an important way of building strong support for the planning effort'. So, planning systems may evolve from systems which are mainly capable of helping the organization to avert threats to survival, into systems which allow the organization to design and implement long-term strategic blueprints.

If organizations have a strategic vision for the next ten years, or longer, they may still have to deal with threats which develop very rapidly and have to be handled immediately, or in the short and medium term. Perhaps, then, organizations need to have more than one strategic management process; perhaps they need at least two processes – one for handling strategic issues and one for implementing long-term strategic visions (Ansoff and McDonnell 1990). No doubt organizations will find various ways to combine strategic management processes. Box 1.2 shows how Kirklees Metropolitan District Council handled the need to combine two different kinds of strategic management: one focused on service improvements, and the other on community issues.

Box 1.2 Kirklees Metropolitan District Council (UK)

Kirklees Metropolitan District Council has gained a national reputation for its innovative management. In 1989 it began introducing strategic management processes. At a council seminar it was considered that council activities required targets and performance measures. Changes were needed to enable management accountability and monitoring, and review processes were needed to inform policy making. Given a clear set of policies made by the elected politicians, the chief executive recommended devolved management as the key to radically improving the situation. He explained the rationale to elected members in terms of increased accountability and flexibility.

> In the past the organization has been controlled by centralized financial and establishment controls and bureaucratic hierarchy. This approach does not permit the customer responsiveness which must now be a watchword . . . The alternative is to give managers clearer accountability for delivering defined outcomes, but greater flexibility over their use of resources to achieve them. There is then a need for a process of performance management and appraisal . . . The key is to translate policies and activities into directorate, sectional and personal goals and action plans, the achievement of which can be monitored and appraised.
>
> (Quoted in Davies and Griffiths 1995: 161)

A vision for Kirklees was produced, with three corporate goals; as was a statement of core values, which were summed up as working for quality and equality. The operational services within the council produced annual service plans describing the service and its objectives.

But the council was not only concerned with using a strategic management process for improving service delivery. Its development of strategic management has been taken forward through both 'policies' and 'strategies'. Policies were defined as involving targets and were to be set for executive directors and operational heads of service. In contrast, strategies in Kirklees were issue-based – such as economic regeneration and cultural strategies (Davies and Griffiths 1995: 165).

The changes in strategic management were made over a two-year period. There were some early indications that some of the changes were working. A comparison of the results of customer satisfaction surveys conducted in 1991 and 1993 showed improved customer care on several measures. Interestingly, the Labour Party lost overall control of the council as a result of the 1994 local council elections – a surprising result, as it might have been expected that the public would reward the party with increased electoral support because of the improvements they had made.

According to Leadbetter and Goss (1998), devolving responsibility for operational matters to line management has enabled experimentation in service delivery at Kirklees. Both aspects of Kirklees' strategic management – that aspect which created a framework for devolved management of service delivery and that which addressed community issues – were credited by them with producing innovation.

We will return to the case of Kirklees Council again in Chapter 4, when we note how they brought politicians and managers together to work on strategy.

In summary, when it works, strategic management is a way of engaging people, getting their commitment, steering the organization into the future, framing efforts at reorganizing and redesigning for greater efficiency and quality, and forming partnerships and joint ventures with other organizations. It is also required to satisfy executive or statutory requirements in a number of cases.

Models of strategic management

It is possible to identify at least four models of strategic management currently being promoted or used in public services organizations. These are:

1 the 'classical' planning model;
2 the businesslike strategic management model;
3 the visionary strategic planning model; and
4 the foresight-based strategic management model.

The 'classical' planning model

Strategic management, or rather strategic planning, is not a choice for many public services organizations. For example, in the UK, National Health Service (NHS) trust hospitals were required by the NHS executive to prepare a strategic direction document every three years. A draft of this was to be submitted in late 1996 and a final summary published in 1997. In addition, the trust hospitals were to produce draft one-year business plans, final business plans and summary business plans according to a centrally determined timetable. England's universities were asked, in 1996, by the Higher Education Funding Council (HEFCE) to provide it with copies of their strategic plans and financial forecasts for the period 1994/5 to 1999/2000. And, according to a consultation document published by the Department of the Environment, Transport and the Regions in 1998, local authorities may be required to bring in a 'Best Value' framework involving the setting of authority-wide objectives, performance measures and performance plans.

Other examples of the requirement for public services to carry out strategic planning or strategic management are also to be found in other countries, such as the USA and Ireland. In 1993 the Government Performance and Results Act was passed requiring strategic plans from US federal agencies (Bryson 1995). In the case of Ireland, the Strategic Management Initiative announced in February 1994 began the process of introducing strategic management processes in all government departments (Boyle 1995a).

It is broadly the case that the model represented by all these developments tends to be what might be called a 'classical' strategic planning model. The approach is essentially an endorsement of a rational planned approach to management. Its assumptions are suggested by the exercise conducted in 1997 when the strategic plans produced by US federal agencies were being judged for compliance by Congress. Compliance was judged in very logical ways. For example, was the mission statement in line with statutory mandates and was it results-oriented? Are strategic goals measurable and linked to the mission statement? Are resource require-ments of strategies described? Are there annual performance goals linked to the mission statement and strategic goals? Are external factors taken into account? Has the plan been discussed and coordinated with other agencies, and has unnecessary duplication been avoided? Has the agency the data capacity to establish baseline data and apply performance meas-ures? Does the plan describe how stakeholders were consulted and their input used? These questions imply that strategies are very straight-forward and logical things. All in all, this model says goal-led planning plus performance measurement is a good idea and should always and everywhere be applied to ensure that public money is wisely spent and used effectively.

Governments are not always convinced of the merits of strategic plan-ning, and politicians in the UK have been fickle in this respect. Public services have had to put up with some relatively rapid changes in political thinking. In the case of the NHS, for example, there has been a succession of political perspectives. In the 1980s there first appeared to be strong political interest in the health services adopting market oriented decision making. But then a managed market emerged. Then the idea was to emphasize local decisions. During this time planning was bad: devolution was good. Then, at a time when some people were saying that devolved decision making had led to paralysis, the idea of planning started to revive. Finally, planning was back in a big way, but, by 1997, there were some murmurs from regional level officials and trust hospitals that the local commissioners were not very effective as strategic planners. This ineffectiveness may have allowed health service providers to pursue quite different and conflicting strategic agendas at the local level.

A policy framework requiring strategic planning may create lots of written strategic plans, but it is not assured that these will express any strategic thinking at all. The bits of paper may keep the administrative oversight bodies happy, but the documents may be worthless in managerial terms.

The rationale for strategic planning in the public services has been given a new twist in the 1990s by the emergence of a popular analysis of the ills of the public sector. This boils down to the argument that the public sector has failed to adjust to new times and the reasons for this failure can be largely placed at the door of its bureaucratic organization. The cure has been seen as a shift to a more entrepreneurial form of government

(Osborne and Gaebler 1992). This involves a whole raft of different measures, including making use of competition, creating mission statements, funding outcomes rather than inputs, and decentralizing authority to empower employees and teams. It also includes using strategic planning, which is valued for the way in which it allows government to anticipate the future and then use preventative measures – which it is assumed is more economical. Strategic planning also helps public services to change and be innovative; under the influence of strategic foresight members of the organization can work towards where the organization will be. This particular view of entrepreneurial government assumes that the main problems are, first, fiscal stress, hence the need to do more with less, and, second, social changes that have meant that consumers expect more choice. The overall implication seems to be that under fiscal pressure, entrepreneurial governments change and innovate (Osborne and Gaebler 1992: 17).

This view of the public services context emerges strongly in accounts of developments in Britain, the USA, New Zealand, Australia and other mature democracies. Legislation and executive action on strategic planning seems mainly framed to ensure managers are accountable, that public services are streamlined, that there is better coordination between public services, and that resource allocation decisions will be informed by better performance data. All of this suggests that the politicians, on behalf of the public, are applying pressure for more performance and cost consciousness.

Not everybody agrees with the emphasis placed on fiscal stress to explain the crisis in public services. There is another view which suggests that the crisis in the public sector, in the UK anyway, 'has been induced by the way in which the post-war social democratic settlement severed the organic relationship between public and service' (Corrigan and Joyce 1997: 417). This indicates that the problem is in the first instance a political and not an economic one, and can be summed up by the concept of the alienation of the public services from the public. This does not deny that there are pressures from the public and politicians, but the argument is that these are not simply pressures to do more with less money.

Nor does everybody agree that innovative public services will emerge from fiscal pressure. American research on the winners of the Exemplary State and Local Awards (EXSL) may be interpreted as casting doubt on the idea that fiscal stress is a cause of innovation (see Box 1.3). It seems that a public service ethic and support for innovation are more important than pressure to innovate because of cut-backs.

However, the idea that strategic planning is part of the armoury which modern public services are using to address problems of insufficient resources by becoming entrepreneurial and innovative is influential. This can be seen in the diagnosis below that South African local government needs strategic management (see Box 1.4).

Box 1.3 The sources of public services innovation in the USA

Holzer and Callahan (1998) describe the results of a survey of two-thirds of 140 winners of the EXSL, which were awards sponsored by the National Centre for Public Productivity. The survey suggested that award winners had a tendency to see themselves as better resourced than similar agencies in other districts or states. However, when asked how important different kinds of resources had been for pursuing the innovation, it emerged that having funds available was much less important than having the support of top agency executives and political officials, and having committed personnel.

The winners were also asked about the motivations for pursuing the innovation for which the award had been received. Motivation 'to save money' was quite important, but it ranked behind a desire 'to do the right thing' and the desire 'to respond to citizen demands'. The motivation 'to respond to budget cut-backs' came very low down on the list of motivations.

Holzer and Callahan (1998: 161) comment on the relative financial situation of the winners, the importance of various kinds of resources, and the ranking of motivations:

Adequate funding can neither be dismissed nor confirmed as a precondition of innovation ... We might, however, question whether inadequate funding limited resources available for experimentation and innovation. The weaknesses associated with funding factors may suggest that the management cutback and privatization proponents are on the wrong path.

Holzer and Callahan argue that a public service ethic which is backed by the support of the top executives and politicians, and support in the form of committed personnel, is needed for innovation in the public services.

It is popular nowadays to imply that rational models of planning do not work. On this basis we might expect simple models of strategic planning to produce poor results or even problems. However, a recent study of UK local government (Flynn and Talbot 1996) suggests that not only did a majority of organizations have formal strategic planning, but also that it provided a wide range of benefits. It was seen by local government managers as helping them achieve goals and objectives, specify milestones for organizational achievement and achieve a better use of resources. These types of benefits are not too dissimilar from the reasons politicians in a number of countries have used to justify the introduction of strategic planning in government and public services. In other words, strategic planning helps to improve the results and efficiency of public services.

The study also found that local government managers appreciated the way in which strategic planning created a unified vision of the organization's future for staff and helped to identify new opportunities and ideas. This suggests that strategic planning may also help to bring about new kinds of innovative and entrepreneurial public services.

Box 1.4 Developing strategic management capacity in local government in the new South Africa

South Africa's local authorities were restructured following an act passed in 1993. As a result of the restructuring, previously racially divided communities were now covered by single local authorities. This had an important effect on the problems facing local government as the country continued its transition to a democratic multiracial society. The May 1997 issue of *Quarterly Trends*, published by the National Business Initiative (NBI) with over 140 companies in membership, reported:

> The stresses of managing cities in transition are threatening the future of metropolitan authorities. The maladies facing Johannesburg – decline of the CBD [central business district], crime, depressed property markets, rates boycotts, poor services and infrastructure and the retreat of business into former white suburbs – are testimony to the difficulties confronting local governments.

A big challenge to local government was to improve services to the black population. The new black councillors elected in the post-apartheid era were facing the difficulty of finding money to spend on improved services in the black areas and townships.

In these black areas and townships unemployment was high, services were very poor, and there was a culture of non-payment. There were many black people who were unable to pay for services. In white suburbs, which had good services, and which benefited from most of the spending on services, many people were resistant to increases in rates to fund improvements in services to black areas.

In the transition from a society based on the apartheid system to one based on democracy, local government was seen as an important institution in delivering services, managing local economic development and redistributing resources. It was expected to work in partnership with community organizations and other organizations, to be creative about financing, and to consult and involve the community.

It is interesting to note just how important strategic planning was regarded for the success of local government. Zybrands (1995: 21) identified what would be needed if local government was to succeed: 'This will require clear strategic and business planning, with clearly defined objectives and goals and a commitment towards achieving those objectives and goals'.

NBI, with a mission which included supporting effective and efficient governance, established a Local Government Facilitation Unit. According to NBI's annual report for 1996/7: p.10, 'The core focus of the unit is to develop the strategic management and service delivery capacity of local authorities'.

It might be inferred from the stress placed on strategic management in local government in 1997 that major issues of societal reconstruction, equity, economic development and the survival of democracy rested upon the effective introduction of strategic management.

The businesslike strategic management model

A national survey of strategic planning in state governments in the USA was carried out in 1992 (Berry and Wechsler 1995). A majority of the respondents said that strategic planning was used in their agency. It had typically been initiated from 1985 onwards, and largely as a matter of managerial initiative. Why had it become important in the latter half of the 1980s? Berry and Wechsler say:

> Since the beginning of the 1980s, state governments have faced increasingly difficult challenges from reduced federal domestic program expenditures, changing demographics, citizen demands for more services without tax increases, and increasing calls from elected officials to 'run government more like a business' . . . in such turbulent circumstances, we believed that state agencies might adopt strategic planning as a tool for responding to intense environmental demands and pressures.
> (Berry and Wechsler 1995: 161–2)

During the 1980s the idea of running public services more like businesses was very popular with politicians in a number of different countries. It was felt that too much money was being spent on public services, and that there could be major savings if services were run more efficiently. This was often described in terms of making public services more businesslike. An Audit Commission report in late 1985 estimated value for money gains from UK local government rising to £2–3 billion a year. Being more businesslike also meant treating clients and service users better; indeed, it was often suggested that service users should be treated as 'customers'. The more businesslike approach was even taken as being applicable to internal relationships, and so hierarchical structures were replaced (or supplemented by) purchaser-provider relations. Planning became, of course, 'business planning'.

The role of political conditions in creating the vogue for this type of model can be seen in Box 1.5, which describes changes in two Australian local councils in the early 1990s. It seems that the businesslike approach followed shortly on the heels of the adoption of corporate planning.

One of the key features of the businesslike model, as can be seen from the details of arrangements in Brent Council (see Box 1.6), is the development of a strategic core within a public service organization at the same time that power is devolved to front-line service managers. The devolution of managerial decision making was usually described as 'empowering' front line managers and staff. It was also clear that the empowered managers were required to be more accountable for the performance of their service units.

The role of senior managers in the businesslike model is sometimes developed in such a way that they feel more distanced from service units with the result that their relationship to service delivery becomes more arm's length. Moreover, this sometimes seems to be a deliberate measure

Box 1.5 Evolving from corporate planning to entrepreneurial strategic planning?

In 1995 Jones and Gross conducted a peer review among the general managers of all the local councils in Australia's New South Wales (Jones and Gross 1996). Two councils emerged from the peer review process as having been the most successful in adapting to changed conditions: Wollongong City Council and Liverpool City Council.

Both these councils brought in corporate management and planning at the end of the 1980s and the beginning of the 1990s. Wollongong City Council brought in a corporate management model in 1988 and corporate planning in late 1989, while Liverpool City Council had also restructured on corporate management lines in 1989–90 and introduced corporate planning one year later.

Then, in both councils, there were changes in the approach to planning and management. In Wollongong Council the focus of reform switched 'to embrace the softer notions associated with the new issues of business planning, community responsiveness, quality and customer service' (Jones and Gross 1996: 130). The council's general manager introduced total quality management (TQM) in 1990. The council defined a vision, mission, values and goals. It produced a three-year corporate plan with objectives, performance indicators and human resource requirements. Jones and Gross report that, 'Business plans began to take shape' (1996: 130). It was claimed that the 'emphasis is now on both employees and managers performing together to realize business plans in order to achieve the objectives of the organization' (Jones and Gross 1996: 131).

At Liverpool City Council the changes followed the appointment of a new general manager, who wanted a purchaser-provider based organization and who recruited a number of private sector managers for middle management levels. He also wanted an outcome-focused, performance management culture. During 1994–5 'meaningful movement' was achieved on: 'costing of different council activities; composition and structure of the purchaser/provider split; financial implications of the new structures and approaches; and the operation of data-driven, output-focused performance management' (Jones and Gross 1996: 138). In other words, in both cases planning and management evolved, arguably, towards a more businesslike format, but this was especially the case at Liverpool City Council.

The important contextual factors were political. A 1993 local government act was reported to have been a catalyst for much change in New South Wales. More particularly, the general manager at Wollongong City Council had forecasted local government reform as likely to stress cost-effective management and accountability, and corporate planning was apparently introduced in 'anticipation of expected legislation' (Jones and Gross 1996: 129–30). In the case of Liverpool City Council, political changes within the council resulted from the local elections in 1991. A set of younger politicians who 'possessed a very political agenda and a vision of where local government should be going' were elected (Jones and Gross 1996: 132). The new mayor had an agenda based on 'notions of contestability and customer service' (Jones and Gross 1996: 133). The new politicians perceived the existing general manager as a 'road block' and replaced him with a new general manager who brought commercial experience to the position. Obviously, the purchaser-provider split which was introduced in Liverpool City Council by the new general manager can be seen as an expression of the notions of contestability and customer service. It looks as though, in this case, the public elected a new set of politicians, who instigated managerial changes and brought about a new stage in the planning and management of the local council.

Box 1.6 The formation of a strategic core and devolution to business units at Brent Council, London

Brent Council, a local authority in the greater London area serving a population of nearly a quarter of a million people, carried out a series of major changes in the 1990s, transforming it from a traditional and hierarchical structure to a strategic and decentralized organization. It formulated a mission statement, which was to be 'simply the best'. It defined a set of core values: to achieve quality, to be efficient, to give customers what they want, and to value and empower the council's staff.

The centre of the council was considerably slimmed down and support services were cut back. After the changes, the council had 11 multidisciplinary strategic units which comprised the council's core. The core units were made responsible for setting strategy.

The devolution programme was intended to eliminate bureaucracy, empower front-line service managers, strengthen accountability, redirect resources to front-line services and improve the responsiveness of support functions.

The council delivered a range of services: education, social services, environmental services, economic planning, leisure and housing. These services had been organized through a departmental structure. After the changes in the council's management structure, there were 80 independent business units, each said to be in complete control of its own budget. The changes also brought in a commissioner-contractor system, with seven commissioners each responsible for specific customer groups. An active internal market was said to have developed.

Early results were very promising. There were reports of savings of £20 million in administration costs and an 18 per cent increase in the satisfaction of residents. The council's director of quality reported that staff were more motivated and satisfied and that services had improved. She also suggested that difficulties in making the changes to a more devolved structure were as often a matter of behavioural and thinking patterns as they were to do with changing systems, but that there had been 'culture change' among front-line service managers who were positive about their increased responsibility for performance.

Source: Management Accounting (1996a, 1996b).

designed to allow a psychological or emotional separation which enables the senior managers to be more demanding in terms of service standards and performance targets. This would be consistent with the idea of making the front-line service managers more accountable for the performance of their units. The role of the executive level of the organization can even be seen as in some way analogous to an empowered 'customer': the strategic core is in a sense buying services from front-line managers who are producers of the service. Perhaps the overlay of a market relationship onto the relationship between senior and front-line managers seeks to use an ideological element to spur a performance culture?

The strategic core is not necessarily engaged in long-term planning or foresight. The core is strategic in the sense that they create mission statements, values, and approve plans which enable the decision making to be devolved.

The visionary strategic planning model

Unlike the businesslike model of strategic management, the visionary model is concerned with the long term. The essential idea in this case is to define a desired future for the public service and then to identify activities which get the organization from its present state to a future one.

While elected politicians or top managers are involved in the strategic management process through brainstorming or otherwise defining the strategic vision, employees are engaged in the process through internalizing a set of values. A large number of public services organizations have spent time and trouble identifying their core values and then promoting their acceptance within the workforce. These values sometimes seem to be close to being a set of objectives, but they can also seem to be a moral statement defining how the organization will behave in pursuing its mission or strategy. A third, and arguably very important, tendency has been to see these values as a way of binding everybody together emotionally. The set of values then represent a unified and unifying cultural glue which may be seen as useful in creating a unity of purpose behind a strategy.

In the Box 1.7 below the case of Islington Council shows how a long-term strategic vision produced by elected politicians is combined with planned activities and core values and aimed at bringing about strategic change. There is no necessary emphasis in this model on devolution, and, indeed, if the desired future state is defined by politicians, then the approach is in at least this sense a centralized rather than a decentralized one.

The foresight-based strategic management model

The foresight-based strategic model might be defined as being based on the idea of the guidance of strategic action by the use of intelligence. This has philosophical echoes in the work of pragmatists who reconcile being

---

Box 1.7 Visions, planning and values in the London Borough of Islington

Leisha Fullick, chief executive of the London Borough of Islington, outlined her approach to strategic management in early 1997. She summed it up as consisting of three elements: a strategic vision; planning to get to that vision; and values for the organization. The starting point was a strategic vision produced by the elected politicians. She said:

> I think you start with the vision. And, in fact we have been going through an exercise here. We went through an exercise with the [elected] members [of the council] about: 'What do you think Islington is going to be like in ten years time?' And they brainstormed . . . And then: 'What do you think are the most important things that this council should be doing in ten years time?' They brainstormed a load of things. And from that we were able to get these longer-term priorities.

Once the vision of the elected politicians was clarified, the managers began planning how the vision could be achieved. This involved looking at how the various parts of the organization could take appropriate actions to bring about the required changes.

Leisha Fullick believed that the strategy had to be underpinned by organizational values which were communicated to the workforce. In her opinion, it was important that employees understand and agree with the values. The consequence for the organization is that employees 'are then more committed to their work, they perform better, and you get better quality outcomes'. If there are no organizational values then there is no framework for employees: 'they don't know why they are there, what they are supposed to be doing'.

Source: Unpublished interview with Leisha Fullick by the author, January 1997.

---

realistic with idealism: they suggest the importance of imagining a future which projects what is desirable in the present and planning a path to that future (Dewey 1993: 9). This model takes a long-term view of strategic change. It also develops a strategic vision, like the visionary model. But planning in this case is not simply about identifying activities that will take the organization towards the strategic vision. A public service organization making use of the strategic foresight model also focuses on developing areas of special expertise or capability, and it develops cooperative ventures with other organizations which it believes will be needed to ensure that the strategic vision is realized.

This type of strategic management is associated with a form of intellectual leadership which is concerned to engage the hearts and minds of managers and employees, and secure their consent to the strategic direction being set. This type of intellectual leadership also recognizes and deals with the uncertainties in building capabilities and moving towards a long-term future. These uncertainties arise in part because the environment will

Box 1.8 The development of King's Healthcare in the 1990s

One long-term issue which chief executive Derek Smith had considered was how King's Healthcare could survive and prosper as a university teaching hospital on its own. He was thinking about a very different environment 'in which academic medicine might be operating in 10 or 20 years'. His strategic foresight was that the future of academic medicine was focused at an international level. His view was that the hospital had to associate with other institutions in quite a different way, and with them the hospital might build a world-class institution. In private sector language, he was thinking about strategic alliances.

He worked with his board and executive to define what strategy meant and to develop a picture of what kind of organization they wanted the hospital to be. (The strategy which emerged offered frameworks for managing three areas: internal processes of the hospital; the King's College medical school; and relationships with external parties, which included the health authorities and other NHS trust hospitals in their locality.) Strategic aims, goals, and finally operational targets were also formulated. A real effort was made to engage senior professional staff and middle management. Business planning, seminars and away days were all used to discuss and debate strategy.

Derek Smith's visionary approach to strategic management was designed to take his organization into planning longer-term and enabling it to build capabilities as well as solve problems. For example, King's Healthcare has been building a core competence in the field of neurosciences. This had a number of potential elements to it: neurosurgery, neurology and other areas of expertise concerned with diseases of the brain, spine and nervous system. Derek Smith identified neuroscience as an important area for the hospital: 'it is very complex, you can't replicate it easily . . . it is the sort of services we should be into . . . It is academically extremely fertile ground. And a lot of future academic work will be in that area.'

It was not certain that King's Healthcare would be able to build up a service in the area of neurosciences, but a strategic view was taken that neurosciences was an excellent fit with the way the hospital wanted to develop. The hospital saw it as the basis of a key area of tertiary service, alongside their expertise gained as a result of having the largest liver transplant programme in Europe. It was decided that these two areas of specialism would be combined with an improving record as a large general hospital serving the necessary requirements of its local population.

The decision paid off. The hospital was given the go-ahead to develop neurosciences. It took over two years to get the services operating at anywhere near the desired level, and the commissioners who awarded the contracts for these services probably wanted results more quickly, but installing the levels of expertise involved cannot be managed overnight.

Derek Smith's hospital has also made radical changes in its relationships with other important local NHS trusts. At the centre of these changes are plans for the merging of medical and dental schools to form the Guy's, King's and St Thomas's Medical and Dental School, creating the second biggest medical school and the largest dental school in the country.

The fact that King's had a strategy has helped them to play an influential role in creating this major cooperative venture. The hospital has, according to Derek Smith, been enabled to act in a fairly open way, and in such a way as to positively advance the change. Prior to the existence of the current strategy to form, using the combined resources of the partners, a very large academic institution, the hospital appears to have been more inclined to choose conservative options. Defence rather than transformation had been the hallmark of the hospital's actions.

Source: Unpublished interview with Derek Smith by the author, July 1997.

create dilemmas or issues – for example, alternative opportunities (or threats) which have to be evaluated for their potential in bringing about (or delaying) the long-term strategic vision. These opportunities (or threats) contain uncertainty too because they are not realized (or deflected) automatically; the outcome contains uncertainty because realizing the opportunity (or deflecting the threat) requires skill and judgement. So, strategic issue-management is subsumed within a strategic foresight model.

This model of strategic management is illustrated by certain aspects of the way in which King's Healthcare was developing in the 1990s (see Box 1.8).

Conclusions

This chapter has explored what strategic management might mean for the public services. The introduction of strategic planning has been placed in the context of pressures of a public and a political kind. These may be seen as essentially economic (i.e. caused by fiscal stress and public demands for better services) or they may be seen as political, and thus the result of a gap between the public and its public services. The pressures appear to be persisting.

This chapter has also reviewed different models of strategic management for use in the public services. These have been described as the 'classical' planning model, the businesslike strategic management model, the visionary strategic planning model, and the foresight-based strategic management model. In order to simplify the discussion these models have contained little about how the public have been involved in strategic management by public service organizations. This important issue is taken up in Chapter 8.

two

Mission statements, performance and situational analysis

Introduction

This chapter begins the job of outlining the basic elements and methods of a strategic planning process. It distinguishes the process of strategic analysis from that of strategic implementation. It then sets out a comprehensive model of strategic planning attuned to current concerns about accountability, performance planning and improving the performance of public services. It moves on to describe key concepts and methods used for carrying out a strategic analysis, including those useful for establishing strategic direction and intent, for assessing current performance, and for making a situational assessment.

Strategic analysis

Strategic analysis is an intellectual process concerned with the formulation of ideas. Strategic analysis can be seen as answering a number of key questions, which vary in their formulation depending on the preferred approach to strategy. For example, an issue-management model of the strategy process might focus on the following four questions:

1 What is the overall purpose of the organization?
2 What are the key strategic issues which need to be satisfactorily managed if the organization is to be successful in terms of the overall purpose?
3 What actions need to be taken to address, and hopefully solve, the key strategic issues?
4 How can these actions be best implemented in the circumstances which prevail?

It is possible to simply brainstorm answers directly to these questions, and, on this basis alone, carry out a strategic analysis. Alternatively, techniques can be used for drawing up mission statements, analysing the environment, identifying strategic issues, generating ideas for strategic action, evaluating these, planning the management of stakeholders, and planning the acquisition of necessary resources. These are tools of the intellectual process, not a replacement for it. As tools, they are selected and used by strategic leaders and managers to get the work of strategic analysis done.

Overall strategy analysis

One of the key reasons for strategic planning is operational planning, or performance planning – as it is now being called in the public services – which sets annual performance targets. So, while there may be a strategic plan covering, say, the next five years, the organization is really held to account for its one-year performance. This kind of planning may be introduced by politicians who feel that there is too much complacency within the public services organization, and that there is a need to counter bureaucratic inertia. The important strategic analysis questions, therefore, are:

1 What is the organization's mission statement and, therefore, what are the associated strategic goals?
2 What opportunities and threats need to be considered in determining performance plans?
3 What annual performance targets (based on strategic goals) are to be defined within the performance plan in order to provide a basis for accountability in relation to the quantity and quality of services?
4 What problems might get in the way of accomplishing these performance targets and, therefore, how can adjustments be made to anticipate them, or what contingency plans are needed?

The fashionable element in this type of approach is to be seen in the prevalence of newly formulated mission statements. It may seem strange that a public services organization which has been operating for decades, such as the UK's NHS, should find itself needing to draw up mission statements. But the reason often given for establishing mission statements is the muddle and confusion which develops when public services organizations have been around for a long time. As different societal problems have emerged, or politicians have made new demands on public services, public services organizations have acquired additional new responsibilities without anyone having made sure that it made sense.

The evolution of public policy and the passing of more laws over time has certainly produced complexity: take the case of the US food safety system, which developed incrementally through 35 laws and was administered by 12 federal agencies. Or consider the case of the US Bureau of Reclamation which has to take account of many different laws to understand its legislative mandate. The Bureau undertakes irrigation works in western states under the Reclamation Act of 1902. More authority – to provide water for towns, for hydropower and for other purposes – was granted in 1906 and 1920. Just before the Second World War, the US Congress gave the Bureau further authority to construct multipurpose projects. Yet further additions to its authority – for municipal and industrial water supply projects – were approved in 1958. After 1969 decision making by the Bureau was required to consider the environment, and from 1973 onwards there has been a requirement to protect endangered species. According to the Bureau, in 1997, there were more than 1400 pages of laws, directives and specific authorizations which defined its mandate.

• • Thus performance planning can be seen as an attempted answer to the muddle and confusion of legislative mandates. But it is also posed directly against the traditional view of measuring public services in terms of inputs.
• • Further, it is seen as instrumental in providing a base for continuing performance improvements. Therefore, clear performance measures are a part of a system for ensuring accountability of managers to politicians, better motivation of federal agencies, and continuing increases in performance.

This model of strategic analysis probably comes closest to one of the most widespread conceptions of strategic planning which, at its most simplified, sees strategy as fitting the organization to its environment. For example, the UK's Audit Commission in the 1980s gave advice on improving UK local government which assumed that the strategy of a council should be determined partly by a vision of what it was trying to do, but also by the need to respond to its external environment. This idea of strategy – adapting an organization to its environment – implies first the need to do an assessment of the environment, then the need to plan a strategic response to threats and opportunities detected in the environment, and finally the need to manage the strategic response.

A strategic planning process for this kind of strategic analysis could be designed by building on Eadie's (1983) proposals. So the process might look something like the following:

- Step 1: formulate mission statement and strategic goals
- Step 2: carry out environmental assessment
- Step 3: carry out a resource audit to determine strengths and weaknesses
- Step 4: cross-tabulate opportunities and threats by strengths and weaknesses
- Step 5: identify ideas for strategic action
- Step 6: carry out cost-benefit analysis to evaluate and select strategic actions
- Step 7: carry out a risk analysis to identify dangers for the strategic plan
- Step 8: draw up implementation plans
- Step 9: incorporate into operational plans (alter current and upcoming annual budgets, define performance indicators, etc.)

In this chapter and the next we will briefly outline some of the key ideas and techniques which are employed in this type of strategic planning process. At times, we will also explore ideas and techniques which would be used in alternative planning processes.

Mission statements

In 1996 the UK's NHS executive identified the national priorities to be taken into account by NHS trusts and general practitioners (GPs) when preparing business and practice plans. The executive also provided guidance on the plans for 1997/8. This guidance included the following statement:

> The purpose of the NHS is to secure through the resources available the greatest possible improvement in the physical and mental health of the people of England by: promoting health, preventing ill-health, diagnosing and treating disease and injury, and caring for those with long-term illness and disability who require the services of the NHS: a service available to all on the basis of clinical need, regardless of the ability to pay.
>
> (NHS Executive Priorities and Planning Guidance
> for the NHS, 1997/98: EL(96)45)

This statement of purpose is more commonly referred to as a mission statement. The statement makes clear what the NHS exists for and what it does. But if we examine this statement further we can see that it has a number of components (Duncan *et al.* 1994).

1 It defines the intended beneficiaries of the NHS as the people of England.
2 It defines the particular service activities it will use to benefit them: promoting health, preventing ill-health, diagnosing and treating disease and injury, and caring for those with long-term illness and disability.

3 It specifies, implicitly, a geographical boundary – that is, England.
4 It specifies a desired consequence, which is that it should achieve 'the greatest possible improvement in the physical and mental health' of the target group of beneficiaries.
5 Finally, it defines a basic assumption of the organization – that the NHS provides a service available to all on the basis of clinical need, regardless of the ability to pay – which is seen to be fundamental to the identity, or concept, of the NHS.

This suggests a fairly basic definition of a mission statement. It is a statement of organizational purpose which sets out:

1 the intended beneficiaries;
2 the main services to be provided;
3 the geographical boundary of the organization's operations;
4 the desired consequences of the organization's services; and
5 a concept which expresses the organization's identity.

Not all mission statements have all the components suggested here, and many may contain other things as well. It may well be that the legislative mandates make it relatively easy to define the intended beneficiaries and the services to be provided. But perhaps many public services organizations are less inclined to spell out in their mission statements their basic assumptions which give them their identity.

The definition of the desired consequence of the organization's services is the element of the mission statement which is most critical from the point of view of measuring organizational performance. Without this, it is hard to see how the mission statement can be used as a basis for performance planning.

One final issue is the extent to which a mission statement should be unique to each public service organization. To some extent of course, the answer depends on the legislative mandates that set out an organization's authority. But, as Bryson (1995: 66) points out, 'Too many organizations think they are more constrained than they actually are'. So, providing the organization does not define its mission in a way which contravenes its legislative mandates, there is scope for mission statements to be made distinctive while conforming to the intention of the relevant laws. A mission statement which is distinctive may encourage stakeholders to see the organization as in some way special and, therefore, as deserving of a special level of support and commitment.

Mission statements are a common feature of public services organizations, and may be seen as the starting point of a strategic analysis. Mission statements should be written in a way that will help the process of strategy formulation.

Legislative mandates are often a key influence on the development of mission statements in public services organizations; hence part of the work of drawing up a mission statement consists of reviewing these mandates. It would be very useful preparation for writing a mission statement to study relevant legislation and other documents to clarify the mandates which apply to the organization. It would also be useful to do a comprehensive stakeholder analysis identifying the expectations each group has of the organization and their relative power or influence. Such a stakeholder analysis might also be useful for identifying who should be involved in strategy formulation.

Goal-setting techniques

Mission statements are meant to be relatively enduring. Strategic goals are derived from mission statements but allow for evolution and innovation in activities.

One approach to developing strategic goals from the mission statement is based on identifying key performance areas (Duncan *et al*. 1995). These may be defined as areas of activity which are critical to the organization's survival and success. The mission statement should have identified a desired consequence, such as in the NHS case above, that there should be 'the greatest possible improvement in the physical and mental health' of the population. The strategic leaders and managers of a health service organization covered by this mission statement need to identify what activity by the public service has the biggest impact – or what activity *could* have the biggest impact – on this outcome. The key areas might be, for argument's sake, reliable assessment of the population's health needs, good access to primary healthcare for the population, and an effective programme of health education.

Key performance areas are difficult to identify. One suggestion for a procedure which may be used is as follows. Chief executives and top managers would first remind themselves of the mission statement and then ask themselves, first, what key problems or concerns they think need addressing by their organization, and second, why it would be important to find solutions to these problems or concerns. The rationale for identifying key areas in this way is that chief executives and top managers have a lot of tacit information and understanding of their situation and can use questions like these to elicit hypotheses about what the key areas are.

However difficult the process of identifying the key performance areas is, it is self-evidently important that they are identified and used for formulating strategic goals. The organization is thereby focused in a way that brings the best prospects for success in relation to its mission. The strategic goals for a five-year strategic planning horizon would then be formulated to ensure that these key areas were being addressed.

In drawing up the strategic goals the usual advice given is that organizations should not formulate too many strategic goals, that they should be stated in a way that means that they are measurable, and that they should be challenging but achievable.

Strategic visions and values

Some public services organizations prefer to create strategic visions and define core values rather than produce mission statements. Some define core values alongside mission statements.

The strategic vision is probably best seen as corresponding to a strategic goal. Not all public services organizations like to set their strategic direction in terms of a number of discrete and measurable goals. It is also possible to use the strategic vision of the future of the organization as a statement of the goal to be pursued. This vision can be expressed as a qualitative statement (Nutt and Backoff 1992). Such an approach may be adopted when the main emphasis in strategic planning is on issue management rather than on implementing strategic goals.

But it is also possible to use a vision of a successful future for yet another kind of strategic planning process. In this case the goal is a strategic foresight of a desired future (not a predicted future) in which new kinds of benefits will be offered to the public through services with new functionalities. The strategic foresight process then involves using the desired vision of the future as a goal from which it is necessary, analytically speaking, to work backwards. The planning involves trying to work out a path which might be taken to produce the future desired state. An example of this kind of goal setting applied to public management is to be found in ideas of the development of desiderative scenarios (Bohret 1993). These have been suggested as a technique which can be used to identify future possibilities for societal development. But the technique could also be used in strategic planning for goal setting. As suggested above, this involves defining a desired future and then working backwards to produce ideas for a possible path from the current situation. Using visions of a successful future either in strategic issue management or in a strategic foresight process are mentioned here, but are not discussed in further depth because the main intention of this chapter is to discuss the results-oriented approach to strategic planning which begins with a mission statement and strategic goals and is used to develop performance plans.

Values may be regarded sometimes as goals. For example, Brent Council (see Chapter 1) specified four core values:

1 to achieve quality;
2 to be efficient;
3 to give customers what they want; and
4 to value and empower the council's staff.

Since the council then set about deliberately trying to pursue them, these values could be seen as goals. Alternatively, values may be seen as complementary to a mission statement or a strategic vision statement, in which case they may be used to stipulate how the organization will conduct itself in implementing its mission or strategic vision statement.

Analysing performance issues

One reason for carrying out a strategic analysis and exploring the need for a change in strategic direction is that current organizational performance, or projected organizational performance, is unsatisfactory. The analysis of performance issues may be seen as peculiarly difficult in the public services because goals are difficult to specify and performance expectations are vague and fluid (Nutt and Backoff 1992). In contrast, it is often suggested that the private sector finds it easy to recognize performance issues and measure performance because it has got the profit figure, which provides a quantitative and universally yardstick by which to measure organizational performance in the private sector.

Many public services in recent years have been confronting the need to measure performance. Measurement of performance is difficult when organizations are unclear about what they are measuring and why they are measuring it. One key issue, which has been discussed in the USA and New Zealand, has been whether organizations should be held accountable for service outputs or outcomes for the public. US federal government reforms have focused on outcomes, but in New Zealand government reforms chose measures based on outputs because government departments were considered to have insufficient control over outcomes (Ball 1994). In the UK it has been argued that outcome measurement is still in its infancy and that too many performance indicators are poorly conceived (Smith 1995). However, in a range of different public services – health, education, local government, etc. – although experience is still limited, considerable progress has been made in deciding what needs measuring and why. Much of the impetus came initially from political and executive pressures, but the habit of thinking about goals and performance and measuring performance gaps is becoming integrated into managerial practice.

Strategic management and planning has played a part in the way in which the public services have responded to the measurement challenge. A recent survey in the USA discovered that the most important objective of the strategic planning process in state agencies was the desire to set programme and policy direction (Berry and Wechsler 1995). Goal setting was a fairly universal part of the strategic planning process used by the state agencies, and establishing the management direction and clarifying agency priorities were seen by many as the most important outcomes. Therefore, where the public services have introduced strategic planning, they are better placed for knowing what needs measuring.

One interesting private sector development in recent years has been the use of the balanced scorecard to evaluate overall organizational performance. Major companies such as Johnson and Johnson, SmithKline Beecham, and British Aerospace are using the balanced scorecard concept to design strategic measures for their strategic management processes. This means defining objectives, targets and measures around four perspectives: financial, customer, internal business process, and learning and growth (Kaplan and Norton 1996). Some public service organizations have also experimented with the use of multiple measures. They measure service efficiency (using benchmarking and performance indicators), and also measure public satisfaction with services. Perhaps they should measure their key internal processes and their performance on innovation as well? If it is assumed that all these things are causally interrelated, and if organizations were able to model these interrelations over a period of time using actual data, they would then be better placed for deciding how to enhance their effectiveness.

If the organization already has a set of strategic goals which are measurable, then analysing performance in key areas is relatively straightforward – providing the necessary management information systems have been set up to enable managers to report and review performance. The identification of performance issues can be found by looking at performance trends over time or making comparisons with similar organizations. Either of these approaches may use data to pinpoint poor performance.

Boschken's (1992) study of public transit agencies shows what can be done with data to produce performance measures (see Box 2.1).

Some public services organizations, even with good reputations for innovative management, have found themselves with clear strategic goals but without data which can tell them how well they are doing (Davies and Griffiths 1995). In the absence of both clear strategic goals and appropriate management information systems, public services organizations may only have ready access to financial data. The reporting systems will then provide information on overspending or underspending. If financial data can be linked to physical output data, it is possible to calculate unit costs. This is recommended for use in monitoring performance plans and, consequently, in results-oriented strategic planning. However, it is important to note that the ways in which costs are allocated within cost accounting systems can distort the results obtained.

Box 2.1 Performance measures and public transit agencies

Boschken's (1992) study was concerned to measure and understand performance of US public transit organizations providing bus and rail services. His data was based on reports they had to make under Section 15 of the Urban Mass Transportation Act. Boschken extracted performance data for the years 1987–90 from these reports for 42 transit agencies in urban areas with populations of above 500,000.

Boschken used 12 measures to create four variables. One variable he defined as the organization's strategic positioning in the industry. It comprised three measures:

1 passenger trips/district population;
2 passenger miles/vehicle miles; and
3 percentage change in revenue, all sources.

Arguably, a transit agency which supplies a relatively high number of passenger journeys for its local population, which has buses and trains that are packed with passengers, and which has a growing revenue base, is a 'star' in terms of strategic positioning, in the same way that private sector portfolio planning regards a business with a large share of a growing market as a star. In the public services case we can speculate that it must be meeting public needs and complying with its legislative mandates for its services to be, apparently, so popular and for revenue to increase. (This logic is clearly appropriate to public agencies providing services when the focus is on organizational achievement by the lone agency. Different measures and different logic would apply if a public services organization was being measured in terms of community goals and on the basis of activities tightly integrated and coordinated with other organizations. Nor would such logic or measures be sufficient for situations in which public agencies were involved in regulatory activities.)

Another variable was focused on operational efficiencies. It comprised the following three measures:

1 operating costs/vehicle miles;
2 maintenance costs/hours of maintenance-free operation; and
3 capital assets used in operating the services/vehicle miles.

The third variable was intended as a measure of social effectiveness in relation to politically mandated objectives. It comprised three measures.

1 passenger miles/service area square miles;
2 the number of off-peak vehicle miles driven as a percentage of total vehicle miles; and
3 annual capital investment per head of population.

The first of these measures is meant to proxy the meeting of needs for access to transit services by the public; the second is meant to indicate the meeting of needs of the non-working poor who use transit systems outside of commuting hours; and the third reflects needs for economic development.

The fourth variable was a measure of effectiveness for various stakeholders (employees, taxpayers, pedestrians and motorists). Boschken used: wage yield for the mileage driven; how much service is rendered per dollar of tax subsidy; and accident rates (which were of interest to motorists and pedestrians).

Benchmarking

Benchmarking involves making comparisons of processes, practices and performance with other organizations – or within an organization. It is about analysing data with the intention of improving performance to match that of the best. Benchmarking, therefore involves comparing data and analysing the causes of any differences which are found. Essentially, an organization is interested in learning how another organization performs the same services or processes better than they do themselves, or how one part of their own organization performs better than another.

Public services organizations may agree to work together on making comparisons of their processes, practices and performance by exchanging data. However, in the public sector, where there is a strong culture of openness and there are legal requirements to publish performance information, the data needed for benchmarking may be obtained in other ways. For example, Pembrokeshire County Council in Wales set up a local government benchmarking reference centre in the summer of 1996, with the aim of providing benchmarking services to local government.

Benchmarking may also be done internally as well as externally. The Further Education Unit advised UK colleges that benchmarking might involve analysing the same processes in different parts of the same college, the same process in other colleges, or the same process in organizations outside the further education sector (Further Education Unit 1997).

Benchmarking may be seen as important for making operational improvements. It can also be very useful as part of a situational analysis of a strategic planning process, because it helps to identify activities which are strengths or weaknesses of the organization. It helps by pinpointing activities which are done comparatively very well or very badly. In this way, benchmarking can be important in identifying skills and core competencies possessed by individual public services organizations. Alternatively, it can help to identify skills and core competencies which need to be developed because of current areas of weakness.

Environmental assessment

Perhaps the only environmental assessment a public services organization might do is a study of its legislative mandates. However, public organizations have set up strategic management processes which involve scanning the environment for demographic, economic, social and legislative trends and events (Davies and Griffiths 1995). In Box 2.2 there is an indication of the demographic and social data which might have been used to plan health services. Public services strategic planners and managers have borrowed from the private sector literature and made use of PEST (political, economic, social and technological) analysis.

Box 2.2 Information available for health district planning

In the 1980s health services management and planning had access to national, regional and local statistics. In assessing the current situation, therefore, planners could make reference to demographic and social trends. Data could be found on the size and distribution of the population, birth rates, death rates, migration, the numbers of single parent families, the numbers of pensioners, the number of unemployed people and types of housing. All these could be used to plan health services.

One approach to assessing the environment, developed by the Harbridge Consulting Group for use with clients, prompts groups of managers in an organization to think about possible changes and then come to an agreement about the importance of the changes and about the organization's preparedness for dealing with them (Hussey 1998). Managers are prompted to think about changes in respect of demographic, social, economic, political, ecological, technological, legal and infrastructure factors.

Public services organizations could also adopt a structural analysis. It can be argued that such an analysis could correspond to Porter's (1980) structural analysis of industry, but with the difference that public services planners and managers should look at political forces rather than competitive forces. Five political forces might be:

1 political oversight forces;
2 professional forces;
3 market forces.
4 citizen forces;
5 service user forces;

At a macro-level of analysis we might argue that different configurations of forces produce tendencies towards different modes of governance and administration (Jorgensen 1993).

Where politicians in oversight bodies (e.g. elected representatives on local government councils) and professionals employed in the public services are the dominant forces, then public service organizations are likely to place the emphasis on strategies and planning which help to implement policies and are consistent with the priorities of expert opinion. Where market forces are dominant, then we may see strategies primarily aimed at results in terms of costs and performance. When citizens and service users are very dominant, then we are more likely to see strategies which give priority to innovation in services and service delivery systems.

The following five questions could be asked by an individual public services organization in order to direct its structural (political) analysis:

1 What directions or priorities are political oversight bodies emphasizing?
2 What pressures are professionals and their organizations creating on public services?
3 What challenges are being formed as a result of commercialization pressures or by the competition of private sector organizations?
4 What concerns do the public have and how powerfully are these being expressed by pressure groups and lobbying?
5 What do service users need and how strongly is this expressed through surveys and complaints?

Market research

The perceived need for using market research has undoubtedly increased in recent years as public services have not only introduced strategic management but also programmes of customer care and quality management. Some public services organizations have even set up marketing units and appointed marketing specialists (Davies and Griffiths 1995).

Market research in the public services often looks at public satisfaction with services. It also covers markets, services, promotion, pricing and distribution. It should also look at what the public needs or desires from its public services.

Data on the public may already exist – for example, in the form of census data and government reports. However, it may be very worth while at the beginning of a strategic planning process to survey a sample of service users to assess their needs. Gatherer (1971) described a survey of health needs in Baltimore in which 100 randomly selected households were visited each month and a questionnaire was used to collect information on the most important health problems. He tried out a similar survey of health needs in a northern UK city in 1961. He concluded: 'It proved to be feasible, not too demanding on the time and effort of the people involved, and valuable in supplying information not otherwise readily available' (p. 74).

The use of surveys by public services to find out what the public wants or needs may seem so obvious that it hardly seems necessary to mention it. But is this really true? How much market research is done by public services? Is there still enormous scope for making greater use of surveys? Buurma (1997) pointed out that the government in The Netherlands constructed a 'car-pool only' lane for one of its motorways. While this was a very expensive investment, it has not provided much benefit to the public. Buurma reported: 'The government failed to measure the demand amongst road users beforehand and it turned out that almost nobody made use of it – car-pooling in the Netherlands is not working (yet)' (p. 4).

Buurma's approach to marketing has the unusual result of requiring governments and public services to think of the public as customers (which is obviously a carry-over from private sector marketing ideas) while at the same time highlighting the obligations of the customer. Consequently, he is not interested in the usual market transactions of buyers and sellers, but societal exchange transactions between a government striving for societal goals and citizens pursuing their own interests. His specific concern is with government provision of free goods such as roads, and with social objectives such as road safety and reducing environmental pollution. He argues that measures regulating traffic behaviour are mandatory for road users, and that obligations are also an automatic part of the package for those who opt to use the roads. This leads, logically, to the idea that market research can be used to assess the needs of road users and 'with the help of proper promotion tools they can be unambiguously called to account for their contribution to safe and clean traffic' (Buurma 1997: 8).

Other methods of data collection apart from surveys using random samples are possible. Qualitative data on service-user needs may be collected using focus groups, questionnaires and neighbourhood meetings. The data obtained need not be restricted to problems and needs. The public services organization may also want information on the perceptions and feelings of service users. Qualitative methods can be extremely useful in not only finding out what the public wants, but *why* they want it. A deeper understanding of the public's motivation and problems enables public services to be more creative in meeting public needs; public services are often not able to just give the public what it demands, because of resource availability. Qualitative methods can also be used to get a better understanding of the 'moments of truth' when service users make their critical judgements of a service. Using a knowledge of the moments of truth the public services are better able to specify the service standards which are important in setting performance targets.

The analysis of the data can be directed towards identifying the most frequently occurring need, but, as Walsh (1989) argued there is an increasing need to segment the market for a public service. While it is no longer good enough to design a general or average service, the basis for segmentation may not be immediately obvious. Streetlighting, for example, does not satisfy the same need to the same degree for all segments of the population in these days when women may feel especially vulnerable to assaults. So, in respect of this service, it is important to segment by gender. In the case of another service, it may be important to segment by age or ethnicity.

Market research firms may be employed to carry out data collection and analysis, but a public service organization can also use exit polls from service delivery outlets, service satisfaction cards which can be left with a household when a service has been provided, or suggestion schemes to obtain data relatively cheaply.

Duncan *et al.* (1995) report a number of questions which can be used for customer analysis in the healthcare sector. These can be adapted for more general application in service user analysis. Questions which might be asked include:

- Who uses the service?
- Who are the most frequent users of the service?
- Who should be using the service but is not?
- How are service users currently segmented?
- Is there a better way of segmenting users?
- What motivates the public to use this service?
- What aspects of the service are most valued by the service users?
- What benefits are the users seeking in consuming this service?
- What changes are likely to occur in user motivation?
- Are users currently satisfied with the service they receive?
- Do users perceive problems with how the service is delivered?
- Are there unmet needs which the users are not aware of?

Stakeholder analysis

Stakeholder analysis can be carried out for different reasons within a strategic planning process. It can be used at the outset to decide who should be involved in the planning process; in preparation for drawing up a mission statement or a strategic vision; and after a decision has been made about which strategic actions are to be implemented and when implementation plans are being drawn up.

If it is used prior to establishing mission statements or strategic visions, then stakeholder analysis might consist of the following steps:

1 identification of stakeholders;
2 identification of how stakeholders influence the organization;
3 identification of what the organization needs from each stakeholder;
4 identification of the criteria used by the stakeholders in evaluating the organization; and
5 ranking of stakeholders in a rough order of importance.

Completing these steps is likely to require some guesswork and should be checked by research (e.g. studies of service users and employees).

When planning the implementation of strategic action, the strategic leaders and managers will want to assess how different groups are likely to react to news of the intention to take specified actions. They will also want to assess the importance of any opposition or support which is proffered by stakeholder groups to planned actions. In consequence of these forecasts of stakeholder reactions, decisions can be made about the tactics of implementation. Some of the tactics which may be considered include persuasion, demonstration projects to show that the ideas are feasible, surprising opponents, negotiating changes to make the strategy more acceptable, etc.

Table 2.1 Values table

Clients	
____ 1	A decent quality of life
____ 2	Living with people he/she gets on with
____ 3	Appropriate help and support
____ 4	Additional needs met
____ 4	Safety and protection from abuse
____ 5	To be listened to

Support staff working in the residential service	
____ 1	Adequate pay
____ 2	Career development opportunities
____ 3	Training in the skills to do the job
____ 4	Job satisfaction
____ 5	Decent working conditions
____ 6	Appropriate management support

The clients' relatives	
____ 1	Confidence in the service and its future
____ 2	Knowing their relative is well cared for
____ 3	To be able to express their viewpoint to staff
____ 4	To see their relative happy

Managers of support staff	
____ 1	Stable contracting arrangements with purchasers of services
____ 2	Less bureaucracy
____ 3	Good staff
____ 4	Adequate financial and other resources
____ 5	To stay within budget

Note: The dash before each item is for the respondent to record their rating of how satisfactory the situation is for the group in question. Score 0 to 10, 0 – not satisfactory, to 10 – very satisfactory.

Tables of values

Bohret (1993) suggests drawing up tables of values to explore the goals and expectations of different social groups. These tables can be seen as a way of presenting some of the results of a stakeholder analysis which can be useful for identifying strategic issues and providing clues for possible strategic actions. A partial table of values for a community-based residential service for people with learning disabilities is shown in Table 2.1.

Each value for each group can be rated in terms of how satisfactory the situation is, thus enabling a profile of how well the values and expectations of clients, support staff and others are being met. Table 2.1 could be extended to include other groups such as professional specialists, neighbours, purchasers/commissioners, and central government.

A values table is custom-made for each public service and each particular organization. Over time the elements of the table will change, as well as the ratings of how satisfactorily the values/expectations are being met. It would not be possible to draw up such a table without considerable familiarity with a service.

A values table can reveal or suggest problems – and the *lack* of such problems in the case of particular groups would itself be interesting. In Table 2.1, the rating of values for clients is probably a useful basis for viewing the pattern of tensions suggested by the table. For instance, a rating of the clients' values might reveal that their quality of life was adequate and that they were reasonably safe from abuse, but that values in respect of living with people they get on with, having additional needs met and being listened to were not being met. This might reveal that services are caring for clients in basic terms but are not ensuring that they are able to exercise much choice. This might be regarded as indicating the existence of a major strategic problem, if the organization considered its mission to be the provision of support to enable clients to live valued lives and exercise as much autonomy in decisions as possible.

The ratings for other groups might supply clues as to the causes of this situation. For example, support staff's values might be rated as not being satisfactorily met in relation to pay and training in skills to do the job, despite management support and job satisfaction being rated as at a reasonable level. The managers' values might be rated as satisfactorily met in terms of stable contracting, good staff, less bureaucracy, and staying within budget, but as being unsatisfactory in relation to resources. This could indicate that the service was only being resourced to provide a basic service, and was not being resourced to enable clients to live a full life in the community or to employ suitably experienced and skilled staff. This might lead to the strategic issue being formulated as a tension between attempting to provide a quality service based on the principles of normalization, and pressures created by financial constraints which worked against the recruitment and development of staff with the skills needed for a high quality service.

Resource analysis

Any strategy will require the reuse of existing resources, the acquisition of new resources and the disposal of resources. An audit of resources is obviously required to ensure that the selection or creation of a strategy is realistic in terms of existing resources and to provide a basis for assessing what resources are required or should be disposed of. The resources may be classified in a variety of ways: financial resources, skills, facilities and equipment, knowledge, goodwill, brand image and so on.

The key resources of any organization are increasingly described in terms of 'core competencies' which are said to provide the real basis of organizational success. A core competence is an organizational ability to do something which results in a product or service which is above the average in terms of the value to the consumer. It consists of an integrated 'bundle' of skills and technologies. Examples from the private sector include Honda's ability to make engines, Sony's ability to miniaturize, and 3M's ability to manufacture substrates, coatings and adhesives.

Core competencies mainly arise from learning by doing. Therefore public services would develop core competencies through new programme or service developments. If there is a connection between the ability to create and sustain core competencies and the effectiveness of the organization at learning by doing, then public services may be able to accelerate the rate of development of core competencies by improving themselves as 'learning organizations'.

Despite the increasing amount that has been written on core competencies, there has been little written on the development of tools for identifying current and required core competencies. A crude preliminary analysis of core competencies might be attempted by reviewing all the main activities of the organization and asking if they are distinctively done and produce high perceived value for the public services consumer. These activities will include those relating to management (e.g. strategic planning, financial management, consulting the public) and professionally-based activities (e.g. particular medical specialties in a hospital, library services in a local authority). This implies valuing and nourishing professional skills within public services organizations.

The preliminary analysis should be supported by:

- conducting research (e.g. large-scale surveys, focus groups) among the public and asking members of the public what they consider to be good about the services offered by the organization;
- reviewing services to see if those that are judged to be excellent by members of the public depend upon any particular skill or expertise which the organization has to an unusual degree; and
- carrying out benchmarking studies with public, voluntary and private organizations to see if superior services exist and why they are superior.

A resource analysis which aims to identify core competencies should also assess the infrastructure which supports those competencies. This infrastructure includes capital equipment and organizational structures and culture (Klein and Hiscocks 1994).

SWOT analysis

This technique, more than most, is identified with the idea of strategy as ensuring a fit between the organization and its environment. The Strengths, Weaknesses, Opportunities and Threats (SWOT) analysis concerns itself with identifying the threats and opportunities of the environment and the strengths and weaknesses of the organization.

The results of SWOT can be used as a platform for determining strategic responses to adjust the organization to its environment. As Bryson (1995: 84) puts it: 'Effective responses build on strengths and minimize or overcome weaknesses in order to take advantage of opportunities and minimize or overcome threats'.

However, Nutt and Backoff (1992) recommend combining SWOT analysis with a strategic issue agenda to identify possible strategic actions. This means looking at how an issue can be addressed by: using the top-rated opportunities, exploiting the top-rated strengths, countering the top-rated threats and rectifying the top-rated weaknesses.

Strategic issue analysis

Strategic issues may be seen as resulting from external developments (events, trends or discontinuities), and could be defined simply as any opportunities or threats posed by such developments. These could be developments in the economic, political, social or technological environments of the organization.

However, there is another view of strategic issues which sees them as being 'issues' because they are especially difficult to manage or handle, and also sees the developments that are creating issues as including both internal and external ones. The difficulty in handling an issue, according to this view, arises from a contradictory relationship between opposing developments. For example, a public service organization may be under a great deal of national political pressure to increase its efficiency and reduce unit costs while expanding its output. At the same time, the same public service organization may be under regional political pressure, say, to develop new programmes which better address the needs of the public in the region. The increasing demand for efficiency and reduced unit costs may be causing the public service organization to streamline its operations and concentrate on delivering programmes in a way which reduces costs, whereas new programmes linked into regional priorities require higher expenditures on research and development, and long-term investments and risk taking. This situation could be seen as creating tensions and confusion, as the organization is pulled in two different directions. This is just one illustration of a strategic issue as a contradictory tension; what is important is the idea that dealing with only one of the developments is unsatisfactory because the effects of the other development create difficulties and blockages.

Another point which may be usefully made is that the strategic issues may be the result of actions by several distinct groups or parties, and the strategic issues will of course have differential consequences for those different groups or parties. So the strategic issues which matter might be discovered by considering all the various stakeholders and looking at their values and aims, and how successful they are in realizing those values and aims. It may also be the case that the issue arises between the organization and one stakeholder group. In consequence, as Heath (1997: 116) puts it: 'One place to look for issues is in any difference of opinion between an organization and its stakeholders'.

Nutt and Backoff (1992) provide some guidance on identifying tensions. First, trends and events are identified. Then the content of a trend or event is described as fitting one of four possible categories: equity, productivity, preservation and transition. This is then paired with one of the three remaining categories by searching for a tension between the trend or event and another trend or event. For example, the issue may be first character-ized as a 'productivity-transition' tension. Nutt and Backoff then suggest considering the presence of the other logically possible tensions. These would include: productivity-equity, productivity-preservation, etc. Up to six dif-ferent types of tension may be identified on this basis, and an organization may have one or more issues in respect of each of them.

This is an interesting technique for generating awareness of strategic issues in any given situation, but we should not rule out the use of brain-storming as a way of identifying contradictory events and trends. If brain-storming is used, it is very important to think through the actual ways in which one development (i.e. trend or event) is related to another. This involves examining the processes involved in one development and assess-ing their effects on the other development. Only if each of the develop-ments have effects on the other which are harmful can we say that there really is a tension.

However the strategic issues are identified, there should be some screen-ing to ensure that they are genuinely strategic and worth consideration. The question to be posed about each strategic issue identified is: why does this need to be addressed? If the answer is that it is seriously damaging to the prospects of the organization achieving its desired future or its key strategic objectives, then it is a strategic issue meriting proper attention from the organization's strategic leaders and managers. Other reasons for concluding that an issue is strategic in nature could be that the issue implies a failure to do what it is required under a legislative mandate, or a failure to achieve results required by a mission statement. These types of criteria for judging that an issue is strategic can be seen in the following statement by Bryson (1995: 109):

Box 2.3 Industry-wide paradox in public transit agencies

Boschken's (1992) study suggests that the idea of issue tensions has some merit when we look at the experience of a whole sector of public service. He discovered what looks like a major trade-off between strategic positioning and operational efficiency. Furthermore, since performance appeared to have this trade-off pattern, it might be deduced that there was a fundamental strategic issue which elicited different types of strategy.

Boschken used the data from published reports to produce four-year averages and then aggregated them to create four variables (see Box 2.1). He also calculated the correlations between the four variables (see Table 2.2).

The data seems to indicate that a good strategic position is associated with good public service (access, etc.) ($r = 0.477$; $p < 0.05$). But Boschken also identified the negative correlation between strategic positioning and operational efficiency ($r = -0.56$; $p < 0.05$) as a significant paradox, and suggested that there were contradictions 'between the long-term aspirations of strategic management and the immediate needs of operations' (Boschken 1992: 280).

It is not clear from Boschken's analysis why this paradox existed but many of the transit agencies either scored high on strategic positioning or high on operational efficiency. He suggested, therefore, that agencies were handling the paradox trade-off by favouring either strategic positioning or operational efficiency. There were some agencies who performed moderately on both variables, and these Boschken described as accepting the paradox (see Table 2.3).

One intriguing finding, which is not really discussed, is the performance of Philadelphia's public transit agency which seems to have scored highly on both variables. Had this agency done something creative and innovative which allowed it to do well on both?

Table 2.2   Boschken's study based on 42 transit agencies, 1987–90

	Strategic positioning	Social effectiveness	Operational efficiency	Effectiveness for stakeholders
Strategic positioning	1.00			
Social effectiveness	0.477	1.00		
Operational efficiency	−0.563	−0.433	1.00	
Effectiveness for stakeholders	−0.217	0.115	0.225	1.00

Source: Boschken (1992).

Table 2.3 Managing paradoxes

		Strategic positioning	
		Low rank-order	High rank-order
Operational efficiency	High rank-order	St Louis Los Angeles Orange County Denver Twin Cities	Philadelphia
	Low rank-order		Washington, DC San Francisco Chicago Contra Costa

Source: Adapted from Boschken (1992), Exhibit 5, p. 281.

An adequate strategic issue description (1) phrases the issue as a challenge that the organization can do something about and that has more than one solution, (2) discusses the confluence of factors (mission, mandates, and internal and external environmental aspects, or SWOTs) that make the issue strategic, and (3) articulates the consequences of not addressing the issue.

Successful strategic action must handle both aspects of the tension contained in the issue. To respond to only one aspect – for example, the need for increased productivity or the need for innovation – risks taking action which will be ineffective because of the effects of the neglected aspect. In the words of Nutt and Backoff (1992: 144): 'Transcending the opposites in a tension produces a win-win strategy'.

Boschken's (1992) study of public transit agencies provides some persuasive evidence for the existence of such tensions (see Box 2.3).

It has been suggested that 'issue briefs' and 'issue position papers' are useful for the processes of identifying and analysing issues (Heath 1997). Issue briefs are 'thinking' documents which '(a) define and explain the issue; (b) explore its various positions, sides, and options as well as the parties that have an interest in it; (c) determine the nature, timing, and mechanisms of the potential impact of the issue; and (d) guide attention to additional sources of analysis regarding the issue' (Heath 1997: 91). Issue position papers are based on the issue briefs, and set out a management position and tactics in relation to the issue.

It seems likely that issue briefs would be useful in a range of situations, but the issue position paper sounds like it could be a stand-alone document. Where strategic issues are handled within a strategic management process the strategic actions to be addressed are likely to be formulated and presented formally within a strategic plan, rather than in a separate issue position paper.

Conclusions

In this chapter we have introduced the strategic planning process primarily as a results-oriented model, in which the mission statement is the platform for developing strategic goals. We have also briefly outlined various techniques which may be used to carry out a strategic analysis. In the next chapter we will explore the process of making strategic decisions and then evaluating the consequences of their implementation. This will then complete a logical framework for strategic planning.

We have discussed in this chapter how strategic goals may be formulated as a set of discrete and measurable objectives. But it was also recognized that public services organizations may prefer to produce a qualitative statement of their strategic vision of a future state of success as their strategic goal. This may be more useful where the public service organization wishes to pursue strategic planning as an issue-management process, and needs a 'vision of success' to sensitize the search for strategic issues. It may also be more useful where the public service organization is experimenting with a strategic foresight process and is going to use the vision of success to identify the consumer benefits and service functionality which it desires to offer in the long term. Then the vision of success represents an end point from which to work backwards in an attempt to discern possible paths to the future.

It should also be noted that this chapter has looked at how an empirical comparison of public services organizations in the USA revealed evidence of performance trade-offs. This suggested that public transit agencies faced a choice: either they could perform well on one dimension, or they could perform well on another. But one organization had managed to perform well on both dimensions and thereby indicated the possibility of organizations which defy the trade-off dilemma. This leads to the idea of strategic planning as a creative process of problem solving, which manages to reconcile what are normally incompatible performance outcomes.

three

Strategic decisions and evaluation

Key learning objectives

After reading this chapter you should be able to:

1 Distinguish between approaches to strategy formulation based on choosing between alternatives and more creative approaches (such as the use of strategic issues).
2 Understand the alternative strategies for dealing with political pressures.
3 Design methods for evaluating strategies.
4 Understand how risk may be taken into account when making strategic choices.

Introduction

In the previous chapter the intellectual activities of setting a strategic direction, assessing current organizational performance and analysing the strategic situation were explored. We complete our examination of the basics of the strategic planning process by outlining the issues and methods involved in deciding on a strategy and evaluating the success of strategic implementation. How this strategic planning is embedded in organizational arrangements and how strategic change is handled are taken up in the following chapters.

Much of what has been written on strategy in the public services has been prescriptive. There are four common propositions about finding strategic solutions in the literature of public services strategic management.

The first is that the rate of change is now so great that bolder strategic changes are needed than in the past. Incremental changes, although more comfortable, are dangerous because they do not measure up to what is needed. The second proposition is that public services leaders and managers must involve employees, the public and others in finding solutions. (How employees and the public can be involved will be taken up in Chapters 5 and 8.) This is, in part, because strategic changes are more likely to be acceptable to those who participate in finding solutions. The third proposition is that public services can no longer think of themselves as self-sufficient organizations, and must work in partnership with others (public agencies, private and voluntary organizations, families and communities) to coalign activities and resources to address community problems. This may involve changes to existing service delivery activities or even modes of service delivery. The fourth proposition is that finding solutions must contain an element of creativity.

In this chapter we will look at some of the techniques used to enhance creativity in finding solutions. These techniques involve *generating* a solution rather than *choosing* one from a standard set of well-known strategic choices. Such techniques for boosting levels of creativity are needed to find answers to the difficult dilemmas and contradictions which organizations now face. However, there can be no guarantee of success even if they are used.

This chapter will also look at evaluation, which can occur at four points at least in a strategic planning process. Evaluation can occur, first, during strategic analysis, as part of assessing the internal environment. Second, evaluation can occur during the strategic choice phase when an organization may have to choose between one of several possible strategies that it has formulated. Thirdly, evaluation should occur during implementation, as strategy is refined and modified as a result of learning. Finally, they occur at the end of implementation, when organizations are concerned with determining whether the implementation has resulted in their strategic goals being achieved.

We will take a fairly conventional look at how to carry out a strategic appraisal. Cost-benefit analysis and risk analysis – two important techniques relevant to the appraisal process – are considered.

Selecting strategic options

Strategy formulation may be seen as the process of making a choice from a set of strategic options. These options are regarded as alternatives which the organization could pursue.

The generic strategic alternatives which receive most consideration in the business literature appear to reflect the nature of prevailing environmental conditions for a given sector at a given time. In the private sector during the 1960s, when there had been a long experience of economic growth, it was perhaps natural to see the alternatives in terms of opportunities for growth, and thus businesses would think in terms of entry to new markets and in terms of investing in new product development (Ansoff 1968). Later, when competition became more intense and there were threats to survival, ideas changed and the generic strategies came to be seen as options that positioned businesses to meet competitive pressures (Porter 1980).

Need volatility

Likewise in the public services, the basic strategic alternatives may be seen as shaped by the most critical feature of prevailing environmental conditions. The most critical feature identified by Nutt and Backoff (1992) is public need volatility, which is transmitted via politicians in the form of pressures on public services to change direction and priorities. This may mean that public services organizations have a basic decision to make about how they will respond to public need volatility and political pressures. Will they seek to resist the political requirement to adapt and innovate, or will they seek to match and comply with this requirement – or even exceed public and political expectations for innovation to keep up with changing public needs and political pressures? To the extent that the activities of public services organizations lag behind the expectations of the public and politicians there is what might be termed a 'legitimacy gap' (Heath 1997). The bigger the gap, the bigger the strategic challenge for the public services. An individual organization that chooses to act to close this gap is aiming to become more responsive to the public and politicians.

Case studies by Wechsler and Backoff (1986) bear out the overall idea in this contention about the need to respond to public and political pressures. They describe four strategic alternatives: protective, developmental, political and transformational. The protective strategy, in the face of a threatening environment, seeks to develop good relationships with political oversight bodies, lowers the organization's public profile and tightens up internal control. (This seems to be a combination of trying to win powerful political friends, keeping your head down, and avoiding doing anything which will give politicians an excuse to cut budgets.) The developmental strategy might be defined as making changes in the organization's resources and capabilities, with management taking pains to appear capable and energetic. (To the extent that such a strategy develops capability and resources without fundamental changes in services and activities, we might say that this strategy makes a 'show' of being innovative.) The political strategy involves making changes in services and activities which reflects shifts of power within civil society, with resources being redeployed to reflect new realities. The transformational strategy is where the organization makes fundamental changes in line with external pressures. In other words, the protective strategy is aimed at maintaining the status quo despite the build-up of environmental turbulence and political pressures, the developmental strategy evidences a willingness to comply with political pressures, and the last two strategies involve significant change and innovation in response to the external developments.

Nutt and Backoff (1992), who, as we have noted, see environmental turbulence as linked to need volatility, set out a range of strategic altern-atives. They do, however, tend to favour an alternative which they call a mutualist strategy. Indeed, they tend to define a mutualist strategy in terms of the capacity to respond to volatile needs. This type of strategy involves developing a dialogue with collaborating parties – which has the effect of bringing about a move towards a shared vision – and then forming a con-sortium. Out of this might come various changes which are instrumental in the consortium addressing the emerging needs.

Nutt and Backoff also consider posture, accommodator and comprom-iser strategies, but see them as less effective than they could be in respond-ing to volatile and emergent needs. In the case of the posture strategy, organizations make statements about planned responses which fail to materialize. Nutt and Backoff define an accommodator strategy as involving a little more commitment to action than the posture strategy. The com-promiser strategy deals with external pressures by 'playing one constituency off against another'. This can be done by meeting the needs of the most important group or meeting the needs of only the most needy. (The posture strategy has some resemblance to the developmental strategy, and the compromiser strategy appears to be similar in some respects to the polit-ical strategy. In fact, the two typologies of strategic alternatives by Wechsler and Backoff and by Nutt and Backoff are quite similar.)

Fiscal stress

Another view of the most critical feature of external conditions is that there is pressure which leads to fiscal stress within the public sector (see Chapter 1). This idea has cropped up in a number of places, but nowhere is it argued so tenaciously as in Osborne and Gaebler (1992). Essentially, they argue that fiscal stress requires entrepreneurial organization rather than bureaucratic organization. It can be argued that there are two broad strategic themes within entrepreneurial government (which Osborne and Gaebler present as complementary components): the use of competition and the adoption of a community enabling role. The latter might be termed a governance strategy. This reading of Osborne and Gaebler's work pro-duces a three-fold typology of strategy:

1 A bureaucratic strategy: in the face of emergent needs, expand public employment, and design and supply new services.
2 A competition strategy: respond to fiscal crisis by using the market mechanism to revitalize the public services, cut costs, increase quality and get the public's needs met more effectively.
3 A governance strategy: respond to fiscal crisis by catalysing changes and mobilizing private as well as public resources to address community problems and needs.

A typology

Perhaps we can combine the ideas of Nutt and Backoff (1992) and Osborne and Gaebler (1992) to suggest that the types of strategy can be classified in terms of the political pressures created by need volatility and in terms of the political pressures created by fiscal stress. Figure 3.1 presents this idea and suggests a fit between the two types of pressure and each type of strategy. This set of options and contingencies is put forward hypothetically, and doubts about the validity of the fiscal stress factor (expressed in Chapter 1) should be kept in mind here.

It is important to point out one hidden assumption of this approach to the selection of strategy. This is the assumption that strategy consists of fitting an organization to its (political) environment. This makes it seem that there is a one-to-one relationship between an organization's activities and its environment. Two reasons exist for doubting this. First, there is evidence to suggest that different organizational patterns may be equally

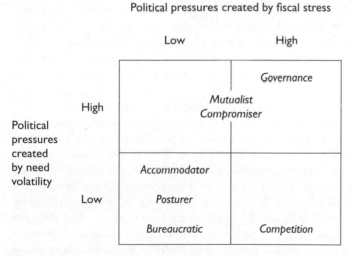

Figure 3.1 Types of public services strategy

viable in an individual industry (Nath and Sudharshan 1994). Second, the fact that industries are dynamic and evolve suggests that any successful pattern is only successful for a limited period of time. In other words, organizations that are innovative and successful in the long term may initially appear to have an incoherent pattern and thus be mistakenly perceived to be wrongly adapted to their environment. This idea has been expressed by Nath and Sudharshan (1994), who, paradoxically, were intent on measuring strategy coherence. Their study was a cross-sectional investigation of hospitals (see Chapter 4), and they warned: 'A longitudinal examination of coherent and non-coherent firms might be illuminating in identifying the evolution of industries as certain firms spin-off in apparently non-coherent patterns which might be innovative responses to the environment (for example) and thus long-term success stories' (p. 59).

Using strategic issues

Selecting a strategy from a list does not seem on the surface to be a very creative approach to strategy formulation. Even if creativity is required in applying a selected strategy to a specific situation, the whole process can seem a bit mechanistic. There is an influential view of strategic management in the public services which tends to assume that issue management and strategic change need to be creative and to result in innovation (Eadie 1983; Nutt and Backoff 1992; Bryson 1995).

If an organization does approach strategy formulation through issue management, then strategic issues need to be identified. Also, the relationships between issues need to be worked out. This is important in deciding on possible action to address the issues. For example, if one issue causes another, then action to address the first issue will also have beneficial consequences for the other, but not vice versa.

Nutt and Backoff (1992), who argue for the need to explore the relations between strategic issues, suggest that a technique called interpretive structural modelling can be used to do this. This involves taking each issue in turn and looking to see if it is linked to any of the other issues, as in a cause and effect relationship. Evidence confirming that the cause-effect linkages exist should be sought. When all combinations of issues have been considered, the cause-effect linkages which have been identified are then considered. If the interpretive structural modelling is done by a strategic management group, then the probability of identified linkages may be decided through voting. The linkages in which more people believe are regarded as more probable, whereas those which have been nominated by just one or two people may be regarded as more uncertain. The linkages may be rated in terms of the importance of the causal issue in explaining the dependent issue. Finally, it can be very helpful to diagram the cause and effect relations which emerge from the modelling.

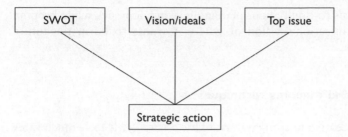

Figure 3.2 Formulating ideas for action

There is contradictory advice on which issues require priority action. The management may be advised to select as a high priority for action that issue which precedes or causes other issues (Nutt and Backoff 1992). Dealing with this issue has a beneficial consequence for all the other issues it produces. If the most serious issue is not dealt with, leadership challenges may also intrude on the process of managing lesser issues. On the other hand, it has been said that it may be best to start with a less important issue in order that those who are involved may gain experience in working together and handling conflict (Bryson 1995).

Having selected an issue which will be addressed, how can possible actions be identified? Bryson (1995) recommends that strategic decision makers think both about alternatives for addressing the issue and the barriers to realizing a solution. They should then generate proposals to pursue the alternatives and overcome the barriers. Next, he advises decision makers to think about actions, assuming existing staff and job descriptions – that might be taken over the next year or two to implement the proposals. Finally, he thinks that decision makers ought to decide on steps, and who will be responsible for the steps, so that the proposals can be implemented over the next six months. As a variation on this, Bryson says that a strategic planning team might decide on alternatives and barriers, and then involve others (individuals, committees and task forces) in formulating proposals, actions and steps.

Bryson's (1995) process is interesting in that it includes a step in which decision makers should think about the barriers to realizing alternatives. This could to some degree ensure that the tension within a strategic issue is kept in mind, providing we assume that the barriers are equivalent to forces which stop the issue being easily handled.

Nutt and Backoff (1992) have a different method for producing ideas for action. They suggest that strategic management groups think about the organization's ideals and then directly suggest actions to manage the issue. This is done by thinking of an action which builds on strengths, overcomes weaknesses, exploits opportunities or blocks or blunts a threat. An action which manages an issue by doing all these things is considered to be especially interesting (see Figure 3.2). In other words, they advise using the SWOT analysis to think about managing strategic issues while keeping in mind the organization's vision of where it wants to be in the future (see Chapter 2).

Brainstorming and mapping techniques

Choosing to be creative in strategy formulation is risky. It feels much safer to consider the selection of a strategy from a standard set of strategy options and simply to evaluate each in turn using some predetermined criteria. To opt instead for a creative, problem-solving approach means looking for some imaginative leaps from issues to ideas for strategic actions. This is hard. Bryson (1995: 137) reports that 'failure in the middle' of the process – failures of imagination between issues and ideas for strategies – occur in many cases. However, there are approaches and techniques which can assist decision makers to be creative.

In the public services, approaches to strategy formulation using groups of people in workshops and participative processes are often favoured. Groups of politicians, managers, professionals and other stakeholders are brought together, face to face, to work on producing a strategy. Facilitators on such occasions have often encouraged these groups to use brainstorming to pool their ideas and experience.

Brainstorming

The general concept of brainstorming is to encourage members of a group to generate ideas by suspending the usual habit of responding to ideas with critical (especially negative) judgements. The absence of any evaluation is considered to be helpful in maximizing the number of ideas volunteered which, in turn, boosts the prospects of creativity.

The silent reflective technique, the nominal group technique and 'cued brainwriting' are further techniques which are useful in generating new ideas. These techniques have the advantages of generating large numbers of ideas very quickly and enabling quieter and less assertive group members to make a contribution to the process.

The silent reflective technique is where members of a group have a period of silent reflection in which they individually think of ideas in response to specially formulated questions (e.g. what are the issues we should be tackling?). The group may be asked to engage in silent reflection, making notes as they think of ideas, and then an open group discussion is held. As Nutt and Backoff (1992) point out, open discussion used by itself has various weaknesses which silent reflection does not. When someone presents an idea in an open discussion they can quickly become publicly committed to it even though they have not had a chance to evaluate it properly. Paradoxically, another problem in open discussion is that listeners tend to rush in with evaluations, which discourages others from taking risks by saying whatever comes into their mind. Thus the silent reflective technique is said to produce a more open-minded discussion and to lower barriers to creativity.

The nominal group technique, as described by Nutt and Backoff (1992), starts off with group members working silently, but face to face, on answering a set of questions. They write down as many ideas in answer to these questions as possible. Then the group members are asked to take turns in presenting their ideas and explaining them to other members of the group. Each idea is discussed and then the group is asked to vote on the ideas to arrive at a group consensus.

Cued brainwriting can be done by sitting group members at a table on which there are several sheets of paper. Each of these sheets may have a question at the top. The procedure is very simple. Members of the group take a sheet, silently read it and write their ideas on the sheet. When they have finished, they take another sheet and repeat the process. This continues for a period of time or until no more ideas are being produced. In this process the members of the group are able to read other people's ideas, which can suggest yet further ideas.

Oval mapping technique

The oval mapping technique outlined by Bryson (1995) is a process for mapping relationships between ideas. It can be used for a variety of decision making tasks and can easily be modified to suit different preferences. For example, members of a strategic management group could be asked to generate ideas in response to the following three questions:

- What should we be concerned about over the next five years?
- Why should these concerns be addressed?
- How can these concerns be addressed?

These questions, in effect, elicit ideas about strategic issues, strategic goals and the strategic actions which might be used to manage the issues. Silent reflective techniques can be used to generate a large number of ideas in a comparatively short period of time. If these ideas are recorded using oval cards or post-it notes and placed on wall charts, then it is possible to group similar ideas into a cluster ('snowballing'), labelling them in terms of the common underlying idea, and then linking the clusters by drawing arrows to show how actions can address issues, and how the management of issues can achieve important strategic goals. The processes of clustering ideas, labelling them and drawing linkages can be done by the group with the help of a facilitator or can be done by the group themselves silently taking it in turns to make the various decisions.

This type of mapping process is easily used for groups of up to 16 people (and even more, especially if the nominal group technique is used to generate the ideas). The required materials are easily available and relatively inexpensive. The whole experience can be enjoyable and very creative.

Mapping software

Eden (1990) has suggested that mapping which produces models with more than 70 concepts is usefully handled using computer software. One well-known software package for this purpose is Decision Explorer, which uses a Windows environment. It was originally developed to support cognitive mapping and can be used for strategy development, stakeholder analysis scenario building, competitor analysis and tracking the implementation of plans.

Carrying out a strategic appraisal

We know relatively little about how strategic leaders and managers in the public services actually appraise strategic proposals, although we do know that it is very rare for the public, employees or other stakeholders to have a direct involvement in formal strategic appraisal. We do not know what criteria are normally used during a strategic appraisal, although, based on anecdotal evidence, the main concern during discussions of strategic altern-atives seems to be with the resultant organizational structure rather than with the service and public needs! We do not know much about the techniques normally used, although a recent survey suggested that cost-benefit analysis is widely used throughout UK local government (Flynn and Talbot 1996).

In one of the rare empirical studies of the appraisal process, Bryson and Roering (1988) found that planning teams in eight government units in Minnesota evaluated statements, documents and recommendations using an informal set of criteria. It appears that planning teams tended to focus on three types of question, asking of a proposal: (a) is it technically work-able; (b) will stakeholders support it; and (c) can it be defended morally, ethically and legally?

Bryson and Roering's research suggests that the evaluation of strategic proposals in these eight government units was not a mechanistic process: 'The frame of reference would shift back and forth among criteria until fin-ally the participants developed a proposal that satisfied all criteria . . . Stra-tegic planning became a kind of planning by argumentation' (1988: 109).

Perhaps evaluation is more elaborate and more formal in public services which have been through the strategic planning cycle several times. Hennepin County in the USA used a large number of criteria to evaluate alternative strategies. According to Bryson (1995) their criteria were:

- acceptability to key decision makers, stakeholders and opinion leaders;
- acceptance by the general public;
- client or user impact;
- relevance to the issue;
- consistency with mission, values, philosophy and culture;
- coordination or integration with other strategies, programmes and activities;
- technical feasibility;
- cost and financing;
- cost effectiveness;
- long-term impact;
- risk assessment;
- staff requirements;
- flexibility or adaptability;
- timing;
- facility requirements;
- training requirements;
- other appropriate criteria.

It is possible to group the majority of these criteria into three logically clustered sets. One cluster might be called 'administrative criteria'. This would include criteria such as: cost and financing; cost effectiveness; staff requirements, technical feasibility, coordination or integration with other strategies, programmes and activities; and facility and training requirements. Such criteria might be suitable when managers are mainly applying strategic thinking to ensure the successful implementation of policy decisions made by the politicians. Another cluster might be called 'results-oriented criteria' and would include: consistency with mission, values, philosophy and culture; client or user impact; and flexibility or adaptability. These types of criteria are very relevant to situations where strategic planning has been brought in at the behest of politicians who want to be reassured that public services are accountable, responsive and efficient. This is strategic planning of the results-oriented and mission-led kind. A third cluster – the 'acceptability criteria' – can be identified as including acceptability to key decision makers, stakeholders and opinion leaders, and acceptance by the general public. This third cluster might be logically associated with models of strategic management which place a lot of emphasis on partnership-based models of planning and governance (see Table 3.1). The list represents a very comprehensive view of all the considerations which might be used to evaluate alternative strategic options.

The rationale for carrying out a formal evaluation of strategic alternatives is obviously to make sure that the 'best' option is selected. What is 'best' depends partly on the dominant meaning attached by a particular public services organization to its strategic planning and management. If it

Table 3.2 Example of a formal evaluation

	Strategy A	Strategy B
1 Acceptability to key stakeholders (score 0–10)	7	5
2 Acceptance by the general public (score 0–10)	7	5
3 User benefits (score 0–20)	10	15
4 Consistency with mission (score 0–10)	7	3
5 Technical feasibility (score 0–10)	2	5
6 Cost and financing (score 0–20)	10	5
7 Cost effectiveness (score 0–10)	5	5
8 Timeliness (score 0–10)	3	7
Total (0–100)	44	50

quality. These have reflected politicians' views of the qualities needed for an acceptable standard of public services, with the implication being that current levels of efficiency and quality were not acceptable to the public which had elected politicians and given them a mandate to streamline the public services.

The mechanics of a formal evaluation are relatively straightforward. A number of criteria are selected as being especially relevant to the choice of strategy, decisions are made about their relative importance, and each criterion then becomes a factor in a points system framework. Each factor is worth a predetermined number of points depending on its importance weighting. The likely performance of each strategy is assessed in terms of each factor and an appropriate proportion of the maximum possible number of points awarded, with a maximum score denoting a likely performance which is highly satisfactory and a score of zero meaning that the likely performance of the strategy is totally unsatisfactory in this respect. This is then aggregated for all factors and the totals for the different strategic alternatives are compared to see which amassed the largest number of points. The bigger the total, the better.

For example, two alternative strategies may be compared using the criteria shown in Table 3.2. In this example, Strategy B would be evaluated more highly. However, it would be a mistake to carry out this evaluation in a mechanical way. As Duncan et al. (1995: 262) point out about the various methods for evaluating strategic alternatives: 'Although the evaluation methods fine-tune the manager's perspective and organize thinking, ultimately, the manager must make the decision . . . the evaluation methods cannot be used to obtain "answers", but rather to gain perspective and insight'. The points system should be used to encourage a thorough and objective discussion of the strategic options, with the participants supporting their evaluations with evidence and arguments wherever possible.

Cost-benefit analysis

The calculation of a rough cost-benefit ratio using quantifiable factors is relatively straightforward in the case of an investment designed to improve efficiency by introducing, say, new equipment or new information technology (IT) systems. It does, however, require some previous experience of similar changes so that various estimates can be made.

Consider the case, for example, of an investment under consideration because it will reduce costs. Based on prior experience of this kind of investment it might be reckoned that there will be staff savings of a certain percentage and this can be used to find a figure for the annual savings in money terms. The benefit in terms of reduced costs over, say, a five-year period can then be determined, bearing in mind that the savings may not materialize until the new equipment or IT systems are effectively implemented, which may take a year or more. The costs will include the one-off investment cost and annual operating costs, and these may also be calculated over five years, again relying on experience to estimate the operating costs. Dividing the benefits over five years by the costs over five years produces a cost-benefit ratio. Such a rough calculation may be used to screen out financially undesirable strategic options.

However, such rough cost-benefit analyses are not always that useful. For example, public services organizations often make changes which clearly increase their costs but improve their services, improve accessibility to services or improve the responsiveness of providers to the public. That is, the non-financial benefits of such changes are valued above the increased financial costs.

Benefits may not immediately improve the financial position of a public services organization but might contribute to the achievement of a state of affairs in which the financial position is more stable or satisfactory. For example, some strategic actions may be aimed at improving the public image of the organization, customer service, public information and public consultation. Others may be aimed at changing public attitudes about when and how to access public services, or at getting others (individuals, families, other public organizations, private sector organizations and voluntary sector organizations) to act differently or to contribute to the solution of community problems. Strategic action which ultimately encourages the public to support increased funding of a public service organization, or reduces the public demand for its services, or generates other providers to meet the public need, implies a beneficial financial impact.

If cost-benefit analysis is to be extended to cover non-financial consequences then either the linkage to a long-term financial consequence has to be assumed, or account must be taken of the monetary implications of the strategic action for others. For example, an analysis of a proposal to spend money on an advertising campaign to stimulate volunteering in the community care field might need to estimate the additional cost that the public service organization would have incurred if more volunteers had not been encouraged. And a proposal to create a strategic forum to discuss a campaign to promote the town centre as a shopping venue might eventually produce increases in turnover for retailers, which are quantifiable on the basis of estimates from similar initiatives elsewhere.

Evaluation using stakeholder criteria

Different stakeholders evaluate the performance of an organization differently (Thomas and Palfrey 1996) and will value differently the criteria for the appraisal of possible strategic actions. There is usually a wide range of stakeholders who will be affected by the outcomes of a strategic appraisal. These include: elected politicians, senior managers, operational managers, employees, taxpayers, service users, other public organizations with overlapping legislative mandates, the business community and so on.

The activities of public services organizations are carried out under legislative mandates. Politicians will be concerned that their legal intent is being respected during the strategic appraisal process. The legislative mandates of several public agencies will often overlap. Consequently, any strategic changes which follow from a strategic appraisal can have consequences for other public agencies. Take, for example, the work of health and social services; these are thought to require coordination in the field of community care. An organization in the health services sector might change its activities in relation to community care in a way which could be of concern to the corresponding social services organization.

Public services are carried out to meet public needs. The public cannot always be regarded as having a homogeneous set of needs. Some members of the public may pay taxes which fund the public service in question but not be among the section of the public which uses the service. Then, the members of the public who are service users may form a number of more or less distinct groupings on the basis of their needs. So, we should not automatically assume the existence of a single standard need amongst service users; there is likely to be a diverse set of needs.

Public services are provided by 'producers' who also have a set of interests. A strategic appraisal may have big implications for the structure of the organization, the number and type of skills required, pay and promotion opportunities, job security, etc. The outcomes of strategic appraisal will obviously be of some interest to those who lead or work in the public service organization.

In consequence, appraisal of strategy may have to deal with the possibility that a strategy appears very satisfactory to one group of stakeholders and very unsatisfactory to another group. Such a skewness in potential outcomes needs to be identified and taken into account when appraising strategic options.

One way of ensuring problems of skewness are considered is to include criteria for each of the most important stakeholder groups and to weight them so that they clearly influence the overall score in any points system used for evaluation. On this basis, the interests of taxpayers, politicians, service users, managers and employees may be taken into account explicitly. Differences of interest and power cannot be abolished, but strategic decision makers can be more explicit about the criteria being used and how they are balanced and weighted (Thomas and Palfrey 1996). If skewness is discovered, then the strategic leaders and managers must decide whether this has to be accepted as inevitable in the circumstances, or whether more work needs to be to done to find strategies which produce more balanced outcomes (i.e. strategies which do not entail skewness).

If this type of problem is not sufficiently considered at the evaluation stage, then it may have to be faced again at the implementation stage, when the feasibility of the strategy is examined in order to determine how key stakeholder groups should be managed to ensure successful implementation. It may be necessary, as a part of stakeholder management, to negotiate changes in the strategy so that a modified strategy can be implemented with extra support won by the changes in the strategy.

It is little mentioned, but the decision on *who* will take part in discussions and decisions regarding the evaluation of alternatives is very important, and thus the decisions on the design and membership of the group, committee or forum responsible for evaluation should not be taken lightly. If the organization needs continuity with its current activities and organization, then the design and membership decisions will need to reflect who has the biggest stake in the current status quo. If major innovations are urgently required for the organization to survive and be successful, then the design and membership decisions should ensure that new arenas are used which involve a critical mass of people likely to favour changes in the status quo. This is, in effect, a matter of balancing the composition of strategic evaluation forums in terms of the representation of stakeholder groups to either maintain existing organizational results or to bring about changes in the results.

Evaluating trade-offs and ensuring deeper appraisals

The evaluation process may be enriched, and deeper thought and debate may be promoted, by use of matrices. For example, two strategies may be placed on a matrix composed of two axes: 'cost and financing' and 'user benefits'

Table 3.3 Evaluating trade-offs

User benefits	Cost and financing		
	Low	Medium	High
Low			
Medium		Strategy A	
High	Strategy B		

Table 3.4 An acceptability-benefits matrix

User benefits	Acceptability to key stakeholders		
	Low	Medium	High
Low			
Medium			Strategy A
High		Strategy B	

(see Table 3.3). (Note that a high score means the strategy performs well in terms of costs and financing, not that the costs and financing are high.)

Piggot (1996) briefly noted the use of a matrix to evaluate plans within the UK's NHS. She suggested a matrix using an axis for 'consistency with the organization's mission' and an axis for 'feasibility' (1996: 35). Such matrices could be seen as enabling strategic management teams to discuss trade-offs in terms of the various strategic alternatives under consideration. For example, should an organization choose a strategy which looks as though it will perform moderately well on two criteria, or should it choose a strategy which performs very well in one respect but poorly on another criteria? The matrix can be used to trigger such a question and lead to a discussion of which is the best overall combination.

Another potentially interesting matrix to enrich discussion and consideration of strategic alternatives would be one which has the two axes 'acceptability to key stakeholders' and 'user benefits' (see Table 3.4). This matrix is consistent with a desire to have a results-oriented approach which is pragmatically focused on mobilizing stakeholders to support change.

A matrix can help to sustain a longer and more thorough discussion of the relative merits of alternatives if used in the right way. Arguably, matrices work well because they use a spatial format for presentation of the relative merits of alternative strategic actions and because they manage somehow to evoke a more intelligent and 'scientific' frame of mind.

Risk analysis

Risk analysis is frequently used as a strategic planning technique in UK local government (Flynn and Talbot 1996). It is tempting to see the use of this technique as suitable for a technocratic, top-down planning system, in which major projects are planned and the planners wish to take account of possible obstructions or threats to the swift implementation of the project. However, it is, in principle, useful for partnership-based strategic planning by a coalition of stakeholders who need to agree a strategy in the light of an open discussion of, and clear appreciation of, possible dangers.

The approach to risk analysis presented here is just one of several approaches which can be used within strategic management. It is based on an approach suggested by Hussey (1994) and is considered here in its stand-alone form.

The first step is to decide on a list of environmental and organizational factors (trends, events or discontinuities) which might affect the implementation of the strategic alternatives being considered. The list can be generated in various ways, but one approach is to carry out the risk analysis in a workshop involving managers at various levels of the organization. The list will obviously be quite specific to the organization in question and to the strategic alternative being considered.

The next step in the risk analysis is to rate each of the environmental and organizational factors in terms of their probability and impact on the strategy under consideration. Probability could be rated from 0 to 10, with 0 meaning that the trend, event or discontinuity is not going to occur, 5 being a 50 per cent probability, and 10 meaning that it is certain to occur. The impact on the strategy can also be rated from 0 to 10, with 0 meaning that there is no impact likely, 5 meaning that there will be an impact of some importance, and 10 meaning that the impact will be very strong. The product of the rating of probability and impact yields a score of the risk from each of the factors considered.

A possible list of factors is shown in Table 3.5, which also shows the impact, probability and risk columns. One list is used for all the strategic alternatives because the scoring system used allows factors to be rated as having probabilities and impacts of zero.

The final optional step is to take 'total risk' and 'overall attractiveness' for a number of strategic alternatives and plot them against one another in a graphical analysis. It should be noted that the overall attractiveness scores may implicitly include some risk assessment (e.g. support of key stakeholders may make the strategy attractive and may, at the same time, mean a low risk of resistance at the implementation stage). If the risk scores and scores for the overall attractiveness of a strategy are banded, the strategies may be placed in a risk matrix such as that shown in Table 3.6 (see Hussey 1994).

Table 3.5 Risks: probability and impact

Environmental and organizational factors	Probability (score 0–10)	Impact (score 0–10)	Risk (probability * impact)
Sudden announcements of cuts	___	___	___
Key personnel leave	___	___	___
Changes in government policy	___	___	___
Key stakeholder may object/resist	___	___	___
Public outcry against the strategic alternative	___	___	___
Difficult to recruit new staff needed	___	___	___
Total score:			___

Table 3.6 Risk matrix

Risk score	Overall attractiveness of a strategy		
	Unattractive	Average	Attractive
High			
Medium			
Low			

   Drawing up such a risk matrix has a number of benefits. There is, potentially, the benefit of involving managers at various levels in thinking about potential dangers to the success of a strategy. A risk matrix provides another opportunity to deepen the appraisal process and to avoid over-hasty and ignorant strategic choices. It allows the trade-off between the overall attractiveness and riskiness to be explicitly considered, with the obvious implication that very risky strategic options should be rejected unless they have outstanding advantages in terms of their attractiveness, and it should lead to further discussion about how the dangers to the chosen strategy can be averted.

Appraisal of emergent strategies

Much of this chapter has presumed a traditional model of strategic management in which analysis precedes the identification of alternative courses of action, and equates the appraisal process with the selection of the most attractive option for implementation. Strategy may involve a one-off big decision in the form of a clear and distinct strategic choice, but it can also involve streams of decisions and actions which cumulatively add up to a major strategic change. Moreover, these streams may include both purposeful actions and emergent actions. For example, Frost-Kumpf *et al.* (1993) suggested that the Ohio Department of Mental Health, which underwent a fundamental strategic change in the 1980s, implemented more than 120 strategic actions in the period from April 1983 to December 1986. The researchers suggest that these actions were often emergent in nature.

With hindsight it is possible to find patterns in the strategic actions of a public service organization and to suggest that emergent actions are constituents of streams of strategic action which produce the overall strategic change. It is, however, by definition, implausible to think of many small emergent actions being subjected to the formal appraisal we have been considering in this chapter.

Does this mean that the public services organizations which have fostered an approach to strategic change which is marked by a profusion of streams of action, and by emergent action as well as purposeful action, must proceed to some degree haphazardly? How can appraisal take place under these conditions? No doubt the bigger and more purposeful decisions can still be formally evaluated in advance, but perhaps another answer is to create continuous collaborative evaluation through setting up forums which involve strategic leaders, front line staff, service users and other stakeholders. If information systems are also set up to support evaluation by these various groups, then the cumulative impact of streams of action can be identified and evaluated by the forum members. If such forums have an input into strategic planning, then the evaluation becomes the basis of strategic learning. All of this would need to take place within a fairly explicit vision of the future of the organization and a shared set of values. The success criteria used by the different groups of stakeholders would stand more chance of being shared by forum members if they have discussed and agreed the vision and values which define the strategic intent of the service.

Strategy evaluations at the end of implementation

Obviously, much strategic planning in the public services is done in the hope that improved services will be the final result. However, the specific evaluation which occurs at the end of implementation depends in part on how strategy was implemented. If the implemented strategy has led to revised operational goals and budgets, and was implemented through operational planning, then evaluation could take the form of evaluating performance using performance indicators and comparing this with performance goals set in the context of the general strategic goals. On the other hand, if strategy has been implemented through project planning and

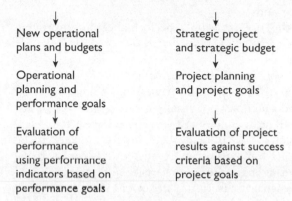

New strategy

New operational plans and budgets	Strategic project and strategic budget
Operational planning and performance goals	Project planning and project goals
Evaluation of performance using performance indicators based on performance goals	Evaluation of project results against success criteria based on project goals

Figure 3.3 Evaluation at the end of implementation

management, the goals of the project should have been clarified at the outset, and these will provide the basis for defining the success criteria for evaluation purposes. Then it is a matter of comparing the project results and the success criteria (see Figure 3.3).

The preceding remarks suggest that the complete answer to evaluation rests on a systematic approach so that goals, performance targets and success criteria are set and then performance is evaluated. However, it also worth stressing the need for a consideration of the possible performance skewness that even a systematic approach may fail to recognize. In the same way that private sector firms may be criticized for short-termism and over-dependence on measuring financial results, so too may public services end up with measurements which suggest a good performance but which are biased in terms of the benefits produced for some of the stakeholders. So, it is a good idea to check out the plans for evaluation at the end of strategic implementation to see if there is any danger of performance skewness. (A similar point was made above about skewness and strategic appraisal.)

One approach which may be useful is the 'balanced score-card' method which was developed in the private sector but has been adapted and used in the public services. This approach involves identifying different perspectives and using them to identify one or more performance measures for each of them. Then the organization looks for good results in terms of each of the perspectives. For example, measures of performance for a public services organization could be based on four perspectives:

- efficiency perspective: producing services at lowest possible cost;
- effectiveness perspective: the degree to which the organization's activities are meeting public needs as defined by legislative mandates;

- user perspective: the value of the organization's performance as perceived by the service user; and
- innovation perspective: the organization's performance in improving services and its service delivery processes.

If these four perspectives were covered in the evaluation of performance at the end of implementation, then it could be argued that a good score on all four would be a balanced outcome, potentially creating satisfaction for all key stakeholders. Other things being equal, we would expect taxpayers to be relatively pleased because cost is being kept low; politicians to be satisfied because their legislative intentions are being realized; users to be pleased because they are getting a good quality service; and managers and employees to be pleased because their future prospects will be better if the organization is successful. Of course, under real conditions, the link between these results and the satisfaction of the stakeholders may not be as simple as this suggests.

The question of who does the evaluation is an important one in public services organizations. In particular, where there are politicians carrying out executive management functions, how involved in the detail of evaluation should they be? Should it be left entirely to the managers of the organization? In recent years there has been some recognition of the benefit of strategic committees composed of both elected politicians and managers. Working closely together in strategic forums can help to break down prejudices which cause friction between the two groups. Elected representatives worry that managers may pursue their own strategic agendas rather than use strategy to implement the policies and priorities of the politicians. The managers in turn may doubt the capacity of elected politicians to think and act strategically (Richards 1993). If both are involved in evaluation there is a chance that the evidence of how strategies have actually worked out will help both to keep focused on the strategic challenges of the situation and develop shared perceptions of how to proceed. Certainly, if joint arrangements have been used to create new strategies, it seems sensible that they should also be used to evaluate the results of the implementation of those strategies.

If the evaluation at the end of strategy implementation finds that the results have not met the expectations of the evaluators, then there needs to be an effort to identify the causes of failure. Various problems may be responsible for poor results (Bryson 1995). For example, insufficient resources may have been mobilized to implement a strategy; there may be unanticipated interactions between policies and strategies producing undesirable effects; and the strategy may have been made obsolete or inappropriate by the emergence of new problems. Obviously, the reasons need to be clearly identified so that the organization can decide what now needs to be done. Even if these kinds of failure have not occurred, the time for a new strategy may have come. Politicians may have new priorities and want the organization to take new directions in strategic terms.

Conclusions

It has been hypothesized that types of strategy can be classified in terms of the political pressures created by need volatility and in terms of the political pressures created by fiscal stress. There may then be an assumption that there is a fit between the pressures and an appropriate type of strategy. Selecting a generic strategic type is then a matter of understanding the contingencies which apply. This can become quite a mechanical way of find ing strategic solutions. The validity of fiscal stress as a contingent factor may also be questioned.

Influential American writers have championed strategic planning processes which strive for creativity. This may be sought by thinking about the barriers to realizing alternatives, or looking for solutions in the intersection between issues, SWOTs and the organization's vision of where it wants to be in the future. The trend towards stressing creativity in strategic thinking for public services no doubt explains the popularity of techniques based on the idea of brainstorming. The clear assumption is that there is a lack of ideas and too much pessimism. Additional assumptions are that strategy processes are needed which allow a lot of work to be done quickly, and that there is a need to boost participation in strategic thinking by enabling quieter and less assertive people to contribute their judgements. Various techniques have been reviewed including: the silent reflective technique, the nominal group technique, cued brainwriting, and the oval mapping technique.

In this chapter we have also reviewed systematic approaches to strategic appraisal. The best strategic option may be seen as offering a combination of technical feasibility, clear connections with the mission and strategic goals of the organization, and acceptability to all those parties who have to be kept on board during the strategy process. This best option would satisfy requirements for a cost effective use of resources, benefits for clients and users and the maintenance of an organizational capacity for flexibility and adaptability.

Of course, there is a danger that the overall tone of this chapter, with its discussion of an appraisal framework and the use of analysis, leads to the idea that selecting a strategy can be done completely dispassionately. Strategic changes have to confront problems of limited knowledge and limited control, and these can make it difficult to see appraisal as a purely decision making calculus. These limits are discussed in Chapter 4, but here we simply note that selecting a strategy must inevitably contain an element of subjective judgement in assessing the position of these limits. This subjective element calls for a quality of what may be described as strategic leadership. This has come to be seen in recent years as involving intellectual foresight about the kinds of strategic directions that should be pursued and the use of challenges to frame the selection of courses of action. The importance of strategic leadership will be further discussed in Chapter 5.

four

Systems and implementation

Key learning objectives

After reading this chapter you should be able to:

1 Understand some of the difficulties of implementing strategic plans.
2 Define some of the issues of budgeting which can create barriers to implementing strategies.
3 Outline some of the methods and techniques which may be used to facilitate the implementation of strategies.

Introduction

This chapter begins to get to grips with strategic management. It starts to leave behind the rather abstract and free-floating conception of a strategic planning process as outlined in Chapters 2 and 3. There, as in many accounts of strategic planning, it is easy to see strategy as the simplest thing going. Each stage of the planning process – analysis, choice and implementation, for example – is logical. They are sequential. So, strategic analysis turns into strategic choice, only to be followed by strategic choice turning into strategic implementation. It all seems obvious – and such a simple and unresisting process.

Only when we begin to discuss who in practice analyses, who takes decisions, and who acts – only, in other words, when the process of planning is seen realistically and concretely – do some of the difficulties become apparent. For one thing, it is not the same person necessarily who analyses, decides and acts. Those who formulate strategies may not be the same as those who fix the budget allocations, and these two decision making processes may be difficult to unite. The problem then is one of ensuring unity of purpose and coordination among all those who need to be involved. Only when we discuss strategic planning in practice does it become clear how real situations may resist the simple logic of the strategic planning process. For example, it may be obvious to the specialists who have examined the new legal requirements and carried out benchmarking that doing more with less is a real strategic issue. But to a line manager asked to implement new performance goals and targets, the logic may be far from obvious. To a member of a strategic management group it may seem a really good idea for the organization to act in partnership to address a neglected community need, but a line manager expected to achieve results by mobilizing private sector or voluntary sector resources may find nobody willing to take on the mantle of partner or willing to contribute real resources to a cooperative venture. And how is all this time consuming work of creating and sustaining partnership arrangements to be fitted in alongside all the other demands on the manager's time and energy? Now, strategy making and implementation appears a challenging and difficult activity.

Many of the practicalities of developing strategic changes are more easily appreciated with the benefit of a good understanding of models of strategic planning systems. These are models of how strategic planning processes are embedded within organizations, and, when presented in detail, how planning processes are integrated (or not) into budget allocation processes and functional strategies. This chapter will look at all these matters.

Another objective of this chapter is to introduce the important idea that pilots and projects may be used to implement strategies. We then discuss the primary features of project management to accomplish the implementation of strategic projects. First, however, we look at the implementation challenge in a little more detail.

The implementation challenge

The implementation of strategy can be seen as getting the organization to perform in the way that a new strategy requires. In the modern public services, with its higher profile management, implementing a strategic change is often seen as involving a comprehensive change, meaning not only changes in the services but also changes in organizational systems. In recent years this has meant the introduction of new management structures, performance management systems, performance measurement, information systems and training. This has been backed up by intensive efforts at management development, meaning selecting and retaining the right people for managerial responsibility and providing training and development opportunities.

One issue that has been behind attempts to implement comprehensive change is the concern that changes in services will not be maintained unless the organization can change the behaviour and attitudes of professional and other employees. The perceived solution is to install these organizational systems (especially information systems, performance management systems and training) so that management can check and ensure that services will be delivered to the quality standards expected, and so match performance targets.

In public services organizations there is often a concern that strategic management will fail at the implementation stage. Experienced chief executives will warn that strategy is all about implementation. It is relatively easy for top managers to talk and write convincingly about their organization's new strategy. Even in these confusing and complex times, many senior managers are capable of the intellectual work needed to produce strategic documents which analyse strategic situations and identify sensible strategic actions. They are also well capable of putting the case for the strategic actions over to staff and communicating it to all concerned. But the problem arises with the need to move from this stage to the implementation stage.

Implementation is very hard work, requiring persistence, attention to detail and resilience to keep going in the face of setbacks. A recent survey of 11 national libraries (see Box 4.1) confirmed managerial anecdotes that implementation is the hardest part of strategic management, and it pinpointed difficulties particularly in respect of changing budget priorities, developing skills, changing the culture, unifying goals and aligning operational processes, actions, information and decisions.

To sum up, in recent years it has been increasingly recognized that implementation of strategy is a severe challenge to strategic leaders and managers in public services. In order to underpin major changes in services, there have been attempts to create the right organizational infrastructure. This has been aimed in part at ensuring that general strategic ideas are translated into very specific operational terms. This has amounted in many cases to an attempt to create a new public service ethos, incorporating a performance culture.

Strategic planning systems

Strategic analysis and strategic planning processes take place in organizations. There is, therefore, a question about how analysis and planning processes are 'folded into' organizations' authority levels, roles, routines and procedures.

We have already made use of the study by Chalmers (1997) to suggest the importance of the implementation challenge. This same study also illustrates how strategic planning in the public services these days is the job of managers rather than specialist planners, and how responsibilities for

---

Box 4.1 Strategic management in 11 national libraries

Chalmers (1997) reported the results of a questionnaire survey of the national libraries of Australia, Britain, Canada, France, Germany, Ireland, New Zealand, Malaysia, The Netherlands, Singapore, and the USA. One part of the questionnaire dealt with key aspects of strategic management and asked respondents to rate their importance to the success of strategic management in their library, and the respondents' satisfaction with their library's achievement of (or progress on) each aspect.

In several respects the libraries appeared to be doing well. Thus, a written mission statement was considered by many to be important, and all but one of the libraries were reported to be satisfactory in this respect. Many considered the identification of clients, consumers or service users to be important, and many considered the identification of external stakeholders to be important. A majority of respondents rated their libraries as having a satisfactory level of achievement in identifying both of these.

There appeared to be several unsatisfactory areas, where gaps between ratings of importance and ratings of satisfactory levels of achievement were identified. First, all but 2 of the 11 respondents considered that budget priorities and strategic priorities should match, but not one respondent reported that their library was satisfactory in this respect. A second example was in respect of making changes in the competencies of staff and managers if required for the implementation of a strategy. A majority of the respondents (7 out of 11) rated this as being important for strategic management to succeed in their library. Again, not one of the 11 respondents reported a satisfactory level of achievement by their library in this respect. Gaps between importance and achievement also appeared in relation to the integration of strategy and the library's culture, and in relation to the unification of goals and the alignment of processes, actions, information and decisions to support the goals.

The overall conclusion seems to be that the thinking and analytical parts of strategic management (mission statements, identifying beneficiaries and stakeholders) were relatively easy to do, but that implementation was more difficult.

---

planning, implementing and monitoring strategy are divided up between different levels of management (see Box 4.2).

A useful tool for thinking about how strategic planning is embedded in organizations is the concept of the strategic planning system. A simple conceptualization of a strategic planning system usefully refers to the location and number of strategic management roles and groups within the organization's structure. It also refers to the existence of strategic management procedures (e.g. monitoring) and the planning cycles which need to be established (e.g. periodic issue identification). It may be extended to include temporary structures and arrangements (e.g. task forces).

Bryson (1995) has suggested a number of different types of strategic planning system. He suggests that a strategic planning system is something

---

Box 4.2 Strategic planning systems in national libraries

The study by Chalmers (1997) of strategic management in 11 national libraries found that strategy was usually formulated at the corporate level.

Chief executives and the senior management teams typically did the strategic thinking for mission statements and strategic documents. The senior management team were often responsible for implementing and monitoring strategic documents. In only two of the national libraries were the planning department or a chief planner among those with a primary responsibility for strategic thinking, planning, etc.

If strategy formulation did occur at the business unit level, then the libraries' middle managers were typically responsible for strategic thinking at this level, for producing the business unit business plans and for implementing them.

Monitoring progress on implementing strategic documents occurred typically on an annual basis, but could be more frequent. Various actions had been taken to follow up the monitoring of plans. As well as fine-tuning and increasing support, these actions included making adjustments and changes to organizational structure, budget allocations, output measurements, time scales and task design.

---

which 'engages the organization in strategic management, not just strategic planning' (p. 40). The 'layered' or 'stacked units of management' planning system involves a framework established by top management and the formulation of strategic plans on a bottom-up basis. The strategic plans are reviewed by top management, and operating plans are then developed in accordance with them. This design of system obviously places great value on a consensus within the management structure at all levels and is geared to linking operating plans with strategic plans.

The 'strategic issues management system' is designed to ensure the management of specific strategic issues, but there is no attempt at tight integration of the strategies developed to address the issues. It is assumed that this is not necessary because different issues apply to different parts of the organization and are subject to different time pressures. We might call this a pluralistic system of strategic planning because it has multiple centres for the identification and solution of strategic issues.

Bryson (1995) also describes a 'contract model' and a 'goal model'. Both these apply to network organizations, either based on purchaser-provider structures or on partnership linkages developed for shared power settings. The contract model assumes that not only the purchaser but also the various provider organizations will be doing their own strategic planning. In other words, we have again a pluralistic system. In the case of the goal model the process is seeking to achieve joint strategic planning and voluntary commitment to a shared issue agenda. This is essentially an integrated design even if it lacks the powerful central control possible within a single organization.

Table 4.1 Strategic planning systems

Number of organizations covered	Nature of the system	
	Pluralistic	Integrated
One	'Strategic issues management system'	'Layered system'
More than one	'Contract model'	'Goal model'

Source: Based on Bryson (1995).

It appears from Bryson's description of these four strategic planning systems that they may be classified using two dimensions: the nature of the system (integrated or pluralistic) and the number of organizations covered (one or more than one) (see Table 4.1).

The best strategic planning systems seem to have to be able to provide: overall coherence to the results of the efforts of different levels of management; effective review of the plans that are generated; and involvement of managers at lower levels in the design of strategies and the planning of implementation (Bryson 1995: 148–9). However, in many public services organizations there is not a system of planning at different levels which is integrated (Flynn and Talbot 1996). Over time, if evidence from the USA can be generalized, we can expect more diffusion of planning downwards in public services organizations, and then perhaps more integrated planning systems will emerge (Berry and Wechsler 1995).

The design of a strategic planning system is important in part because it influences the precise nature of the forums and arenas in which strategic matters are considered and decided. Indeed, we can see the forums and arenas as being an aspect of the design of the strategic planning system. Changes in them, such that new participants are introduced, may mean that there will be greater willingness to perceive a need for change in organizational strategies. This suggests that it is possible to bias the degree of change perceived as needed by review groups simply by decisions made about the design of forums and arenas and their membership composition.

One issue which emerges distinctively in public services organizations is the question of how politicians and managers are involved in forums for strategic decision making. It has been said that policy making and policy implementation are becoming more interactive, and so some politicization of the managerial role may be inevitable, reflecting changes in the way in which government and society relate to each other (Kooiman and van Vliet 1993). Indeed, it may be this development which has caused a shift from public administration to public management. But, there is still a need for the managers' strategies to be consistent with the policies and laws of politicians. Managers must still ensure new strategic ideas are ratified by

Box 4.3 Kirklees Metropolitan District Council (UK)

Davies and Griffiths (1995) described decision making in Kirklees Council during the 1980s in very unflattering terms. Strategic matters did not receive sufficient attention, reports were 'clogging up' the council's committee system, the members of the management team were locked in interdepartmental battles and relations between elected politicians and the managers were very formal and, apparently, devoid of trust.

In 1989 the chief executive presented the elected councillors with proposals for the management of the council. He was critical of, among other things, the lack of strategic thinking and the failure to implement the policies of the elected councillors. He proposed that a new management structure be established, with an executive board led by him, and new functional units each led by a head of service. He also proposed a new policy board comprising senior elected councillors from the Labour Party and the executive board. The policy board was an informal body in the sense that it could not take decisions officially.

The head of the council's Policy and Performance Review Unit, in a personal appraisal of the changes, believed the policy board 'had become a more effective strategic forum' (Davies and Griffiths 1995: 171).

Nearly ten years later, Kirklees was reckoned to be a highly innovative and entrepreneurial local authority. Leadbetter and Goss (1998) have suggested that part of the explanation for the innovation and entrepreneurship is the way in which political leaders and senior managers have focused on strategic issues. The council's political leaders and executive management team have worked on strategic issues (e.g. environment and community safety) through the policy board where strategy ideas were developed. The executive managers then organized the cooperation of operational departments to deliver the strategy. This focus on strategic issues is praised by Leadbetter and Goss for renewing the council's sense of purpose by highlighting outcomes rather than outputs.

politicians before they move to strategic implementation. So, managers must ensure that the linkages between their strategy and the policy and priorities of politicians are clear (Leach *et al.* 1994). One way of doing this is to create strategic management forums involving both politicians and managers so that these linkages are discussed and made clear. In many UK local authorities, for example, politicians have informally moved towards an executive or cabinet type of system and these would seem to have the potential for acting as a strategic decision making group. In Chapter 1 the case of Kirklees Metropolitan District Council was outlined, noting its introduction of strategic management and consequent improvements in customer satisfaction and innovation. In Box 4.3 the case of Kirklees Council is again examined, but this time with the focus on how they brought politicians and managers together to work on strategy.

Perhaps each type of strategic planning system is prone to different problems. Nutt and Backoff (1993) have identifed problems where there are multiple centres of strategic issue management in what they termed an 'empowered organization'. This type of organization has strategy being created simultaneously at all levels by self-managed work groups and, according to Nutt and Backoff, this poses problems of integration and communication. (However, Bryson (1995), as we noted, considers there to be situations where tight integration is not needed.) The contract model system might also be prone to fragmentation if provider units are excessively maximizing their own interests and the purchaser organization has serious weaknesses in its ability to plan and manage strategically.

The different strategic planning systems might not only differ in the types of problems they suffer, but also in the types of functionality they offer. For example, a layered model may offer better support to performance planning or more long-term planning based on a strategic foresight process, whereas the issue management model may provide more suitable support to reactive and short-term strategic action in a turbulent and threatening environment. While it is possible that different types of strategic planning system perform differentially in terms of short-term performance (or issue management, or long-term organizational innovation) the fact is that this is an area where more research is needed. We are beginning to be able to describe public services' strategic planning systems, but we are not yet able to describe confidently their consequences.

If there are linkages between types of planning process and types of strategic planning system, then as organizations pass through different phases, requiring different types of strategic management and planning, they may need to change their strategic planning systems, or they may need a more complex strategic planning system which accommodates elements of different types of strategic management. Again, this must be largely a matter of conjecture at the present time, since we lack the research findings to be more definite.

Budget setting and operational planning

The extensive writing on programme budgeting in the 1960s and 1970s revolved around the notion that there had to be a better way of allocating resources to meet the goals implied by public policy (Steiner 1979). Even in the 1990s there has been continued concern about budgeting and how strategic planning processes can help improve the government budget process.

The information contained in strategic plans on missions, goals and performance can be seen as a way of making public services activities more transparent to politicians and thus assisting them when fixing budget allocations. In a sense, the language of strategic planning provides a vocabulary for discussing how politicians' intent (expressed through laws, directives, guidance etc.) is being understood by managers, how the managers intend to achieve the results desired by politicians, the resources they require to achieve these results, and how well they have done.

The desire to move public services away from a bureaucratic and complacent culture to a more entrepreneurial one is also the source of a desire to closely link strategic planning and budget systems. Advocates of entrepreneurial government actually want to interrelate mission statements, budget systems and performance measurement and management. This represents a new twist in the older story of corporate planning since there is a clear concern to allocate resources in line with public policy goals, but with the added idea that the spending of public money should be results-oriented. Consequently, the advocates of entrepreneurial government want to see budget holders focused on the translation of budgets into required levels of performance, which are themselves determined on the basis of the mission statement and general strategic goals formulated within a strategic planning process.

On the other hand, one problem for any strategic planning process is the acquisition of resources needed to implement a strategic change, and this means very often the problem of ensuring that the strategic plan influences the budget allocation process (Miesing and Andersen 1991; Berry and Wechsler 1995; Goodwin and Kloot 1996). If strategic planning is not effectively integrated with the annual budget process (and with other key management systems), then it is likely that the implementation of strategy is ineffective. There is, in other words, strategic planning but not strategic management. (We assume therefore that strategic management is the successful combination of both strategic planning and strategic implementation.)

One reason why strategic planning sometimes cannot achieve much influence in an organization is because the budgeting process continues to sustain an incrementalist ethos. For example, Eadie (1983: 449) comments that: 'the extent to which planning influences resource allocation decisions is impossible to pin down. I would regretfully guess that traditional incremental decision making – often of the gross, across the board percentage type – still holds general sway'. It can also be argued that this incrementalism is the result not only of cautiousness but also of a long 'war of position' by competing interests. The established budgeting processes have long been marked by internal wrangling for resources, and the etiquette of overt and covert conflict between departmental interests, and between resource controllers and departments, is so deeply ingrained that planning finds it difficult to get a purchase within the process. The struggles between interests become geared to blocking others and protecting positions, and ideas of taking action to bring about radical improvements through strategic changes are difficult to import into them (Bryson 1995).

In organizations using long-range planning, the budget process has sometimes influenced planning, as in the case where the budget process has been the basis of annual operational planning, and the annual operational plan is projected into the future to create a long-range plan. Such a plan has little in common with what are today regarded as strategic plans, whether they are mission driven or based on strategic issue management models of planning.

Integrating budgeting and planning processes

Bryson and Roering (1988) studied the initiation of strategic planning by eight governmental units in Minnesota. Their research concentrated on the formulation of strategies, rather than their implementation, but they did observe that 'the efforts at the initiation of strategic planning were almost always out of sequence with the unit's normal planning and budgetary processes, so that it was difficult for most to integrate strategic with exist-ent formal processes' (p. 1000).

While there is a general disquiet about the weak or non-existent linkages between strategic planning processes and budgetary processes, it would be wrong to assume that public service organizations never manage to build a close link between the two. Goodwin and Kloot's (1996) study found a tight linkage in three New Zealand local authorities. They reported that these organizations conducted a strategic review in which changes were made to the strategic plan, and then budgets for the next financial period were decided.

Goodwin and Kloot's research provides an important insight into how strategic planning processes can impinge on operational management. Details of their research are provided in Box 4.4, but the key findings related to a comparison they made of their sample of New Zealand and Australian local authorities. In the case of the New Zealand middle man-agers, they found that their 'budgetary response attitude', which might be seen broadly as a proactive and positive attitude or a negative or even sabotaging attitude to managing the budget effectively, was adversely affected by budgetary role ambiguity (defined as managers lacking adequate relevant information to carry out their role). This is a plausible finding. It is hard to be positive and proactive about managing a budget if you have not been given the information you need to manage it. Goodwin and Kloot also found that budgetary role ambiguity was less where decisions within the strategic process had been communicated to the middle managers. However, in the case of the Australian middle managers, budgetary role ambiguity did not seem to vary significantly with strategic communication nor with budgetary response attitude.

It is possible to draw some important conclusions from these findings. However, this requires an understanding of the context in which these two groups of managers were operating. The managers in the New Zealand local authorities were in a situation in which there was a tight linkage between the strategic planning process and the budgetary process. The

Box 4.4 Role ambiguity and strategic planning

Goodwin and Kloot (1996) surveyed middle managers in three New Zealand local authorities and three Australian local authorities; they repeated the survey twice during a two-year period. In total, 241 usable responses were obtained (and the lowest response rate was 72 per cent). The questionnaire produced data on strategic communication, budgetary response attitude, and budgetary role ambiguity, as well as biographical data. Strategic communication referred to the process of informing managers about decisions made within the strategic process. The budgetary response attitude was the predisposition to support, withhold support or sabotage the budget. The role ambiguity items were concerned with having the information needed to carry out the budgetary role. The items used in the survey were drawn from instruments developed and reported in the litera-ture by other researchers, but, nevertheless, Goodwin and Kloot checked their data for unidimensionality and reliability.

Interviews with staff in the local authorities in Australia and New Zealand were carried out and revealed that the linkages between strategic planning and budget-ary processes were quite different in the two countries. In the Australian local authority cases, the linkages were loose, with a time gap and often with no link at all reported. In the New Zealand cases, the strategic planning process was tightly linked with the budgetary process: first the strategic plan was revised, and then budgetary decisions were made.

The survey data was analysed using correlation coefficients and path analysis. Goodwin and Kloot found that the New Zealand data showed a direct but neg-ative link between strategic communication and budgetary role ambiguity, and a negative link between budgetary role ambiguity and budgetary response attitude. The Australian data suggested only a positive link between strategic communication and budgetary response attitude.

Goodwin and Kloot's interpretation of these results was as follows. First, strategic planning provides an information framework that supports budgetary responsibilities. Second, a loose linkage of strategic planning and budgetary pro-cesses meant that planning was incremental and budgetary decisions led strategic decisions. Third, if the linkage is tight then a lack of strategic communication will have an adverse effect on budgetary attitudes.

budgetary decisions were made once a strategic review had revised the strategic plans. The situation of the Australian managers was quite differ-ent. In their case the two processes were separated by quite a time gap and the managers said there was often no linkage between them. So, in one case the linkage was tight, and in the other it was loose.

It looks as though a tight linkage might create a problem for middle managers. They experience the strategic planning as creating budgetary role ambiguity. This can be reduced as a result of good strategic communications, which involves explaining to them what the strategic decisions are. Where the linkage between strategic planning and budgetary decisions is loose – as it was in the three Australian authorities – the decision making would appear to be of the traditional incremental kind. The managers in this situation presumably know that they will be doing much the same as they did in the previous year with some marginal changes.

The following important conclusions might be drawn from this research. First, the effect of strategic planning, which has an impact by being tightly linked to the budgetary process, is to create higher levels of uncertainty for middle managers. The middle managers know they have to pay attention to a strategic planning process as well as budgetary process decisions. Second, and this is a point made by Goodwin and Kloot (1996), good strategic communication to these managers, ensuring that they are informed of decisions made within the strategic process, is essential to reduce their budgetary role ambiguity. Third, making sure that there is good strategic communication to middle managers will obviously require effort, time and expense; but if this is not forthcoming the organization will fail to implement its strategic planning and leave the middle managers experiencing higher levels of budgetary role ambiguity!

Strategic budgets

One way of ensuring that strategy influences the budget process is to use dual budgeting to create a budget for strategic initiatives separate from the operational budget. This makes most sense where the strategy is leading to strategic innovation and the implementation action takes the form of strategic projects. The organization simply decides to set aside a corporate reserve fund for investment in strategic projects in each budget year, and a management committee is charged with responsibility for appraising alternative options for the investment of the fund in strategic projects.

This idea has been used by public services organizations trying to remedy a lack of strategic thinking and action. Kirklees Metropolitan District Council (which was briefly discussed earlier) created corporate revenue budgets. Davies and Griffiths (1995) reported that corporate budgets had reached £3.4 million by 1992/3 to fund inititiatives on the environment, a corporate discount card, child care and other things. The council was also trying to allocate resources generally on the basis of corporate priorities.

Of course, strategic projects are closed and control passes to operational managers when the new services or activities are fully established and are no longer in their developmental phase.

Strategic changes which involve the expansion of current services, or cost reduction changes, can be handled through changing operational plans and budgets. Strategic changes which involve the development of new services, or the extension of existing services to new client groups, can be handled through strategic projects and the strategic budget. Strategic changes which mainly affect the organization, its culture, its skills and technological capabilities might also be handled through strategic projects and the strategic budget.

As stated above, one reason for dual budgeting is to ensure that strategic change is resourced. This rests on the assumption that operational planning and management may be powerful enough to ignore strategic planning and management and earmarking at least some of the total budget for strategic budgets provides some protection for strategic agendas. It also helps to make more visible the trade-offs and tensions between spending to keep current services and activities well resourced, and spending to bring about strategic change.

Functional strategies

It is normally assumed that functional strategies should be aligned with the overall strategy of an organization. This means that the nature of the overall organizational strategy determines the importance and activities of the main functional areas. A study of two samples of firms from private industries and a sample of hospitals in the USA by Miles and Snow (1978) broadly concluded that this was the case. Some of their data was drawn from voluntary (non-profit) hospitals, which were the pre-eminent type of organization within the US healthcare system at that time.

We can illustrate their findings with two of their cases. First, there was the Pioneer Community Hospital, which appeared to have had stable goals, structure and performance over a five-year period: 'Low labour costs and efficient operations have generated an operating surplus during each of the last 5 years, allowing Pioneer to accumulate comfortable financial reserves' (Miles and Snow 1978: 35). The hospital was aiming for a well-defined and restricted market. Miles and Snow classified Pioneer Community Hospital as, therefore, pursuing a defender strategy, which was focused on the issue of producing services as efficiently as possible. In the hospitals with a defender strategy, the tendency was for them to rely on a limited set of services and markets and therefore marketing activities were relatively unimportant. The financial function was, however, very powerful. At Pioneer Community Hospital the chief administrator and the hospital's controller were the two key decision makers.

The second case, Riverside Hospital, was described by Miles and Snow as providing surgery and short-term medical care. It had extended its mission to cover health needs of people living in its locality, and was pursuing problem-specific healthcare programmes. It had 'a strong emphasis on identifying new needs and developing innovative delivery systems' (1978: 55). The overall strategy at Riverside Hospital was termed a prospector strategy because it was focused on finding new services and new opportunities. In consequence of this strategy, it appeared that medical staff

---

Box 4.5 Aligning human resource strategies and long-term organizational strategies

McHugh (1997) found that the Social Security Agency in Northern Ireland initially concentrated its strategic planning on efficiency improvements through rationalizations and technological change: 'Human resource strategies in the organization had not been developed as an integral part of the main business strategy' (McHugh 1997: 438–9). It appears that the agency subsequently decided that it had to link its human resources strategy to its long-term organizational strategy.

The agency developed a human resources strategy which had the following themes: competitive restructuring, continuous improvement, proficient and valued staff and delegated personal responsibility. Priority areas for action were specified as: restructuring, cultural change, gaining staff commitment and organization development. The strategy was reportedly aiming at the development of flexibility, teamwork and innovation.

It is clear from McHugh's analysis that the Social Security Agency had come to espouse a familiar set of ideas which place a great deal of faith in the efficacy of a culture of empowerment.

---

who were important for developing a new service were influential, and control functions (e.g. around quality) tended to be weak. So, in private sector parlance, production and finance functions were relatively weak, and market and product development functions were relatively strong.

The implication of these findings would be that different overall organizational strategies create different kinds of issues for different functional areas (e.g. finance, human resource management, marketing, etc.). In the light of different issues for each functional area, managers would need to develop appropriate functional strategies to address the issues. Consequently, it might be assumed that functional strategies should be selected so as to be consistent with the overall strategy.

Human resource strategies have been given attention in recent studies of public services management. McHugh's (1997) study provides an example of an analysis which assumes that human resource strategies need to be aligned with the overall strategy (see Box 4.5). The usual assumption is that strategic changes aimed at developing more efficient and consumer-focused organizations will require decentralized structures and participative management in order to foster employee commitment, productivity and innovation (Osborne and Gaebler 1992). Key goals for human resource strategies are cultural change, decentralization, empowerment and training of employees.

Relatively little systematic evidence is available on the design of functional strategies. One exception is the Nath and Sudharsan (1994) study of acute care hospitals in the USA (see Box 4.6). They found that organizations with

Box 4.6 Functional strategies in US acute care hospitals

Nath and Sudharshan (1994) attempted to measure strategy coherence and validate this measure using performance data from 71 acute care hospitals. They defined strategy coherence as being the alignment of the overall strategy of the whole organization with the functional level strategies.

Nath and Sudharshan treat strategy as being an actual pattern in the activity of a hospital, rather than as being a decision about strategic options, or a plan to achieve a strategic intent. To look at patterns of activity, they used data on the hospitals' size, provision of medical education, service portfolio (services being offered were classified as either basic or wide in scope, and case mixes were simple or complex), and patient base (location of the hospital in: the outer suburbs, the city and close suburbs, the suburbs, the city and inner suburbs, or the city; the numbers of medicare and medicaid discharges as a proportion of the total discharges of patients from the hospital). They identified five different strategies (i.e. patterns).

They considered using different performance indicators but ended up using the occupancy ratio of the hospital, defined as the average daily census of patients divided by the available beds. When they examined performance differences across the five strategies, Nath and Sudharshan could find no significant differences in terms of occupancy rates. In other words, each of the five patterns of activity described in terms of services, location, clients, size and involvement (or not) in medical education were viable and successful.

Each of the five strategies was associated with a different profile of activity in terms of marketing, finance, human resources and operations. These patterns were more or less what the researchers had expected on the basis of their knowledge of the hospital market in general. So, the city-based teaching hospitals, which were large and had a wide range of services and a complex case mix, focused their marketing on physicians, were relatively high cost providers, had high capital costs, high ratios of medical staff, and had a relatively high length of stay for inpatients. The small community hospitals located in the outer suburbs were quite different. They focused their marketing on the community, they were low cost, their costs of capital were low or medium, their medical staff ratios were low, their total outpatient visits were high, and the length of inpatient stay was relatively short. (As can be seen, the operationalization of the concepts of marketing, finance, human resource management and operations was very specific to the hospital sector, and was again based on a pattern of activity rather than seeing strategy as a choice of a course of action.)

Nath and Sudharshan carried out a bivariate analysis of the relationship between the performance indicator (occupancy of beds) and a coherence score. The latter variable was based on the degree of alignment between the overall strategy and the hospital's functional activities. A hospital in which the profile of functional activities matched the typical profile for its overall strategy was classified as having a coherent strategy. Only one hospital had a completely coherent strategy. Nath and Sudharshan reported a positive correlation between strategy coherence and the bed occupancy ratio used to measure performance. In other words, the more coherent the hospital was in terms of strategy and functional activity, the more successful it was measured in terms of bed occupancy.

the same overall strategy tend to have similar functional strategies and that there were different but equally viable configurations of overall strategy and functional strategies. This is an interesting study because it suggests that the idea of strategy coherence needs to be treated seriously. It also suggests we need to keep in mind that each industry may accommodate a number of viable strategic patterns. However, it is also possible that organizations need to be alert to changes in the successful patterns of overall and functional strategies, such that an apparently incoherent set of strategies in one organization turns out to be prototypical.

Strategic implementation

Some descriptions of strategic planning – the abstract picture in Chapters 2 and 3, for example – imply that implementation is of secondary importance compared to the need for a correctly formulated strategy. The tendency in recent years has been to denigrate such ways of thinking about strategic management and to insist that implementation is the most important part of the strategic planning and management process. We certainly saw evidence at the beginning of this chapter that implementation often posed the greatest difficulties for strategic planning in national libraries (Chalmers 1997).

The main advice on implementation tends to be couched in terms of the rational steps to be taken. The strategic planners should design action plans, assign individuals specific responsibilities for implementation, calculate the costs of implementing new strategic actions and ensure they are included in the annual budget-setting process, set up information and monitoring systems to track the achievement of milestones on the way to implementation, and ensure that control systems for correcting deviances are in place.

What else apart from these rational steps is there for management to do to ensure implementation? The answer usually boils down to the need to provide inspiring leadership (which we discuss further in Chapter 5). In addition, top management may be advised to keep staff informed, to manage stakeholders so their support for implementation is won and sustained, and, possibly, to involve service users wherever possible to counter the cultural effects of professionalism and bureaucracy.

It may also be suggested, reflecting increased scepticism about the ability of strategic leaders and managers to know what the future holds, that implementation needs to be guided by formative assessments – that is, by learning. This is consistent with the idea that the process begins with an emphasis on the formulation of strategy and over time gives way to an emphasis on implementation, rather than the idea that there are discrete, successive stages. One way of operationalizing this change of emphasis is via the use of small-scale pilots as part of an implementation approach. Managers can learn from the pilots and use this knowledge to refine their formulation of strategy before moving the organization more fully into an implementation phase. This is a more pragmatic approach than that of a simple linear model since it uses experience to shape the formulation of strategy prior to using strategy to create improved performance.

It is perhaps worth noting that we will not be discussing how organizational structures should be redesigned to assist the implementation of strategies. This may seem an important omission. However, there is surprisingly little known about the design of organizations to suit new strategies in the public services (O'Donovan 1990). There has been some analysis of the experience of decentralizing structures to enhance service delivery (Burns *et al*. 1994), and delegation to empower lower levels of management and employees. But, as yet, there is little which can be said on organizational structures and implementing strategies.

Pilot and demonstration projects

Implementation can run into difficulties because a plan is wrong, maybe because it is based on insufficient information or incorrect assumptions. It can run into difficulties because individuals or groups oppose the implementation. These are the reasons why many people feel that it is important to use strategic management rather than just strategic planning.

One way in which strategic planning becomes strategic management is by using implementation to further refine strategy. The implementation process becomes an opportunity for strategic learning. Another way strategic planning becomes strategic management is by carrying out implementation in a way which builds a wider base of support for the overall course of action. Thus we find many public services organizations using a pilot project to discover more about the strategy and its application so that the strategy can be refined and made more feasible before implementing it on a wider scale. We also find many public services organizations seeking demonstration projects to show waverers in the organization that the strategy is feasible, and that across the board introduction of the strategy is going to work.

In a sense, a project is a synthesis of strategy formulation and strategy implementation. In a pilot project the project is a mini-implementation exercise to help strategy formulation because more experience is needed to know what is best. In a demonstration project the project is a concrete form of strategy formulation to help strategy implementation because the formulation of strategy as a set of ideas is not enough to convince waverers that the strategy can work. Knowledge of when to use pilot projects and when to use demonstration projects is clearly very important for designing the implementation strategy. We must emphasize that pilots are not simply ways of enabling strategic learning by the architects of strategy – they are also ways of building bigger coalitions for change.

Bryson's (1995) advice on the selection of pilot and demonstration projects both crystallizes and extends the preceding remarks about the limits of knowledge and control. He suggests that pilot projects are suited to technically difficult situations when it is helpful to become clearer about the relationships between solutions and effects: 'The more technically difficult the situation is, the more necessary it is to have a pilot project to figure out what techniques do and do not work' (Bryson 1995: 183). In the face of political difficulties, Bryson recommends the use of demonstration projects to show that the solutions do work. However, he warns that 'Demonstration projects are most likely to work when existing or potential opposition is not well organized' (Bryson 1995: 184). When the opposition is strong, Bryson suggests attempting to overwhelm it by direct and massive implementation. To use demonstration projects in such circumstances helps opponents by giving them a point at which to concentrate their opposition. Bryson also recommends direct implementation – that is, not using pilot or demonstration projects – when the technical and political situation is simple or when there is a crisis. Finally, Bryson considers that in the face of technical and political difficulties, it is worth trying a pilot project followed up by demonstration projects.

In large measure, therefore, the planning of this aspect of the strategy of implementation needs to appraise the situation in terms of only two dimensions: technical difficulty (which can be defined as uncertainty about what effect the attempted solutions will produce) and political difficulty (that is, the scale and degree of organized opposition to the change being implemented) (see Figure 4.1).

Project management

Projects – pilots or demonstrations – are managed using project management rather than the operational management system.

The usual descriptions of project planning and management can make implementation seem simple and mechanical. As a process, project planning directs the attention of those involved to the following key tasks: clarifying the project's goals, identifying project activities, allocating responsibility for each activity, setting start and finish dates for each activity, and budgeting for the project.

The project manager should clarify the project's goals. This is important for ensuring that those who are involved know what they are doing, for setting boundaries to what must be done, and for providing a basis for monitoring progress. The next step by the project manager is usually

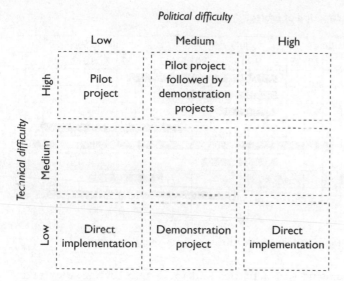

Figure 4.1 Pilots and demonstration projects
Source: Based on Bryson (1995).

considered to involve analysing the activities which will be needed to achieve the results indicated by the project's goals. The analysis proceeds in a way which creates a hierarchy of activities. This means that each of the main activities are analysed to identify the sub-activities which are needed to complete them. Then these sub-activities are analysed into their component sub-sub-activities.

The project manager should then identify a person to take responsibility for each activity (or sub-activity, etc.). Those responsible for the activities estimate the time needed to complete the activity, the personnel required for carrying it out, the equipment needed and the cost associated with the activity. The project manager, or someone else, then schedules the activities to minimize the time taken for the project.

Gantt diagrams may be used to check out the feasibility and logicality of the scheduling (Figure 4.2). These diagrams are used to show which activities are planned to take place in which blocks of time (which may comprise a week or a month, etc.). The obvious issues here include whether the time-scales look feasible, whether the sequencing of activities can be improved, and whether the scheduling of activities creates an unnecessary strain on resources in any period. The Gantt diagram can also be used to select milestones which can be monitored to check whether the project is making its expected progress towards the achievement of its goals.

Project planning may make use of supplementary techniques, such as network planning and responsibility charting. Network planning can be used to work out the critical path of a project. This is based on the identification

Title of strategic project/period of project

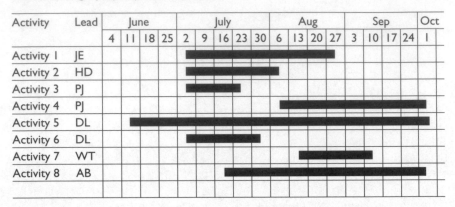

Activity	Lead	June				July					Aug				Sep				Oct
		4	11	18	25	2	9	16	23	30	6	13	20	27	3	10	17	24	1
Activity 1	JE																		
Activity 2	HD																		
Activity 3	PJ																		
Activity 4	PJ																		
Activity 5	DL																		
Activity 6	DL																		
Activity 7	WT																		
Activity 8	AB																		

Figure 4.2 An example of a Gantt diagram to plan project activities

of the necessary sequences of activities and the length of time they take. As might be guessed, problems in keeping activities on the critical path to the timetable are most serious for the completion of the project on time. Responsibility charting involves cross-tabulating those involved in the project and the project activities. Each individual's relationship to responsibility for implementing each activity is shown; that is, they may be the person responsible for its progress and successful completion, or it may be that they must be informed or consulted, or they may be responsible for taking some action as part of that activity. Project planning may also make use of computer packages for use on personal computers (PCs). These may help with the production of Gantt diagrams and network calculations.

In effect project management sets up a temporary organization to work alongside the normal operating organization. When a project planning approach is used to make a major strategic change (e.g. decentralization of service delivery), the project may be staffed by people who have been released partially or totally from their normal activities. The project manager may also be working on the project full time or part time. The effectiveness of the project organization depends to a large degree on the competence of the project manager who is ultimately responsible for the project's success. The project manager must have the ability to ensure the feasibility of the project plan, the availability of the required resources (especially the availability of staff who need to be released from other work), and the effectiveness of the working relationships within the project team.

Effective project management seems to require a strong emphasis on those responsible for activities having regular meetings at which they report to the project manager. This allows actual progress to be tracked against the planned progress, and enables follow-up action to make corrections in a timely manner.

This is the usual view of how project management works. There is no doubt that a project organization and a project plan together provide an implementation structure. But this formal framework, as much as anything else, creates a context within which those committed to implementation must continue to advocate for change and maintain the momentum so far achieved by the coalition which favours the implementation of the strategy. The project planning and management create forums for discussion and problem solving. It must also be capable of coping with conflicts of interests and the negotiation of compromises which may, and probably will, arise during any important strategic changes. It is easy to lose sight of these political aspects of implementing change in the discussion of Gantt diagrams, critical paths and corrections to any deviations from the project plan. The informal aspects of project planning and management, which focus on problem solving and conflict management, are probably very important influences on whether a critical mass inside the organization develop new sets of expectations and understandings which legitimize the post-change situation, and whether new roles and procedures become stabilized and institutionalized.

Conclusions

We have considered in this chapter how strategic planning is actually embedded in organizations and reviewed how strategy may be implemented.

We have reviewed a number of research studies, each of which have contributed to this overall conclusion: strategic management is hard because it needs effective leadership, management action on aligning resources, strategies and activities, and the bringing together of different individuals or groups in effective ways in order to formulate and implement strategies. In particular, we have underlined the need for leadership and management action to:

- bring together politicians and managers in strategic forums;
- align operational activities managed by middle managers with overall strategies;
- integrate planning and budgeting activities;
- align functional strategies with overall strategies;
- win over and bring together interest groups to support strategies.

We have also noted how pilot and demonstration projects may be used to achieve more effective implementation. There has also been a brief outline of the way in which project management can be applied to strategic projects.

In summary, we have seen that strategic planning and strategic management are two very different matters and that between them stands a whole series of different implementation issues. In Chapter 5 we turn to strategic leadership, a process which is critical to the use of strategic planning as a tool of strategic management.

five

Strategic leadership

Key learning objectives

After reading this chapter you should be able to:

1 Identify some of the key demands of a strategic leadership role.
2 Understand some of the issues and methods of involving employees and professionals in strategic management processes.
3 Suggest how strategic leaders operate in learning organizations.

Introduction

As the infallibility and power of strategic planning has been increasingly questioned, the need for good strategic leadership has been given more attention. Strategic leadership is seen as a key element in effective strategic management. Strategic leadership makes the difference between planning which is barely noticed and planning which shapes and makes the future. The concepts and the techniques of strategic planning are increasingly seen as useful intellectual tools which are used to support the strategic thinking of leaders, but they are not a substitute for intelligent and imaginative leadership.

The first objective of this chapter is to consider the qualities and skills required by strategic leaders. The next objective is to look at how strategic leaders, primarily the political leaders and chief executives of public services, operate in relation to their responsibilities for strategic management, notably their responsibilities with respect to mission statements and their participation in policy boards. The third objective is to look at leadership and the consent of employees and professionals, and how consent is obtained through the strategic planning process itself. Finally, we explore the role of strategic leaders in learning organizations, which can be seen as an extension of the idea of including employees and gaining their consent to strategic change.

Leadership qualities

The theory and research of leadership in public and private organizations isolates various characteristics of leadership. In recent years, these have centred on leaders as good at articulating and communicating visions, good at empowering people and good at developing the trust of their followers (Peters and Waterman 1982; Bryman 1992). To these qualities might be added those of a good sense of timing, personal 'drive' and an ability to handle the emotional aspects of strategic change.

Visionary leadership

Leaders focus their organization on a strategic direction. They create an agenda for strategic change. The ability of strategic leaders in public services to do this seems to depend on their ability in the sphere of symbolic- or language-action. Leaders are seen as spreading their ideas through speeches and writing strategy documents. Frost-Kumpf et al. (1993), who researched strategic action in the Ohio Department of Mental Health, have argued that symbolic actions were important in signalling a break with the past and the transformation of the organization. They said that the director of the department gave form to a new strategic direction through the language she used. Furthermore, it is claimed that: 'Through such language, numerous opportunities were opened for new ideas, actions, policies, and programs' (Frost-Kumpf et al. 1993: 151).

This emphasis on the power of leaders to manipulate symbols and language and to create visions of the future may seem nothing more than a postmodernist gloss on the story of organizational leadership. The emphasis on the role of the language of visions and values for creating new strategic moves is also very much in keeping with the spirit of postmodernist thinking, which lays great emphasis on language games and the importance of acting in new ways outside of the existing rules.

However, the Ohio Department of Mental Health in the 1980s is better understood as a case of transformational leadership rather than an example of postmodernist leadership. This is because leadership provided a genuinely intellectual function. The point that must be made about such transformational change is that it does demand a strategic vision. Since such a radical departure from traditional practices is being attempted, the leadership must either rely on spontaneous and haphazard departures from past habits, or it must hold up a vision presented symbolically in words which acts as a plan for the future. They must also present ideas of a possible route for achieving the plan. To move from a traditional public services design to a totally new one must be, in the latter case, a move based on ideas. Of course, the wise leader, intent on a vision-led transformation, will test the ideas as they move forward. The ideas have to be tested to see if they produce the practical consequences claimed. Nevertheless, the strategic vision is indispensable for this approach to transformation.

Conversely, it might be argued that the emphasis on visionary leadership and the symbolic actions of leaders is misplaced when strategic action is not aiming at transformation.

Finally, leaders must also use their skills in symbolic action to orchestrate the ending of implementation. Stakeholders need a sense that implementation has come to a satisfactory conclusion.

Empowering leadership

As ideas of strategic planning evolve, we are becoming more aware of a leadership role in guiding the organization through the strategy formulation and implementation phases. This means empowering others in relation to strategic formulation and implementation.

This empowerment may be achieved in formal terms by delegating strategic decision making through the appropriate design of strategic planning systems. Or it may be achieved by including others in the strategy process. In this latter case, the leader empowers others by acting as a guide and enabler in the decision making process, as well as acting directly as a strategist. This type of behaviour can be observed in terms of the immediate relations of a chief executive and their management team, but can be extended to other levels of the organization through the use of task forces and workshops.

But formal mechanisms for empowering leadership throughout an organization are probably not sufficient. Success may well depend on effective leaders who have the knack of instilling confidence in their managers and employees.

Trust

Leaders generate trust. Bennis and Nanus (1985) interviewed 60 private sector leaders and 30 leaders from the public sector, and found generally that trust was the emotional glue holding leaders and led together. They also claimed that trust in a leader has to be earned. In Chapter 1 it was noted that issue management may have to be given primary attention in the early days of a new leadership, and only when successes have accumulated can the leader move on to installing a more visionary approach to strategic management. In other words, by successfully tackling strategic problems the leader gains the trust of managers and employees, and this enables an ambitious strategic intent to be established.

As well as earning trust through success, leaders earn trust through leading by example and showing consistency. Leading by example includes the idea that leaders share the hard work of making strategies work, and share the disappointments and adverse consequences of setbacks. So, it is corrosive of trust in leadership when leaders get big pay increases while the pay of others in the organization is frozen or where jobs are being lost through budget cuts.

And people like to feel that they they know what their leaders stand for and can be counted on to handle situations accordingly. A leader may need to be around for some while, and continue making their position clear, for an awareness of their consistency to build up. Consistency may also imply a degree of persistence. According to Bennis and Nanus (1985: 52–3), effective leadership achieves change and innovation through 'keeping at it' and 'staying the course': 'Any new idea looks either foolish or impractical or unfeasible – at first. It takes repeated attempts, endless demonstrations, monotonous rehearsals before innovation can be accepted and internalized by any organization'.

Timing

Leaders have to be good at judging the ripeness of a situation for fundamental strategic changes. For much of the time a leader may feel that only small incremental changes are possible. If they seek to instigate the implementation of major strategies at very unpropitious times, then they court the dangers of a serious failure. Leaders who fail to recognize the capacity for major strategic changes when it is there are also making a serious leadership error. Bryson (1995: 213) suggests leaders need an intuitive sense of when the time is right for making major changes: 'Without some intuitive sense of whether big or small changes are in the cards, strategic planning might be used quite inappropriately. Hopes for big changes might be raised when such changes are not possible, or time might be wasted in reprogramming strategies that ought to be drastically changed'.

Drodge and Cooper (1997) report the results of a research project in the British further education sector in 1994–5 (see Box 5.1). They found that the three colleges on which the research was based were positioned quite differently in an organizational 'life cycle'. One college was in a period of incremental change, another on the edge of rapid change, and the third implementing discontinuous change. This idea of a life cycle provides another way of emphasizing that timing is important. Leaders need to be attuned to these cycles.

Box 5.1 Change and organizational life cycles

Drodge and Cooper (1997) interviewed senior managers at three British colleges of further education to find out about planning in these organizations. The background to this was that the Further Education Funding Council (FEFC), after the Further and Higher Education Act 1992, identified the strategic plan as 'pivotal' in the management of a college and established a strategic planning framework.

One of the findings of the research project was that the mechanics of planning were similar in all three colleges. Drodge and Cooper reported: 'We have seen that the planning frameworks of the colleges are not dissimilar, influenced, of course, by the FEFC and its requirements' (1997: 216).

However, there were differences. The colleges varied in terms of the nature of consultation, the freedom allowed to staff in target setting, the commitment to personal growth, and getting commitment or compliance. The researchers identified the importance of variations in managerial ethos and concepts of planning. They also reported that the three colleges varied in terms of an organizational life cycle:

It might be argued that, in the three colleges, we merely observe the results of one college (Southam) being secure within a period of incremental change, one (Easton) possibly just leaving such a period and about to change rapidly, and the third (Norbury) in the process of implementing discontinuous change through swift action.

(Drodge and Cooper 1997: 216)

Box 5.2 Paul Tellier

Schacter's (1994) review of Canadian public service reform included the following anecdote about Paul Tellier who had been in charge of the public service in Ottawa from 1985 until 1992. Tellier's self-appraisal on leaving that post was self-critical. He had failed to lead:

On the plus side was his ability to create a more collegial atmosphere in the top ranks of the federal and civil service . . . But . . . he had become a prisoner of collegiality, expecting the team to make the decisions on modernizing the public service . . . And when his instincts told him to push, he was too easily persuaded by those colleagues to move cautiously. As a boss, he didn't drive the system.

(Schacter 1994: 38)

Drive

Leaders change things. Change can, and does, induce resistance from interests that prefer the status quo. Consequently, leadership may be seen as needing to challenge and drive innovation. Managers who are just team players may be seen as lacking the necessary quality or skill needed to drive change (see Box 5.2 on Paul Tellier, a high-ranking public official in Canada).

Managing the emotions of change

Another reason why strategic leadership is important appears to be the way that good leaders handle the emotions and tensions which accompany strategic changes. Strategic leaders make critical decisions about how much a strategy needs to be modified to ensure its implementation though making it more acceptable to resistant groups, and about how much a strategy should be maintained in the face of such opposition in order to achieve important strategic purposes. These leadership calculations must allow groups supportive of the status quo to vent their tensions and emotions. Consequently, the ability to give emotional forces an outlet, and the ability to make judicious modifications of the strategy, are important leadership capabilities that are required to create and sustain a coalition for change through an implementation phase.

Strategic leaders, mission statements and strategic documents

Wilkinson and Pedler's (1996) case study of Walsall Metropolitan Borough Council illustrates a common concern about strategy documents in general – the worry of leaders and strategic managers that they have a planning or strategy document which, although they may have taken great pains to circulate it as widely as possible throughout their organization, is ignored. Apparently the chief executive and the head of policy at Walsall Council questioned whether the corporate business plan was 'owned' by anybody or whether anyone actually cared about the plan. Did the plan, they questioned, mean anything to anybody, or was it window dressing, or even just the product of 'ivory tower' writing?

These kinds of concern ought to prompt the question: exactly what is the functionality of a mission statement or strategy document in practice? Are mission statements used as the starting point for strategic leaders and top managers to select strategic actions? Is the idea of agreeing a mission statement to provide the basis for coherent direction of the organization by the leaders and top managers? Are strategy documents meant for operational managers, as a framework for their decisions and action, and therefore do operational managers need to keep such documents to hand when making decisions? These uses within the management structure would need to be taken into account when deciding on the content, layout and presentation of such statements and documents. Presumably, the pay-off for a well-designed document from this point of view would be better decision making leading to better organizational performance.

It is apparent, however, that many strategic leaders and top managers have hopes of mission statements and strategy documents in terms of the general understanding, and inspiration, of employees at all levels of the organization. They think that if they circulate the mission statement to all employees, then each and every person will become much clearer about what they have to do. And if the mission statement can be made inspiring, either through its uplifting sentiments or through the passion with which it is communicated by leaders, it is hoped, presumably, that employees will become committed to the general purpose laid down, and work with a higher level of motivation. This would also have the benefit of ensuring the organization becomes more united and cohesive, because everyone is committed to the same general purpose and overall strategy. If there is an assumption that poor performance reflects a widespread lack of clarity about purpose, or a general lack of commitment to that purpose, then a written mission statement could seem like a fast route to success.

Mission statements may also be communicated to the public and to service users, presumably with the intention of inspiring confidence and convincing them that the public services are well managed.

There is another point which bears serious consideration. This is the idea that there may be times when leaders and strategic managers should delay presenting a strategy in a document. Quinn's (1980) study of ten large private sector organizations certainly found this. The reason was the organizational and power relationships in which top executives operated. Quinn suggests that decisions may be delayed or kept vague so as to encourage lower level members to participate, to allow more time to get more information, and to develop commitments. In crisis situations executives will want to consider how power bases and how different groups are being affected and so will keep their options open until they have a better appreciation of these factors. So, we should not assume that effective strategic leaders always rush to bring out formal statements of their strategic thinking and plans.

Bryson (1995: 151) also points out the complication of political considerations in issuing strategy documents:

> It is conceivable, of course, that preparation and publication of a formal strategic plan would be politically unwise. Incompatible objectives or warring external stakeholders, for example, might make it difficult to prepare a 'rational' and publicly defensible plan. Key decision makers will have to decide whether a formal strategic plan should be prepared, given the circumstances the organization faces.

In other words, there are situations where it would not be useful to have a strategy document. This may seem odd, but only from a very technical perspective which sees decision making as an information processing and

problem solving activity and the strategy document as the formal statement of a solution. If decision making is seen, instead, as the interplay of
actions between interested parties trying to maximize their own utilities,
then the document is something to be fought over. The implication is that
the power of an information process and problem solving approach to
enforce rational decisions has its limits, and beyond these limits strategy
takes its chances in the manoeuvres of competing interest groups.

Strategic leaders and policy bodies

Traditionally public services have been run on a model of policy making
and implementation in which the policies are made by politicians and then
implemented by appointed public officials. The growth of strategic planning and strategic management has raised the interesting questions about
how policy making and strategic management fit together, and who should
be the instigator of strategy? Indeed, who should be the strategic leader –
an elected politician or an appointed manager?

Obviously elected politicians may feel that they are the policy makers
and that strategic planning and management is something that managers
do. In practice, public services may arrive at all sorts of settlements between the words 'policy' and 'strategy', between the associated processes
of policy making and strategizing, and between the roles of politicians and
managers. For example, the elected politicians may make policies and the
managers may use strategies to ensure their effective implementation (see
Eadie 1983). Then again, strategy may be seen as an over-arching idea (or
set of ideas) which provides a framework for policy making. Less obviously, it may even be agreed that policies relate to service delivery, and
that strategies relate to community problems requiring community leadership (Davies and Griffiths 1995).

The most we can attempt to do here is sensitize ourselves to some of the
variations in leadership which are currently on offer in public services.
First, leadership may be policy-oriented, strategy-oriented, or both. If
leadership is both policy- and strategy-oriented then policy making and
strategizing must be articulated in some way or other. This is complicated
by the fact that leadership may vary between, or be unified across, the
service delivery and governance activities of individual public services
organizations. How politicians and managers position themselves and
combine together in relation to these options is likely to result in quite different styles of overall leadership.

In Box 5.3, a study into policy boards in the US healthcare sector is
reported. The main line of development in this sector seems to be for
strategizing to displace policy making and for the chief executive to take
on the mantle of leader.

Box 5.3 Policy boards and strategic direction

Delbecq and Gill (1988) report the results of a year-long study of US healthcare organizations. They interviewed chief executives from 13 multi-hospital healthcare delivery organizations and, to provide a comparison, eight chief executives from private sector high technology firms. The interviewees were selected by means of peer nomination to ensure that the two samples represented chief executives who were highly successful.

The interviews with the healthcare chief executives highlighted a number of problems and concerns. First, the chief executives thought that it was difficult to get their boards to be strategic. They were concerned that their boards were short term and operational in their focus. The research also revealed that the boards had lots of subcommittees, and these too were often concerned with operational issues. The interviews with the private sector chief executives suggested that policy boards should not be dealing with operations, cost effectiveness, quality control and resource management, but should stay focused on strategic direction. There is some implication in the arguments of Delbecq and Gill that an emphasis on operational matters derives from having too many internal members on the policy board.

The chief executives were concerned that their policy boards were too big to be strategic. Over half of the interviewees reported policy boards with 11 to 15 members, and they felt that the size of board was twice as large as was desirable for the demands of strategic policy formation and a competitive marketplace.

A third issue was the role of the policy board member. Essentially, the board members were tending to operate a 'constituent representative model' and thus saw themselves as representing a group interest. They focused on ensuring assets were used accordingly. This implied an adversarial role with respect to the chief executive and other board members. The typical policy board member was not operating a 'strategic director model'.

There was also a consideration of the role of the chief executive within the policy board. Is the chief executive a leader of the board or subordinate to the board? The healthcare chief executives denied wanting a rubber stamping policy board, but they did want a policy board that supported innovative ventures. There was an acceptance of the idea that the chief executive should be subject to annual evaluation by the policy board, although there was also a need to provide the chief executive with a contract which was fair in terms of the personal risks of leading in competitive times.

An obvious assumption running through the whole analysis is that policy boards should respond to a transition to a competitive environment by abandoning a representative model and adopting a strategic director model. It is also clear that the researchers favoured a policy board consisting mainly of external people who are experts and primarily see themselves as supporting the chief executive in the role of primary strategic leader. The policy board is conceptualized as focused on providing support for risky, entrepreneurial and innovative strategic moves required by the transition to competitive markets.

Strategic planning processes and the inclusion of employees

Strategic leaders sometimes conceptualize their aims as moving their organization from a bureaucratic culture to a more flexible culture based on managers and employees being empowered to use their ability to solve problems and take the initiative. This idea of leaders empowering others was briefly noted earlier in this chapter.

But how can employees be encouraged to produce new ideas? How can top managers ensure that these ideas reach them? How can a more positive approach to change, flexibility and creativity be encouraged among employees? How can they be empowered to use their initiative?

Strategic planning can be used by leaders to empower employees. The main requirement of this kind of strategic planning is that there should be forums for discussion of strategic issues and strategies which enable the employees to contribute their ideas and enable top managers to hear them. Forums for strategic discussions and participation in the process lie outside the usual hierarchical lines of decision making and communication, and allow a more problem solving and open-minded exploration of issues and possibilities for action. Forums may be called workshops or vertical or diagonal teams (Berry and Wechsler 1995; Flynn and Talbot 1996). In such settings leaders and senior managers behave in ways that signal to lower level managers and employees that their ideas are positively valued and should be discussed openly. Forums may involve the use of strategic planning techniques which encourage more creative thinking and problem-solving analysis (Nutt and Backoff 1992; Bryson 1995).

So, strategic planning can create additional communication channels to those in the hierarchical line, enabling more ideas to be generated by employees and heard by leaders and top managers, and encouraging a more positive culture in terms of flexibility and innovation.

Involving professional employees

It is often said that there is a problem about professionals in public services. Critics of public services, reflecting all shades of political opinion, have pointed to the way that 'professional bureaucracies' decide what the public needs (Leach *et al.* 1994: 34). One of the most pithy criticisms of the 'professional problem' was provided by Osborne and Gaebler (1992: 66): 'Professionals and bureaucracies deliver services; communities solve problems'.

Osborne and Gaebler's terse comment suggests that professionals are a problem because they are an interest group which has an interest in the bureaucratic status quo of public service delivery. The assumption, which is increasingly made these days, is that communities need problems solved, and that it is not in the community's interest if professionals always diagnose the need for more public expenditure and new services every time there is a problem.

Even worse accusations may be made, such as that professionals define the public's needs to suit themselves and are inward-looking. The charge made is that professionals are busy empire building and aggrandizing their own status, and are not really concerned with meeting the needs of the public. Their influence over politicians is assumed to mean that this insularity and self-interested professionalism helps to create a democratic deficit (Clarke and Stewart 1992). This means that the public's voice is muffled and the professionals, and the politicians, have the loudest voices. This point has been made about the public's interest as service users: 'It requires an imaginative leap to consider consumers as equals in a three-cornered exchange with politicians (who possess the power) and professionals (who possess the skills and the expertise, and any delegated or assumed power as well)' (Potter 1994: 262).

Clearly, professionals can be seen as a barrier to responsive public services, and strategic leaders may well feel tempted to bypass the professionals when formulating strategies. However, professionals are experts; they are important because of their knowledge and expertise which are key organizational resources. Professionals should not be seen simply as a problem for managers (Metcalfe and Richards 1990).

Top management, therefore, needs to give a lot of thought to the expectations of their professional staff, and have to be prepared to expend time on discussing and debating changes with them. The problem is attitudinal rather than intellectual. Career, professional and client interests are densely and complexly knotted together in these attitudes. Management communications cannot be based on a simple model of leaders informing professionals.

The professional outlook also prizes the possession of an independent expert status. This means that there is a preference for management styles which are oriented to persuading and convincing. There has been a tendency for professional members of staff to be sceptical of the managerialism which has swept through all the different sections of public services. Management jargon and techniques are regarded with distrust and managerial plans treated with cynicism. This puts a premium on a managerial style which is evidence-based. Managers have to win the support of professionals for strategies (and for strategic management) not by asking for the benefit of the doubt, but by establishing a track record of successful change. Experienced public services managers have sometimes developed repertoires for trust-building with professional groupings. They make clear commitments to achieve specific targets or solve particular problems, and then ensure that they deliver.

If this argument is accepted, then it may be suggested that strategic planning processes can be used to build an internal consensus within an organization and legitimize strategic decisions. Denis *et al.* (1991: 72), referring specifically to planning in the health sector, remark: 'most writers have recognized the futility of attempting to carry it out without the involvement of medical staff and have recommended a much more participative process than the type of planning usually observed in business firms'. They report that many hospitals they had observed did have lengthy and elaborate consultative processes. In a study of 11 Montreal hospitals they found a strategic plan took over 16 months to complete on average. They said: 'A good part of this time was required to complete consultations with medical staff' (p. 72).

So far we have been discussing how professionals can be included in managerial strategic plans. Arguably, many strategic changes occur as a result of a multitude of minor adjustments and innovations made at the behest of professionals operating at 'street level' – that is, operating within the service delivery context. This is what has been called 'emergent strategy' to distinguish it from the top-down grand strategic plans usually considered to be the normal type of strategy. Leadership skills may involve leaders in knowing how to use and integrate this type of emergent strategy with their own efforts at strategizing. A process known as 'backward mapping' could be seen as a recognition of, and an attempt to formalize, this 'natural' approach to strategic change.

Bryson's (1995) description of backward mapping suggests there are four main steps. First, desired changes in service practices to minimize problems for service users are identified. The emphasis may be put on the service users' definition of their problems with the current pattern of service delivery, but the professionals who deliver the services might be expected to have a strong say in what the desired changes are. The second step, according to Bryson, consists of the planners formulating an objective for organizational action at the lowest level to bring about the desired changes in services. The third step involves the planners going up the implementation structure, or going to the implementation agencies, with the aim of identifying the changes required to support the changes in services. In the fourth step, policies and strategies are formulated to direct and provide the resources needed.

This obviously reverses the usual way in which strategy is thought to work, ending with a new policy and strategy, rather than beginning with it, and starting with the identification of operational changes to be made in the service delivery processes, rather than culminating in the identification of operational changes needed to implement a new strategy. The implication is that you start with those who have the most concrete experiences of service delivery, and strategic leaders are placed in the role of supporting and resourcing the changes identified by those at the lowest level.

Strategic leadership and learning organizations

As already noted, there is criticism of strategic planning which assumes that it is possible to plan everything in advance. More and more people take the view that implementing strategic decisions involves trying things out and adapting early attempts to install new services and structures. This is the idea that implementation should involve learning. So those involved in implementing strategy will often need to operate in a learning mode when implementing strategic changes.

There is also a link being made between learning and the implementation of strategic directions based on foresight and the development of core competencies. In particular, the speeding up of learning by doing could be seen as very valuable for creating and evolving core competencies.

Osborne and Gaebler (1992: 150), who have argued for entrepreneurial public services organizations, have claimed that entrepreneurial organizations are learning organizations: 'They constantly try new things, find out what works and what doesn't, and learn from the experience'. Osborne and Gaebler see performance planning and measurement as essential for the realization of a learning organization. Performance measurement means that the organization can know when it is successful, and without it, how can learning take place? Obviously, the more that writers like Osborne and Gaebler stress the governance role for government organizations, defined as catalysing problem solving efforts by others and mobilizing private and voluntary resources to address community problems, the more likely it is that a learning organization rather than a bureaucratic organization will be seen as desirable.

A learning organization might be defined as one that has enlisted the intelligence as well as the effort of all those employed within it. A true learning organization would by definition draw on the intelligence and ideas of all the sections and levels within it when developing strategies and planning implementation. After all, a formal organizational strategy is one of the most explicit attempts that an organization can make to apply intelligence to its activities with the aim of surviving and being successful not only now but also in the future. So the production and application of a strategy becomes a patently valid test of claims by any organization to be a learning organization.

The idea of the learning organization is an ideal that more and more organizations aspire to, even if few would be happy to claim they have achieved it in practice. Organizations, including many in the public services, seem to find it difficult to elicit or make use of the potentially enormous contribution of intelligence by their ordinary members.

One reason for this difficulty appears to be the set of weaknesses which can develop in large centralized public organizations. To explain these weaknesses, we start with an appreciation that those at the top of bureaucratic public organizations have the formal power to make strategic decisions but lack the knowledge of services possessed by service users and employees involved in service delivery. The knowledge cannot get from those who have the experience to those who have the formal power because each strata of the organization becomes isolated from those above it and below it. According to Crozier (1964: 190), 'A bureaucratic organization, therefore, is composed of a series of superimposed strata that do not communicate very much with each other'. As well as this, the isolation enables each stratum to develop its own goals and ignore the corporate ones. In consequence, employees do not try to help the organization to adapt to its environment, but instead develop rigidities which protect them from the public.

There has been some work on how leaders can facilitate organizational learning, but this is based on private sector experience, and may need to be modified before it can be used in the public services. Essentially, it is argued that leaders must be involved in the learning process. They must be a visible and active participant in learning: 'Only though direct involvement that reflects coordination, vision, and integration can leaders obtain important data and provide powerful role models' (Nevis et al. 1997: 46). Individual chief executives have been praised for the way they engage with learning in their organizations, which is demonstrated, for example, by being out learning in the 'field' and by being available and ready to meet and talk with employees at all levels of the organization. The implication seems to be that leaders of learning organizations not only engage very visibly *in* learning, they also engage *with* employees in learning.

In the public services, strategic leaders may be able to encourage a culture of learning and innovation through the development of mission statements and strategic visions. Leaders may provide an inspiring message of how the organization needs all its employees to demonstrate an entrepreneurial and innovative attitude and to assume more responsibility for implementing strategies and modifying them to work better. But strategic leaders will also have to model learning as well. In recent years, strategic leaders have been encouraged to allow employees to take more risks and resist punitive responses to failed experiments. They can symbolize their support for this by also making more open admission of their own mistakes. However, if this openness and honesty is not matched by success as well, the strategic leadership may find its position untenable. So, strategic leadership can only support a learning culture, and thereby gain more input from employees at all levels, if it is willing to risk being more open and honest about leadership mistakes.

Conclusions

In this chapter we have taken on the difficult task of attempting to look at strategic leadership in the public services. We have noted the way in which leaders are seen as having vision and personal drive, but we have also seen how leaders have to have other qualities and abilities, such as a sense of timing and skills in symbolic action which open up possibilities of strategic action and change. We have looked, albeit briefly, at the complicated relationship between those in leadership roles who represent interests, and those in leadership roles who take on a strategic executive function. We have, above all, stressed the role of leaders in including employees and professionals in strategic thinking and action, and in creating a learning organization by becoming involved in learning and engaging employees in the learning process.

The lessons of this chapter for strategic management in the public services may be summed up as follows. First, the very strong emphasis always put on visionary leadership surely supports the critical role of leaders in the strategic management task of focusing their organizations on strategic goals or direction. Second, the emphasis placed on qualities which engender trust in leadership surely suggests, among other things, that strategic management in the public services also requires consistency and persistence. In the previous chapter the challenge of implementation was interpreted as demanding action which brings people together behind a strategy (getting commitment) and aligning resources, activities and strategies with the overall strategy. The need for leadership to achieve focus, consistency and persistence can now be added, therefore, to the need for implementation to achieve commitment and alignment.

The third and final lesson for strategic management in the public services is the need for a style of leadership which wins consent and active support, rather than a style of leadership which simply imposes a direction on the organization. This is made especially important in the public services where there are powerful professional cultures.

Learning Resources
Centre

six

Coordination and cooperation

Key learning objectives

After reading this chapter you should be able to:

1 Anticipate the problems of different forms of joint and cooperative strategic planning.
2 Identify behaviour which increases the chances of successful joint planning and strategic forums.
3 Understand the characteristics of effective networks in the public services.

Introduction

It is now assumed, after some years of thinking otherwise, that coordination and collaboration between public services organizations and with other organizations is desirable. One example of this is the expectation that health and social services organizations will cooperate and even develop joint strategic plans.

Sensitivity to the public desire to limit the tax burden may be an important factor in the political pressure on public services organizations to collaborate: concerns about wasteful duplication which leads to inefficient services are logical. But there are other concerns. Poor coordination leads to gaps and burdens on users who are thought to be looking for more seamless services. There is also pressure for more collaboration as the argument for innovation and public sector renewal leads to complaints that too many public services and public sector managers are handicapped by being trapped within departmental and organizational boundaries: 'An organization can easily fail to recognize the range of other agencies and actors it needs to collaborate with to understand and tackle the complex problems it faces' (Leadbetter and Goss 1998: 61).

Unfortunately very little guidance is provided on how coordination and collaboration can be achieved in terms of the strategic direction and planning of public services organizations. It would be a mistake to believe that such strategic cooperation is without its difficulties. In the case of joint planning and commissioning by health and social services, for example, there may be differences of perspective due to differences in mandates, themselves the result of different statutory responsibilities. Then there are the problems of developing a shared vision and strategic agenda which originate in quite different relationships to the public, different professional cultures and different relationships to political authority and budgetary systems. The evaluations that public services managers in different organizations make of the success or otherwise of strategic action could well give rise to further difficulties of maintaining a joint strategy.

In this chapter we will explore various types of joint planning and also look briefly at joint planning forums.

Joint planning by health organizations

Although there are plans to change the situation, the management of the UK's NHS has been based for a number of years on an internal market system which achieves coordination through contracting relationships. Even a simplified presentation of the situation in the NHS (see Box 6.1) makes clear that strategic planning was being used to shape the internal market and was in this sense, if no other, the means of creating a managed market.

The main participants in this system – health authorities and trust hospitals – had different roles within the internal market. Health authorities, which covered the whole country, were charged with commissioning and purchasing services for their local population and had responsibility for monitoring health services contracts. Trust hospitals had responsibility for providing health services and managing their income from contracts to cover their expenditure.

It is clear that both the purchasers (the health authorities) and the providers (the trust hospitals) could have strategic plans and be following their own individual strategies. Indeed, Perkins (1996: 203) suggests that they do have different concerns:

The purchaser's strategy will be concerned with the balance and availability of services for its population and with obtaining the best volume of quality services possible. As a secondary concern it will be

Box 6.1 Strategic planning and internal markets: the UK's NHS in the mid-1990s

A new system of business planning began in the NHS in December 1995. It commenced with a statement of aims and medium-term objectives for the Department of Health. The NHS executive were given eight development objectives which were:

* to implement the Health of the Nation strategy;
* to ensure quality and responsiveness;
* to ensure effective partnerships to meet the needs for continuing care of elderly, disabled and vulnerable people in the community;
* to develop a primary-care led NHS where decisions involve patients and their carers;
* to ensure comprehensive services for people with mental health problems;
* to improve the cost effectiveness of services;
* to ensure effective management of people; and
* to improve communications in various ways.

The NHS executive set six medium-term priorities for the health authorities, and its regional offices were to make sure that the health authorities took responsibility for developing their healthcare strategies. The regional offices of the NHS executive had to agree with their health authorities as to how the latter would incorporate the guidance in their purchasing and business plans, and to agree success criteria and milestones against which to evaluate performance. The health authorities were asked to develop purchasing and business plans which reflected their own local priorities, agreed with GPs and other local agencies.

The national planning cycle in 1996/7 required the following sequence of actions by health authorities, regional offices of the NHS executive and trust hospitals:

1 Health authorities were to publish their initial purchasing plans by the end of September 1996 and submit their commissioning intentions to the regional office in the following month.
2 Regional offices of the NHS executive were scheduled to review trust draft strategic directions and health authority contracting intentions in October 1996.
3 The trusts were required to submit draft business plans in November 1996 and provide finalized prices to purchasers in the following month.
4 In January 1997 regional offices were to review trust draft business plans.
5 In March 1997 health authorities were to agree and sign NHS contracts with providers and make their purchasing plans public.
6 In March 1997 regional offices were scheduled to conciliate and arbitrate on NHS contracts.
7 Trust hospitals were to publish their strategic direction and submit their financial plans to the regional office in March 1997.

The contracting process was not occurring throughout the year but concentrated in just a few months. There was, in some regions, a tendency for the contracting to be a very pressurized event in one quarter of the year (January to March).

keen to ensure the continued viability of the providers with whom it contracts. The provider will be primarily interested in the viability and development of the services which it provides. It will not be interested in the questions of equity and community need except in so far as it might persuade the purchaser to contract with it for further work.

There is a recognition in Perkins' remarks that the internal market, by creating purchasers and providers, has produced two distinct sets of interests, and so it can be expected that a health authority might find it difficult at times to pursue a strategy based on its assessment of local health needs because its trusts are pursuing strategies to maximize their interests.

Also, a health authority, in contracting with several trusts, might find itself trying to coordinate providers through the contracting process who are pursuing quite different strategies. These different strategies might represent an attempt at strategic positioning in the face of competitive rivalry between trusts within that locality. This might create various problems for the health authority such as the trusts pressing for contracts which allow them to build up a national specialism but which represent a very big investment relative to that specialism's importance from the point of view of local needs. Or, a trust hospital might be seeking to keep a comprehensive portfolio of services whereas the health authority is looking to eliminate duplication with another local provider.

One of the most important issues in the effectiveness of this strategic planning process concerns the degree to which the health authorities' plans really were taking into account local priorities, and then the extent to which these priorities were formed by the needs and aspirations of the local community. It is important to underline that one of the six medium-term priorities set for health authorities concerned giving greater voice and influence to users of NHS services and their carers not only in respect of their own care and service standards, but also in respect of NHS policy locally as well as nationally. If service users and their carers were influential in setting priorities locally, then these could become very important in terms of commissioning intentions, purchasing plans and contracts with providers. There is evidence that in one locality at least (Pratten 1997), the local voice was not heard in this way, and that consultation ended up being a search for community approval for health authority plans (see Box 6.2 which summarizes Pratten's study). This suggests that the reality of strategic planning in this internal market was strongly influenced by the power of national priorities and the power of providers.

Pratten (1997) made it clear that she saw this as a case in which decision making was being dominated by the purchasing process. It is also clear that she saw the scope for genuine public consultation as dependent on commissioning triumphing over purchasing, so that the latter process realizes the intentions of a strong and independent commissioning role.

Box 6.2 A case study of a UK local health authority

Pratten's (1997) case study in a London district health authority explores community involvement in commissioning healthcare. It also provides useful evidence on the conditions and consequences of local strategic planning by health authorities within the internal market of the NHS in the mid-1990s.

Officially, health authorities were meant to draw up local plans in consultation with the public and other agencies. Their development of local strategic and purchasing plans was expected to take account of the views of local GPs. With respect to mental health services, there was to be partnership with local authorities, GPs, and service providers in terms of reviewing and progressing purchasing and provision of services. Continuing healthcare for elderly, disabled, vulnerable people and children was to be provided through integrated services in collaboration with local authorities and other organizations. The NHS executive also advised health authorities to pay attention to variations in health between areas, social groups, ethnic groups and men and women. That was the theory.

This implied what might be called a commissioner-led model of strategic planning and purchasing. The health authority as the commissioner of services would assess the health needs of the local population. They would then develop purchasing plans and finally agree NHS contracts with providers which would ensure the most effective meeting of the public's health needs.

The evidence from Pratten's detailed analysis of how the health authority set about consulting the public suggests that strategic planning worked in quite a different way. This can be summed up by saying that a combination of central government's top-down planning and the providers' *de facto* powers left the health authority little scope to consult the public. The health authority was primarily seeking support for purchasing plans which were largely determined by government and providers. The health authority was, it might be said, operating as a purchaser but not as a commissioner.

An interpretation of Pratten's detailed conclusions follows. As we noted above, there was an official expectation that health authorities would consult their local publics. This appears to have been taken seriously by the health authority in question; it appeared to have had a strong commitment to engaging with its communities and had invested resources in doing this. Because the members of a health authority board are appointed by central government, they are not representative of, or accountable to, local people. They cannot, therefore, claim to know what local people want on the basis of a system of local representation, and a special attempt at public consultation is required. Also, as part of the background to this case, Pratten refers to the government's broader managerial agenda, which in principle required the health authority to challenge the influence of service providers by assessing needs, purchasing services and obtaining better services in a more cost-effective way. Obviously, consulting the public would be one way of assessing local needs. These background factors probably go some way to explaining why consulting the public was being attempted by the health authority.

The health authority could have carried out a thorough consultation process in order to complete the assessment of the local community's health needs before it firmed up its purchasing intentions; or it could have developed purchasing plans and checked out, through public consultation, what the local community thought of the plans. The first approach might have led to the health authority becoming a champion of local people's interests, whereas the second approach could end up with the health authority looking for support and rubber-stamping of its plans.

In the context of an anticipated long-term reduction in resources and its weakness within the internal market relative to both providers and government, the health authority seems to have mainly opted for looking for support for its purchasing plans. It seems that it had not planned how it would respond to public views which emerged through the consultation process; this suggests, of course, that there was no real interest in discovering through consultation any needs or issues of which it was not already aware. This lack of planning as to how it would respond to public views reinforced the nature of planning by the health authority as being led by government and provider needs.

The consequence for the system of local strategic planning and purchasing by the health authority was most obviously that plans were not influenced by the public. There were other consequences. A body which was set up to facilitate public consultation became a proxy for the local community. The nature of purchasing was also fundamentally affected. Instead of first identifying needs and then identifying alternative ways in which services could be provided to meet those needs, there was a tendency for needs to be understood immediately in terms of the type and quantity of services required. This made it difficult to imagine service options and carry out creative problem solving and negotiations with providers in the interests of the local community.

Two other points are worth making. First, this whole analysis seems to be incomplete without a recognition that the lack of effective public pressure, possibly due to the relatively passive and acquiescent nature of the public, was a critical contextual factor, alongside the budgetary problems and the weak position of the health authority within the internal market. Second, the case study presented in Box 6.2 not only explains the lack of public say in the planning and purchasing process but also suggests that joint planning with providers and other agencies can be a very contradictory experience and involves issues of interests, power and influence. It is not a simple process of making plans through rational and orderly decision making within a framework of agreed objectives. This is so even when there are official expectations of consultation, partnerships and integration of services between agencies.

Joint planning by professionals in primary healthcare

In a number of European countries, including the UK, there has been an interest in developing a stronger emphasis on primary healthcare. In 1982 the director of the European region of the World Health Organization (WHO) presented draft targets giving priority to primary healthcare to the ministries of health in Europe. Abel-Smith (1994) suggests that this

Table 3.1 Evaluation criteria clusters

Model of the strategic planning process	Criteria
Application of strategy to implementation of political directives	Coordination or integration with other strategies, programmes and activities; technical feasibility; cost and financing; cost effectiveness; staff requirements; facility/training requirements.
Results-oriented, mission-led planning	Consistency with mission, values, philosophy and culture; client or user impact; flexibility or adaptability.
Partnership-based strategic planning	Acceptability to key decision makers, stakeholders and opinion leaders; acceptance by the general public.

is seen as ensuring that political directives are implemented, then the best strategy is technically feasible, involves a cost effective use of resources and is consistent with the implementation of other political objectives and directives. If the strategic planning and management is results-oriented and mission-led, the best strategy will be clearly consistent with the mission statement and values of the organization, produce the biggest benefits for clients and users and will reinforce attempts to maintain the flexibility and adaptability of the organization. If the strategic planning and management is partnership-based, then the best strategy is one that creates the best possibility for sustaining a coalition for change and maintaining a momentum behind collaborative efforts which address community issues; therefore, acceptability to partners, stakeholders and the public is a very important consideration in selecting the best strategy.

Overall attractiveness of each strategic alternative

One approach to appraisal involves a table of criteria and a points system to score each strategic option being considered.

The three clusters suggested in the previous section might be used to select or weight the criteria to be used to match the function of the strategic planning. Alternatively, the relevant decision making criteria might include, broadly, the costs and the benefits. In recent years, most evaluations of public services have revolved around issues of efficiency and

priority for primary healthcare could be seen as useful for containing costs at a time when governments in Europe were concerned about public spending.

In the UK, the movement towards developing primary healthcare has continued. In 1994, the government stated its aim of moving towards primary-care led purchasing in which GPs would do the purchasing of secondary and tertiary care. Implementation of this via GP fundholding was begun, and it was anticipated that health authorities would increasingly become responsible for strategy, monitoring and support – as they gave up a purchasing role. In 1997 the government announced that Primary Care Groups were to be set up and would be involved in commissioning care for their local areas. This indicates the end of GP fundholding but not the end of a policy of creating a primary-care led national health service. It is envisaged that health authorities will over time hand their commissioning role over to the Primary Care Groups.

One issue which arises from this development in health services is the degree to which GPs are able to balance their operational focus on meeting the immediate health needs of their patients with a strategic capacity for healthcare planning (Hodgson 1996: 250). This is an issue in part because GPs are suspected of not having much of a strategic analysis of their local community's health needs and may not even be that responsive to their patients' wishes. Another issue is the concern about the ability of GPs and other professionals in primary healthcare to work together because of poor communication and mistrust.

It has been argued, however, that getting healthcare professionals to develop and use practice-based information systems can be useful for creating the conditions needed for effective health planning in primary care. Newchurch and Company (undated) recommended a planning process which draws on existing data generated at primary-care level, but which turns it into a 'usable form'. The data relates to GP practice populations. Newchurch and Company suggested that this should be done by 'liaison between all those generating data, first to determine the extent to which existing systems can be co-ordinated to produce practical information and second, to prioritise future data collection, IT was to be used so as to bring together data from disparate sources and convert them so that they can be readily understood by those responsible for delivering healthcare on the ground'. A comparison of data on needs and the services actually delivered would then be the basis for service enhancement plans.

This process was seen as potentially useful for bringing about cultural changes, creating a shared language and building effective primary healthcare teams. It was claimed that 'the GP practice can be confirmed as the focus for healthcare delivery' and 'those responsible for delivering healthcare are encouraged to pull together rather than pull apart'. In other words, what might seem like a technical process of pooling existing data, planning to upgrade the available data, and analysing data using IT is really a team-building process leading to focused and cohesive primary health teams.

Joint public service planning in community care

Public services managers and professionals often express commitment and goodwill towards the idea of working with others in different public services organizations (Cox 1996). Cross-agency strategic planning is supposed to be taking place, especially in services in the welfare field in the UK and the USA (Berry and Wechsler 1995). But, just because a number of public services organizations have intersecting mandates, this does not mean that they are able to cooperate effectively. The experience of collaboration by health and social services organizations in community care in the UK suggests that there is still much to be done to achieve coordination and coalignment.

The background to the emergence of joint planning by social services departments and health services in the field of community care is quite well known. In the mid-1980s the Audit Commission suggested the existence of confusion and problems with the services in community care, and at the end of the 1980s a government White Paper – *Caring for People: Community Care in the Next Decade and Beyond* (Department of Health 1989) – talked about the production of community care plans which would be submitted to the social services inspectorate. The NHS and Community Care Act of 1991 established a legislative mandate for social services departments to take the lead on community care. At about that time, social services departments were being advised to become more strategic, to develop partnerships and to adapt organizationally and culturally to a role of purchasing and enabling alongside a direct involvement in service provision.

The first community care plans were prepared for 1992/3. Knapp and Lawson (1995: 191–2) outlined the requirements of these plans as follows: 'Each social services department must build up a population profile identifying need and available supply, and produce three-year community care plans which are updated annually. These plans must be produced in consultation with users, carers and the independent sector, and collaboratively with local DHAs, FHSAs and housing authorities'.

The course of joint strategic planning has not been a smooth one. There have been tensions in the general relationship between social services managers and professionals on the one hand and health services managers and professionals on the other hand. Heginbotham (1997: 1) nominated 'mutual suspicion of each other's motives, values, objectives and approaches' as the key problem in two cases of local authorities working with health services. The first case briefly reviewed by Heginbotham was focused on the relationship between Westminster City Council and Riverside Mental Health Trust, which was based on the council awarding a five-year contract to the trust to deliver services to mentally ill people. As a result of this contract, staff were transferred from local government to the health services. Heginbotham reports that some of the Westminster staff were sceptical of the ability of the trust to ensure 'social' care continued to be delivered and that other members of staff did not want to be part of the NHS. The second case concerned Stevenage Borough Council and East and North Hertfordshire Health Authority which together established a joint health services committee. Some degree of mistrust might be seen as normal between buyers and sellers of services in a contractual relationship. But why was the second case also marred by suspicion? Heginbotham reported:

> The perceived reason for the development [of] the committee was a lack of effective local accountability of the health service for the significant developments of health and healthcare in the area. Stevenage Borough Council had established a monitoring commitee which was concerned with health service matters but had no direct management relationship with the health authority. The Authority was perceived as rather distant, bureaucratic, hierarchical and democratically unaccountable. The Stevenage Health Services Committee . . . has been one method by which the Authority can be held to account by local people . . .
>
> (Heginbotham 1997: 5)

Although this point is not explicitly made by Heginbotham, it is possible to draw the inference from these two cases that some of the legacy of mutual suspicion between local government and health services arises because of the way in which marketization was the midwife to some of the 'cooperation' between them, and because local government has tended to criticize health services organizations for their lack of local accountability (and democracy).

Marketization has meant that social services are not expected to be so heavily involved in direct service provision, and that they will be more concerned with assessing needs and contracting for services. The result is a mixed economy of community care, with public, private and voluntary sectors all contributing to social care. At the same time there is the pressure for social services, as the leading agency in community care, to promote partnerships. Langan and Clarke (1994) argue that this creates two versions of the social services department's role which have to be handled. These are, their role in contracting and getting value for money, and their role in enabling and partnership working.

> It is not clear that these two versions of the local authority role sit comfortably together. It may be that they become distributed to different levels of the partner organizations, such that competition and

---

Box 6.3 Working in partnership: an ideological blockage?

In December 1997 a UK health minister announced plans to replace the Central Council for Education and Training in Social Work (CCETSW) with the Social Care Council. CCETSW had been formed in the early 1970s and was concerned with the training of social workers, whereas the Social Care Council's scope was to cover social workers and workers in residential and domiciliary care.

A newspaper report said that the minister 'has let it be known that he wants to "break the mind-set" of social workers and social services departments who believe that they are "the only ingredient" in the care of children, the elderly and the disabled' (*The Sunday Telegraph* 21 December 1997).

The newspaper report went on to say that there were ministerial concerns about the failures of social services departments to work with organizations in other sectors.

---

contracting become 'strategic' issues while lower levels of management busy themselves with building partnership bridges – or vice versa, depending on which version is given strategic priority.

(Langan and Clarke 1994: 88)

The antipathy which is sometimes apparent between the two public services, however, is not purely a result of experiences of tendering, cultural changes brought about by social services' purchasing role, and the arguments about the health services' democratic credentials. Social services personnel are sometimes regarded very critically by health services personnel: they are said to lack expertise, to be arrogant and have management structures which function poorly. The health services personnel are regarded by social services personnel as lacking real democratic legitimacy and as not being very accountable to people in the locality. Social services may appear to be very arrogant because they assume they have the sole right to speak on behalf of local people and their needs, and may be disparaging about the public consultation efforts of the health services. These frictions may cause either or both to wish that they could just get on with the job and not have to bother with working in cooperation. However, there are signs that national politicians will not tolerate professional hostility to coordination across organizational boundaries (see Box 6.3).

Other problems for joint strategic planning have stemmed from the funding situation. There has been a perception of continuing pressures of budgetary restraints at a time when demand for community care is seen to be expanding. Langan and Clarke (1994) quoted evidence suggesting that half of all councils were reporting a standstill or reduction in social services budgets in 1991/2 and plans for 1993 showed an intention to cut personal social services budgets by 87 per cent. This was at the time of the implementation of the community care policy, and in the midst of severe

Box 6.4 What is strategy in community care services?

Cox (1996) carried out a study of joint commissioning of a community care service in London. He quotes an official definition of joint commissioning which suggests that this is a process in which two or more commissioning agencies coordinate their commissioning, taking joint responsibility for translating strategy into action. As part of this study he interviewed a number of social services and health professionals. His respondents' answers provide some interesting insights into how public services managers within community care viewed strategy.

As might be guessed, there was no common or universal definition of strategy. At least three different conceptions were apparent. First, there was a conception of strategy as a process of agreeing a plan. Second, there was a view of strategy as a process which consists essentially of setting and realizing objectives. Third, there was a view of strategy as a solution to a strategic issue.

The first conception of strategy was suggested by a local authority respondent, who saw strategy as a plan agreed with health services: 'It means we sit down together and decide where we are going over a period of three years – where we should be going in the future. So it's . . . a plan of the direction in which we're going – it's quite a vague plan'. The British government required local authority social services departments to prepare and submit community care plans and had subsequently advised local authorities to prepare community care plans on a three-year basis.

The second idea of strategy was articulated most clearly by a respondent who stated: 'Strategy . . . is having a set of objectives and a way of getting to them. So, when you talk about strategic planning or whatever, it's being clear where you want to get to and having an ordered path for getting there'. Where were they trying to get to? One health services respondent said that the aim was 'to provide more health services to people in or near their own homes'. This is indeed a summing up of the community care strategic change agenda over a decade or more – moving various client groups (e.g. people with mental health problems and people with learning difficulties) out of hospitals and into the community so that they can lead ordinary lives, and helping clients (e.g. elderly people and people with disabilities) by supporting them in their own homes so they do not need residential services.

One of the health professionals said: 'Strategy for us is eight objectives'. This last curious explanation of strategy probably reflected the approach to planning which had been promulgated at national level in Britain's health services, and which had been relayed down to health authorities through the guidance of the NHS executive. Perhaps the reference to eight objectives derived directly from the fact that, in late 1995, the secretary of state had issued a statement identifying exactly eight objectives for the NHS Executive (see Box 6.1)?

It seems from Cox's findings that public services managers may be inclined to conceptualize strategy in ways which reflect official managerial frameworks for planning public services. Consequently, the difference between health and social services definitions of strategy, as noted above, reflects the variation in managerial frameworks set for the two public services.

The third conception of strategy articulated by health services respondents. was that strategy was concerned with big issues and dealing with contradictory requirements. As one health services respondent put it: 'So a strategy for us

means having to cope with purchasing the same amount of healthcare, or changing or improving the healthcare over time, while we're losing money in real
terms'. One respondent discussed the problem from the local authority point of
view. The problem was described in terms of the level of resources needed and
the limits on the amount which could be spent on care packages for individuals.
This may explain the concern among social services managers about individual
eligibility criteria for access to services. Such criteria are, of course, one way of
handling a situation in which resources are limited and demand is going up.

These different problems reported by Cox's respondents suggest a very difficult general strategic issue: how do you successfully transform public services to
provide effective community care while managing government pressures to be
very economical with resources? This was an issue for both social services and
the health services. Strategy, therefore, was having to cope with the dilemmas of
a situation that had been created by the framework of public policy In terms of
how the public services should be developed and about how spending on services
ought to change.

Another important glimpse into what strategy meant to practitioners concerned the balance between a strategy imposed from above and a strategy produced by managers at their own discretion. Cox quotes one respondent as
estimating that, in the health services, only about 20 to 30 per cent of strategy
was a matter of local freedom. This reflected the fact that planning was being
used in quite a major way to manage the internal market created within the NHS,
and that, consequently, strategic planning was being experienced predominantly as
a top-down imposition on managers at local level.

All in all, managers in these public services were not free agents in terms of
how they saw strategy Their definitions of strategy reflected managerial frameworks created ultimately by government, and the issues that strategy addressed
were created by the policy frameworks also set by government. This may be
taken as a clue to the overall pattern of strategic planning and management in the
public services: they are closely connected to political processes and the actions
of elected politicians.

---

problems in the economy, which could be expected to generate more
demand for social services. In such situations the two sides may see a logic
in cooperating to protect services, but there is the problem that one side or
the other will try to export the pressures to the other party.

We should not underestimate the effects of different managerial arrangements for creating different ideas of what joint strategic management and
planning should be. A study by Cox (1996) shows not only the existence
of varied ideas about strategic management and planning among social
services and health services personnel, but also reports findings which suggest that these differences are grounded in different managerial contexts
(see Box 6.4).

What can be done to create the conditions for effective joint strategic
planning? One popular idea in the late 1990s was the formation of joint
commissioning structures with local authority and health authority money

pooled into one budget for purposes of strategic planning and joint commissioning. A single manager is appointed to head up such an organization, but the staff are drawn from, and still employed by, the separate health and local authorities. The rationale often presented was simply that this is the easiest way of getting a seamless service.

Developing strategy for networks

Boundaries between public, private and voluntary sectors are blurring. This has occurred as a result of governments opening up public services to competition from private sector providers. It has occurred in some cases because the voluntary sector has been preferred as a provider of services previously provided exclusively by the statutory public services. This blurring has been the result, in other words, of competition between the three sectors.

It has also occurred when governments have encouraged public-private partnerships, and where government organizations have taken on a community leadership role and brought together organizations from all sectors to tackle emerging community issues. This blurring is the result of greater cooperation for purposes of problem solving.

To take one example of the move towards cooperation, strategic leaders at Kirklees Metropolitan Authority (UK) in recent years have endorsed the importance of partnership. This has led to managers seeking access to resources, expertise and ideas in the private, voluntary and community sectors. Leadbetter and Goss (1998: 36) have referred to the council as having a 'burgeoning network of relationships with private, voluntary and community partners'. The result has been innovative developments. A new sports stadium, opened in Huddersfield during 1994, is one of the tangible results of Kirklees council working in partnership with others. Leadbetter and Goss remark: 'The stadium, which has a worldwide reputation, is a modern monument to civic entrepreneurship . . . Kirklees brokered a highly creative public-private partnership which has built a stadium that is neither purely public nor purely private: it is a community asset' (p. 36).

In the context of cooperative problem solving, there have been attempts to forge agreed (collective) strategies to address issues of concern to the community which are not being tackled adequately by existing provision. The overall style is one of using strategic planning to bring about innovative alliances to achieve innovative solutions. The issues are increasingly visible and well-known – economic regeneration, crime, community safety, traffic congestion, environmental problems, drugs, and so on. These issues have been seen as sharing a common characteristic: they cannot be solved by one government department or public service acting in isolation. Provan and Milward (1995: 2) make this point in relation to community care:

While focus on organizational effectiveness is clearly appropriate when outcomes can readily be attributed to the activities of individual organizations, not all problems can be solved by the actions of individual organizations. Particularly in the areas of community-based healthcare and social services for such groups as the homeless, people with severe mental illness, drug and alcohol abusers, and the elderly, a focus on organizational outcomes is insufficient, because such outcomes reflect only how well individual providers are performing their particular component of the many services needed by their clients. If [their] overall well-being is a goal, then effectiveness must be assessed at the network level, since client well-being depends on the integrated and coordinated actions of many different agencies separately providing shelter, transportation, food, and health, mental health, legal, vocational, recreational, family, and income support services.

The truth of this and similar arguments for better coordination and integration of the activities of public, private and voluntary organizations is often assumed. Instances of waste and overlap are often adduced to back up the requirement to attempt better coordination and networking of organizations, but rarely have the benefits of integration been systematically measured. And in the absence of systematic study, ideas about coordination and integration can be fuzzy.

For instance, are networks totally different in principle from market and hierarchical systems of coordination and integration? In ill-defined ways there tends to be a positive feeling about networks. Perhaps they are seen as inherently more democratic, cooperative or even humanistic? Frances *et al.* (1991: 14) say: 'A network is often thought of as a "flat" organizational form in contrast to the vertically organized hierarchical form . . . It conjures up the idea of informal relationships between essentially equal social agents and agencies. The collegiate organization is a classic example of a network. These kinds of organizational units are often cooperatively run'.

But as Frances *et al.* (1991) also suggest, the informality of a network may be associated with unclear accountability. Managers in public services who have had experience of marketization, competitive tendering arrangements and a contract culture may even express some dismay at the thought of having to operate within the context of a loosely coordinated and informal network of providers.

Research carried out in the USA on networks involved in delivering services to clients with mental health problems suggests that there is a need to consider how well different types of networks perform. Provan and Milward (1995) looked at the effectiveness of services in four cities: Tucson, Akron, Albuquerque and Providence. Data collected from nearly

140 clients and their families indicated that the most effective network was based in Providence, whereas the network of providers in Tucson were the least effective. Provan and Milward collected data on service and organizational links. Informants in each of the agencies surveyed were asked about five different types of service links: referrals sent, referrals received, case coordination, joint programmes and service contracts. The organizational links within a network were measured by the average number of agency links (based on links of the five types). The network of providers in Providence, the most effective of the four, actually had fewer service links and organizational links than the others.

Provan and Milward (1995) also collected evidence from each agency on whether they considered the needs, goals, decisions and expectations of others in their network. In Providence the core agency was much more of a focus for links and for influence than was the core agency in Tucson, even though the network links were greater for Tucson than Providence.

Provan and Milward sum up their findings by saying: 'When influence over mental health decisions was highly concentrated in a single core agency, as in Providence, client outcomes were strongest. At the other extreme, when influence was widely dispersed among a number of agencies, as in Tucson, effectiveness was lowest' (1995: 16).

These two cities provided examples of very different types of networks for the same client group. Arguably, there is support in these findings for concern that a shift in public services from hierarchical coordination or from a contract culture might end up producing networks in which decision making is informal and there is an absence of clear leadership by one agency. However, the move towards network arrangements could well produce better outcomes for the public if there is one organization at the centre of each network providing influential leadership.

How does, or how should, a network plan? No definitive answer is attempted here, but one key question must surely be: can joint strategic planning emerge when organizations lack effective strategic planning and management within partner organizations in the network? In the case of UK local authorities, corporate planning for the organization seems to have often preceded attempts to develop strategies involving the community and partners. Perhaps this allows an increasing or progressive commitment of time and resources to joint strategic planning. For example, as a first step a public services organization might invite some external people onto one of its strategic forums or working groups. At this first stage, the external people may be able to bring insights and opinions from other public, private and voluntary organizations, without there being any intention that they should act as representatives of their respective organizations. The focus is likely to be on the achievements of the organization which are to be enhanced by involving others in discussions to produce more effective strategies.

At a second stage, perhaps the focus shifts to an attempt to influence the actions of partner organizations by using strategic forums or working groups to discuss goals or problems which might be addressed by each organization separately. It may be hoped that discussions and analysis persuade partner organizations to reconceptualize their own priorities and actions in a way which helps the organization to be more effective. In this case, the members of the forum or working group are selected as key people within their own organization who can influence the strategic direction of that organization. However, all partners remain working within a framework of organizational achievement.

The final stage might occur when a strategic forum or working group takes on a supra-organizational identity, works towards community or interorganizational achievement, and searches for explicit agreements on the respective contributions of each individual organization to community or interorganizational achievement through coordinated action and pooling of resources. At this point, each organization has developed strategic intentions beyond its own limited capacity and is committed to deploying its abilities and resources as part of an overall effort for the greater good (however that may be defined). The members of the forum or working groups at this stage would need to be the strategic leaders of their organizations, or people with a clear mandate to negotiate on behalf of their organizations, with good access to their organizational leaders for the approval of matters which lie beyond their powers of decision making.

Such a process for the development of joint strategic planning presumably has the virtue of building on pre-existing commitments by partner organizations to being strategic. To become involved in joint strategic planning when such a commitment is uncertain may be just too complex to manage. It also has the virtue of evolving a more ambitious form of strategic planning out of the quite modest step of involving others in an internal planning process.

The action of elected politicians is an important factor in the development of joint, or even coordinated, planning by a network of organizations. In some cases elected politicians are requiring the leaders of public agencies to demonstrate that they have developed organizational strategies which have been coordinated with those of other public agencies to avoid unnecessary duplication of effort. Resource allocation processes can be shaped by politicians to motivate and reward joint strategic planning, and agencies which fail to demonstrate a willingness to coalign and work in partnership with other public services organizations could find future funding decisions favouring others. This may encourage a more coordinated approach to strategy formulation, but it is an arm's length one. Alternative forms of political intervention exist which may provide good prospects of effective, coordinated and joint strategic planning. For example, politicians may set up inter-agency forums in which policy ideas and cooperative

---

Box 6.5 Ohio state's inter-agency task forces and cabinet-cluster work-ing groups

In the 1980s, the Ohio Department of Mental Health undertook a whole series of strategic actions in cooperation with other state agencies. This seems to have been facilitated by the appointment of the department's top managers to inter-agency task forces and cabinet-cluster working groups by the state's governor. The clusters were useful in enabling the top managers to talk to other agency leaders, and ideas emerged which led to 'cooperative demonstration projects and other ventures', so that 'the multiple needs of people with mental illnesses could be met through coordinated interagency and interjurisdictional actions' (Frost-Kumpf et al. 1993: 141).

---

projects can be discussed (see Box 6.5 on Ohio state's inter-agency task forces and cabinet-cluster working groups).

Networks, forums and teams

In a network context, the problems of making joint forums or strategic teams work well partly depend on why and how the forum is brought together. If one organization takes the lead in convening a forum of agency leaders, or their representatives, then the other forum members may ask themselves if the motivation of the initiating agency is to offload problems. For example, in the case of community care in the UK, the voluntary sector may feel that 'partnerships' are really the local authority seeking to walk away from some of its responsibilities and 'dump' its problems back on the community.

In general, until there is trust and agreement that a forum is not a one-sided bargain, then the other forum members may hold back in discussions and become rather passive observers. Since they have no real resource stake in the forum, they will politely approve any operational decisions being made by the initiating organization.

Of course, the act of initiating a multi-agency group may not be intended to create a strategic planning forum. The initiating agency may have no real desire for joint strategic planning, but simply like the idea of a forum because it is seen as fashionable or in keeping with the idea that it is good to talk to other agencies. It may be that the initiating agency is intending to use the forum merely as a sounding board, and is seeking approval for the overall strategy it is pursuing and for the measures used to implement it. It may not welcome full-blooded debates to establish a shared strategic agenda, and may wish to conduct forum meetings as a series of formal reports on its thinking and actions, punctuated by invitations to others attending to express approval for what is being planned or done.

For a forum to work effectively as a consortium of strategic partners the strategic issue agenda has to be established by all participating organizations bringing their problems to the forum. Bargaining must then take place over what precisely constitutes the issue agenda and what resources the various stakeholders will contribute to the solution of these issues. The obvious problem at this point is achieving a sense of equity in terms of the costs and benefits this joint strategic planning will offer to all participants.

In order to begin the necessary bargaining over the strategic agenda, forum members need to be encouraged to place on the table their own concerns. Discussions of the forum members may suggest the existence of a variety of concerns, but the chair of the forum must be attentive to the expression of such concerns, welcome them, and seek to induce fairly full statements of them. If inattentiveness becomes the pattern of the early meetings of the forum, then attendance may fall away, and is unlikely to be improved by pleas to forum members to attend because their presence is considered important. Forum participants are much more likely to feel their presence is regarded as important if their attempts to place their concerns on the table are recognized and supported.

Another potential barrier to an effective strategic planning forum is created by jealousies and rivalries between agencies in terms of status or resources. For example, a public services organization aspiring to a community leadership role may antagonize another public agency. There may be counter claims between organizations about the real needs of the community which may become destructive when one organization impugns anothers' credentials in terms of public involvement in its decision making processes. There are difficulties about who most represents the community between the public services and the voluntary sector, with the latter sometimes believing that local elected representatives are just politicking rather than truly speaking from a close knowledge of what ordinary voters want. Some jealousies spring from past public spending decisions which took resources from one agency and gave more to another, especially where the second agency is seen as a quango and not really accountable, or is seen as being too responsive to central government and insufficiently oriented to the needs of the local community. Such jealousies and rivalries are a challenge to the effective working of a strategic planning forum for a consortium of bodies. If the challenge is not recognized, or not met, then the forum can become paralysed by animosities and distrust.

When a range of issues and concerns from all organizations have emerged, then the difficult job of constructing a shared agenda becomes crucial so that a coalition for change can be established. As we saw above, empirical study suggests that all the partners in the network cannot be equal in influence – there needs to be an organization providing a sense of strategic direction and operating as the hub of the network of organizations. Any organization which carries out a leadership role is bound to be accused of being arrogant or bureaucratic, which happened, for example, in the case of the core mental health agency in Providence studied by Provan and Milward (1995) (see p. 116).

Conclusions

This chapter has examined various forms of joint strategic planning. It considered joint planning by different health services organizations, by professionals in primary healthcare, and by social services and health services in the field of community care. Joint strategic planning is difficult. There are tensions. This is reflected in antagonistic attitudes and a lack of mutual trust and respect. Other problems for joint strategic planning have stemmed from budgetary pressures at a time when demand for services is seen to be expanding. There can be fears that one side or the other will try to export the pressures to the other party.

What can be done to create the conditions for effective joint strategic planning? Joint commissioning structures may be thought of as a solution to the problems of strategic planning and joint commissioning. Another answer is to place the development of joint planning in the context of a long-term commitment which can be developed progressively. This approach may start with one organization inviting representatives of other organizations to join in an internal strategic planning process. Then the organizations may seek to influence the actions of partner organizations by using strategic forums or working groups to discuss goals or problems which might be addressed by each organization separately. Finally, trust may be developed to a point where coordinated action is possible. To become involved in joint strategic planning when a full commitment to it is uncertain may be just too complex to manage.

The problems of making strategic forums work in the context of networks of providers reflect the intentions of the respective organizations. The way the problems present themselves also depends on how the forum is brought together. If one organization takes the lead in convening a forum of agency leaders, or their representatives, then the other forum members may ask themselves if the motivation is to gain their support or resources for priorities or aims held by the initiator agency. Yet, there appears to be a need for one organization to act as the leader in a network. The evidence to date suggests that networks which are too collegiate may be ineffective when judged in terms of the outcomes for the public. So, leadership is needed for effective strategic and operational management of networks.

Will the growing experience of public services with networks and forums for planning mature into effective coordinated and coaligned action for the public? Or will the move to partnerships and networks falter as its champions encounter the mundane difficulties of getting people to co-operate who do not yet trust each other, and do not yet have the confidence that cooperation can pay off? The political climate nationally and locally may be all-important in determining how much pressure there is on forum members to overcome these problems of joint working and to develop effective relationships for concerted analysis and action.

seven

Strategy and crisis

Key learning objectives

After reading this chapter you should be able to:

1 Describe and apply the concept of crisis appropriately in the public services.
2 Identify suitable approaches for anticipating, preparing for, and handling crises.

Introduction

The effective handling of a crisis, or potential crisis, is rarely examined in much depth in strategic management theory. This is surprising. Of course, it might be hoped that strategic planning and management can handle crises. For instance, good planning might foresee potential problems, and action can be taken to avert crisis situations long before they materialize. Planning techniques such as scenario planning seem to offer useful tools for anticipating crisis situations which might lie ahead. Monitoring and control systems should deal with crises arising during strategy implementation. And strategic plans might include contingency plans which can be activated if a crisis develops. Despite all this, there are still situations in which crises do develop fully and have to be managed.

In this chapter we briefly review the use of scenario planning and open simulation to anticipate crisis situations, the use of monitoring and control systems to prevent crises developing during strategic implementation processes, the design and use of contingency plans, and the strategies and tactics for handling crisis situations which have not been expected. First, however, we look a little more closely at the nature of a crisis and how different organizations respond to it.

What is a 'crisis'?

The idea that some public services organizations are in a state of crisis has been quite popular in the media in recent years. According to Heath (1997: 294): 'Crisis occurs when an organization actually or seemingly loses control of its operations and the consequences of that action appears or actually does have dire consequences'. This definition seems to fit a number of public services industries in recent years.

The crisis label has been attached to hospital and other medical services because of perceived failings such as lengthening waiting times for operations, poor services in casualty departments and blunders in health screening programmes. The prison services in the UK have been seen as in a state of crisis because of the rising prison population, overcrowding, and, some years ago, a spate of prison occupations. Again in the UK, there have been claims of a crisis in the education services evidenced by poor literacy levels, poor performance judged by international standards and high exclusion rates for some categories of the population. A very specific crisis in welfare services has been associated with the community care policy implemented in the 1990s. Media concerns in this case have sometimes taken the form of accusations that people with mental health problems have been dumped in the community without adequate services being in place, and with consequent risks to the public. Some well-publicized cases of ex-mental health patients attacking and killing members of the public placed the spotlight on the performance of public services in relation to community care.

Common to all these examples is the general idea that there is a crisis in terms of the operational results of the public services. The cause may be disputed. It may be argued that resources are wrongly allocated and targeted. It may be said that public services simply lack a performance culture and waste the resources provided. It may be argued that the whole system of public service provision needs overhauling and modernizing, and that innovative thinking is needed to address community priorities in partnership with the voluntary and private sectors.

Applying the concept of crisis at the level of the individual public services organization can also start with the idea that there is a problem concerning the results being achieved by the organization. This might seem to suggest that we are talking only about operational crises – when organizations are delivering low levels of service output or the service is not achieving the intended outcomes. But a crisis is not immediately to be equated with an operational crisis measured in terms of a lack of results.

Box 7.1 Crisis-preparedness in the UK prison service

Smith (1993) reported the results of a survey of 59 prison governors within England and Wales. Their responses were interpreted by him as showing that 'despite adverse media attention, the Prison Service could generally be considered to be taking the process of crisis management seriously and was not crisis prone as suggested by media reports' (p. 163). Smith detected a good state of preparedness in terms of organizational strategies for crisis management and organizational culture. He suggested that the governors saw some scope for improvements in relation to the core beliefs of individuals and the dedicated structure for crisis management, however these areas were not assessed by him as showing serious deficiencies.

The implications of this research are not clear. Had a crisis of legitimation been created by the media's attention? Should public confidence in the management of the prison service be high on the basis of these findings? Had a good state of crisis preparation been achieved as a result of a lot of experience of dealing with crises? Or can crisis preparedness only be properly validated by the ability of the organization to respond effectively prior to, and during, an actual crisis?

There are some public services which have a reputation for crisis which may be ill-deserved (see Box 7.1 on UK prison services). In the public services, a crisis often has a very political or public nature, too. If a public service organization is not achieving its main strategic and performance goals, as set or agreed by elected politicians, there is often no automatic mechanism by which this becomes a crisis. Unless a system has been set up whereby funding is closely tied to results, then politicians must intervene when a public service appears to be failing to perform adequately. This requires that they must first become aware of a problem and then decide to intervene in the situation (e.g. by threatening to close down the organization or halt public funding for the organization). At this point, there is a threat to the survival of the organization and there can be no mistaking that a state of crisis exists.

The will of politicians to act in this way depends to a considerable degree on the state of public opinion. If a public service organization is not satisfying the public's expectations then politicians are more likely to regard that organization as in a crisis. So, public dissatisfaction may hasten political intervention, just as public confidence and support for a public service organization may deter political intervention. This factor may be used to justify the argument that public services managers need to pay attention to a 'crisis of legitimation' which may intensify the difficulties of dealing with an operational crisis (Smith 1993). Organizations in the public services may need to give attention both to solving the problems behind the operational crises they are experiencing and to regenerating public confidence in the services they provide.

We can speculate that there are important variations in the vulnerability of public services organizations to becoming a target for political intervention. Organizations which are delivering services of central importance to the political agenda of a government ought to be more vulnerable as they are more critical to the overall performance of government. For example, a government which makes education its main priority should be highly critical of teachers, schools and educational institutions which perform poorly. On the other hand, it may be suspected that politicians are more lenient towards services which are closer to their heart. Then again, perhaps organizations which deliver large-scale, complex and integrated services are less likely to be targets for political intervention because it is more difficult to know how to intervene. Finally, it may be that some organizations have highly effective coalitions of administrative and professional interests to lobby politicians on their behalf and head-off political interventions.

The causes of crisis

Most of the explanations for the occurrence of crises in public services organizations locate the source of the problem in the poor fit between the organization and its environment. This can develop because the organization has not kept up with the changes occurring around it. Of course, in the case of the public services, a failure to keep up with external changes tends to mean that a gap opens up between the organization and the public it is meant to be serving. This is one sense in which an organization may be accused of being bureaucratic – that is, failing to observe changes in its environment and make adjustments in strategy, resources, activities, etc. which are required for it to continue serving the public effectively.

Crozier's (1964) investigations of the branch of a large public agency in Paris and a state-owned French production organization offer a number of detailed insights into how large public sector organizations can develop qualities which are dysfunctional for serving the public. Crozier suggested that every organization 'must continually adjust to some kind of change. It must be flexible. To achieve this vague but primary end, it must rely on individual and group ingenuity and cannot discourage it too much' (1964: 186). He believed that it was not possible under normal circumstances for an organization to evade for long a requirement to adjust its behaviour to changing realities. The gap between the organization and its environment meant that it would make errors in serving the public and this would produce feedback that would lead the organization to correct its behaviour. However, based on his two case studies, Crozier suggested that there were four factors which inhibited this error-information-correction loop to close the gap between the organization and its environment. First, if impersonal rules do actually determine all behaviour within an organization, then hierarchical superiors lose their power over subordinates, and vice versa. Second, if decision making is centralized to eliminate the personal element (i.e. so that the decision makers are not affected by those who are affected by the decisions), then those who have first-hand knowledge of problems are excluded from decision making. Thus, a desire to reduce the personal element reduces the ability to adjust the organization to its environment. Third, as an associated feature of the weakenening of hierarchical power by impersonal rules, the peer group formed by individuals at the same strata becomes very powerful. Crozier commmented: 'A bureaucratic organization, therefore, is comprised of a series of superimposed strata that do not communicate very much with each other' (1964: 190). As a result, goal displacement occurs as peer groups protect themselves against other groups in the organization. Fourth, to the extent that areas of uncertainty remain which cannot be subjected to impersonal rules, the experts who handle such remaining areas of uncertainty become privileged and independent.

In summary, Crozier believed that all people in an organization tend to act to further their own privileges, creating these bureaucratic characteristics, which then work to block communication with the environment and communication within the organization. The power struggles within the organization were thus ultimately responsible for the failure to adjust behaviour to changing external realities.

Two views

The general idea of organizations needing to adjust to changing environments is commonly found in contemporary strategic management texts. It is assumed that an organizational response to environmental developments is often made only when a crisis has occurred. This implies that organizations may vary along a continuum in terms of their handling of a trend or event. If the organization has a good environmental scanning system and early warning signs of a problem are picked up quickly, then it may have ample time to analyse the emerging threat and prepare plans for countering the development. This may be done so well that the potential problem is not only neutralized but some advantage is obtained from it. At the other extreme, where an organization is very internally focused, then an event or trend takes the organization by surprise, and the leaders and strategic managers may find themselves assessing the situation and making plans for a response in the midst of a crisis. The implication of this view is clear: the variations in organizational response to events and trends are attributable to different capabilities in environmental surveillance, accurate assessment of the consequences of an external threat, contingency planning and effective implementation of adjustments.

In contrast to this capability-based view of organizational differences, there is what might be termed the 'pathology' view of crisis proneness. While this approach accepts that there is an external trigger to a crisis, explaining a crisis is mainly based on identifying the role of pathology in the organization's design, culture or strategic posture. The grounds of the crisis are located in 'the values and beliefs of managers, the communication processes within the organization and the decision making procedures' (Smith 1993: 146). Given the existence of 'resident pathogens' it apparently only takes a small trigger event to 'propel the organization into the throes of a crisis' (Smith 1993: 146). In less emotive terms, this approach suggests that it is the organization rather than the environment which needs attention, and that crisis-prone organizations need to be changed organizationally so that they are better prepared to cope with external events. This pathology view could be illustrated by the work of Crozier (1964) which we reviewed above – at least in the sense that organizations might be seen as developing bureaucratic rigidities, although, of course, Crozier saw these rigidities as normal consequences of people pursuing privilege.

Research by Miles and Snow (1978), based on a small sample of hospitals during a specific crisis episode, seems to show that the effective management of a crisis depends on following an approach which is consistent with the ongoing strategy of the organization (see Box 7.2). The rationale for this link seems to be that the ongoing strategy requires certain organizational capabilities (e.g. environmental surveillance and contingency planning, management of efficiency and low costs) which are then applied to the handling of the crisis. This implies that there is some basis for the capability-based view of crisis management. In sum, different strategies imply different approaches to crisis management, and both the capability-based view and the pathology view of crisis management have some merit in explaining how crises are handled and what their impact is.

Crises, strategic networks and joint planning

How to develop an effective response to a crisis event in the context of a strategic network or joint planning situation needs some consideration, even if we can only mention it here briefly. Take, for example, the case of the increasing expectation that social services departments will work with health services providers, the voluntary sector and private businesses. How would two partners in such a coalition develop an effective response to a crisis impacting on an area of shared concern or responsibility?

Five points can be usefully made about the complex issues involved in developing effective strategic responses in such situations. First, the different parties in the coalition may not be aware of, or agree on, the early

---

Box 7.2 A capability-based view of crisis management

The study by Miles and Snow (1978), which included an examination of the way in which 17 non-profit organizations reacted to a crisis in 1975, provides one of the few academic analyses of crisis management in a public service industry. The trigger for the crisis was the decision by a large US insurance company to increase medical malpractice insurance rates. This meant that doctors in California were faced by a nearly fourfold increase in their rates, which many of them resisted by going on strike, in the hope of government intervention. The cash flow of many hospitals was immediately hit as non-emergency surgery and bed occupancy levels were cut. The hospitals were forced to draw on their financial reserves. Longer-term effects troubled a number of them.

Interviews with hospital administrators in the affected hospitals revealed quite different responses to the crisis. Some hospitals anticipated the strike well before it occurred, made contingency plans, and involved administrators, medical staff and other employees in making necessary adjustments. They sought to maintain service effectiveness rather than merely to cope with the cash flow problem. They directed some of their actions towards groups and organizations beyond their organizational boundaries. Their actions included communications to the public, influencing political bodies and setting up shared services and linkages with other hospitals. In contrast, there were hospitals that had been surprised by the crisis; that had sought to deal with it mainly by cutting costs to deal with the cash flow problem; and had relied on top down decision making by the administrator.

While there was some evidence that hospitals which had been quicker to pick up the warning signs of the crisis and make contingency plans were quicker to recover from the crisis, it appears that there was no clear implication that this was a better strategic response. The nature of the response to the crisis appeared to be correlated with the general strategy of the hospital in more normal times. Some hospitals were generally successful because they were innovative and possessed a greater capability for environmental surveillance. Others were successful because they were good at defending a low cost position. The former group were more likely to anticipate the crisis, develop contingency plans, use collaboration to make adjustments, seek effectiveness and take actions in relation to external stakeholders. The latter group concentrated on reacting to the crisis once it developed and aiming at cost reduction.

One hospital at least did not come though the crisis so well. This was a hospital that experienced protracted effects of the crisis. It may be significant that it was a hospital which lacked a consistent strategy prior to the onset of the crisis. If we accept the researchers' judgement that this hospital had an inconsistent strategy – which implies a dysfunctional one in their terms – then this provides some support for the pathology view of crisis management.

warning signs of a crisis developing. This will lead to differences in their anticipation of a crisis. Since contingency planning and having responses to the development of a crisis are expensive in terms of managerial time and can entail expenses in terms of service delivery costs, some inter-organizational conflict over the acceptance that there is a crisis on the way can be assumed.

Second, different public services organizations may pursue different strategies in terms of service delivery reflecting their legislative mandates and budgetary allocations. One public service organization may be pursuing a strategy of maximizing resource utilization and targeting of services which leads to great attention to costs and efficiency; another may be more entre-preneurial and seeking to develop new services and new client groups. With such different strategic agendas, public services organizations engaged in joint planning and partnership in service delivery may disagree about the basic approach for handling a crisis, since each has a different conception of how successful management of the crisis is to be judged.

Third, the organizations may differ in their judgement of the long-term significance of the crisis. For one organization, it may be that the crisis must be managed so that it can get back to business as usual. For another, the crisis may represent a watershed, and may be the basis for an acceptance that long-term adjustments need to be made to adapt the organization to the conditions which will prevail after the crisis is over. This will lead in one case to temporary measures which are discontinued once the crisis has passed, and in the other case to fundamental and permanent changes in the services of the organization.

Fourth, managerial cultures and structures will be significantly different between, say, a social services department and a health services provider. These differences will influence how decision making during the crisis is approached. There is obvious scope for conflict where one organization takes a very centralized decision about how the crisis will be handled, and the other organization expects to involve more of its members at all levels in deciding on the response to the crisis. This difference between the organizations in the decision making constituency is very likely to result in different criteria being used when deciding how the crisis is to be managed. Centralized decision making might, for example, have more regard for the protection of the organization's interest, whereas involving professionals and others could lead to more emphasis on the interests of, say, clients or service delivery.

Finally, even though public services organizations are increasingly expected to work in partnership and practice cooperation with other organizations, past traditions of bureaucratic self-sufficiency live on. Even where organizations are involved in formal systems of joint planning, some conflict can be expected on the basis that one organization might attempt to deal with the crisis by making purely internal adjustments, whereas another organization will want a joint approach to the crisis, sharing risks and resources in a bid to provide an effective total response.

Scenario planning to anticipate crisis

Old-style strategic planners were aware that their predictions and forecasts of the future could be in error and that unexpected events might threaten their plans. However, it was only with the development of scenario planning that the difficulties of knowing the future were placed at the centre of strategic thinking and judgements.

One model of the strategic planning process as involving scenario formulation defines a scenario as a 'depiction of the way things could be' and as aiming 'at sensitizing decision makers to the potential outcomes of events and trends' (Grewe et al. 1989: 112). This process requires that top managers conduct 'futures research', which will clarify the issues or events that are important in terms of the directions into the public service agency's future environment, and that they then draw up the scenarios which will be confronted at the end of the time frame being considered. Having drawn up scenarios, this process requires the managers to consider revising their strategic goals based on the scenarios. Opportunities, problems and actions based on these scenarios are then identified. The scenarios may offer opportunities which the public services agency can use to achieve its strategic goals. There may be problems in the scenarios which require management, avoidance action or solution. The scenarios may suggest actions both to adjust the organization to the scenarios, and actions to change aspects of the scenarios. This generates a lot of ideas about what might be done, and the final steps of the strategic planning process involve selecting and thinking through the sequencing of specific action proposals.

On paper at least, this type of strategic planning process, centred on scenarios, emphasizes the need to develop data useful for thinking imaginatively about future conditions and ensuring that all sorts of problems (as well as opportunities) which might materialize are given detailed attention. The limitations of scenario planning can be seen if we look in a little more depth at the mechanics of constructing a set of scenarios.

The development of a set of scenarios is based on constructing stories about the future which weave together events and trends which look as though they may be safely assumed, with unpredictable variables. If this is done using the various combinations possible, then multiple scenarios are produced. Some of these stories may present worst-case scenarios, which although not very probable, could be quite disastrous for the organization. The advantage of having developed such scenarios is that strategies may be evaluated for their robustness even under the worst-case scenarios. The consequence might be that the organization selects a strategy which it thinks may not produce the maximum possible benefits, but which looks like it might produce satisfactory results in the context of a wide range of scenarios and has the advantage of being more effective if the worst-case scenario does materialize.

So, scenario planning assumes that there are a relatively small number of important environmental variables which are highly unpredictable. The organization may know that such variables can have a critical impact but be quite unable to predict with any confidence how the variables will turn out. If there are only a few such variables, then the number of scenarios to be considered can be handled. If there are a large number of such variables, then scenario planning becomes unwieldy in the practical circumstances of a strategic management group working participatively on them.

Open simulation

Open simulation is a 'soft futures' modelling technique which is considered by some people to be superior to scenario planning (Timmins 1997). Whereas scenario planning involves people imagining future situations, open simulation can involve large numbers of people in an exercise to model how strategic changes might develop. The people involved in the exercise are the people who will be involved in implementing and reacting to the strategic change. Within the exercise, people can test out their plans and have others in the exercise react on the basis of their experience. In consequence, the simulated effects of the change unfold with participants being affected by the dynamics created by the reactions of others. The technique has been used in the public sector, where it is useful for exploring large-scale changes in which there are complex interplays between the various interest groups (see Box 7.3).

Using monitoring and control systems

Monitoring and control systems are intended to counter the development of a crisis during the implementation of a strategic plan.

If strategic planning has produced a strategy which is then implemented through a performance plan or through strategic projects, then, in both cases, there should be a clear basis for monitoring and control. In the case of the performance plan the general goals of the strategy will have been used to generate annual performance goals which can then be monitored using performance indicators. If a strategic project is used to implement strategy, then there will be project goals and milestones can be set to monitor the progress of the project. In both cases, there can be a comparison of what has actually happened with what was planned. If there are

---

Box 7.3 An open simulation exercise run by Wakefield Health Authority (UK)

In early 1997 Wakefield Health Authority ran an open simulation exercise on locality commissioning. Just afterwards a new Labour Government won power in the general election and announced that locality commissioning would replace the internal market in the NHS.

The exercise lasted for two days, and brought together 70 participants (GPs, staff from trust hospitals, health authority officials, private providers and others). The simulation of locality commissioning – GPs working in groups as commissioners – produced: the closure of a hospital; a deficit; no local maternity, accident or emergency services; destabilized mental health services; more costly management structures; and less public involvement.

The exercise was useful in pinpointing issues needing attention. These issues included the fact that there seemed to be an absence of direction or leadership. It was not clear who was in charge in the new system of commissioning. Other issues highlighted included the need to make GPs more accountable and the importance of getting a stronger planning framework. Laurie McMahon, a director of the not-for-profit consultancy which ran the exercise, said: 'You have a large number of people who play out what could actually happen and who can ask themselves, when things go wrong: "What are we going to do in management and policy terms to stop this happening?"' (Timmins 1997).

Apparently, the participants were still supportive of locality commissioning despite the problems.

---

deviations from the performance or project plan, then follow-up action is needed to take corrective action. This is, essentially speaking, a control loop to put the strategy's implementation back on course.

Sometimes, however, the deviations may be valuable and they become the basis of strategic learning. In this case the deviations prove to be more useful than the original plan in realizing the mission of the organization or in solving the strategic issues which the strategy was designed to manage.

Of course, not all strategies are implemented according to textbook directions. So, what if there are no annual performance goals or project milestones? A process for these circumstances could involve several steps. First, there would need to be a review of politicians' priorities and key policies, including whether these had changed since the strategy had originally been formulated. Second, it would be useful to design or select a forum for reviewing the results of the current strategy and to decide on the membership of the forum. Third, suitable success indicators would need to be identified, based on the indicators that were used to decide the need for strategic change in the first place, and based on indicators important to each of the key stakeholder groups. Fourth, further indicators would be needed which could be related to specific aspects of implementation effectiveness. Finally, it would be necessary to search for, and collect information on, the process and results of the strategy. The aim would be to then make a judgement about whether the strategy should be maintained, modified or replaced (Bryson 1995: 200–1).

The belated development of key success indicators (in the absence of performance plans and project plans) may in practice be achieved simply by the use of brainstorming. If this is done within a forum which has been designed or selected specially to review the results of the current strategy, then serious thought should be given to the inclusion of representatives of key stakeholder groups within the forum membership.

Monitoring and control is considered best practice even in the absence of crisis. However, when there is a developing crisis, monitoring is important so that management gets an early warning of its likely development and is alerted swiftly to the damage it is producing. This monitoring should provide an adequate basis for corrective action and decisions about communications to the public.

Contingency planning

Contingency planning may be framed by an awareness that the current strategy presumes certain environmental conditions which may change, or it can be geared to possible failures to achieve desired or planned results, and thus be activated by reporting systems which show that the results being obtained are unsatisfactory. This is in line with Duncan et al.'s (1995: 556) definition: 'Contingency plans are alternative plans that are put into effect if the strategic assumptions change quickly or dramatically or if organizational performance is lagging'. However, contingency planning may also address 'problem areas where crisis could occur' (Heath 1997: 302).

If the contingency planning process is conceptualized as a form of strategic control, then it represents a corrective action taken on the basis of planned monitoring. To set up contingency planning as strategic control, the leaders and strategic managers of an organization need to identify potential developments that could be problematic for the current strategy. They then need to define trigger points for reacting to the occurrence of the developments. Presumably, there might need to be a range of contingency plans for each of the possible developments. They may even need to be matched to the strength of the developments. A monitoring system would be needed to not only monitor the results of the strategy, but also to monitor the developments themselves. Corrective action would consist of selecting the contingency plan which corresponded to a development which had been anticipated, and which was appropriate for the strength of the development.

Contingency planning in the public services may not be as elaborate as this. It involves, however, at a minimum, thinking about potential problem areas where a crisis could occur. Piggot (1996), for example, suggests that NHS business plans can usefully include a section that provides answers to 'what if' questions. This requires that leaders and strategic managers identify events or developments which might be a surprise, and formulate some ideas about what the best reaction might be. The implication is that this increases the readiness of the strategic leadership to recognize and react to developments which might occur. The risk analysis technique described in Chapter 3 provides one tool for carrying out this kind of institutionalized contingency planning.

In some cases advance preparation of contingency plans may be difficult because of the rapidity with which a crisis situation develops. If the event or trend causing a crisis is very sudden, then the organization may be forced to develop a contingency plan outside of the planning cycle. Miles and Snow (1978) describe how one hospital handled a crisis with only 65 or 70 days anticipation of that crisis. The hospital's chief administrator felt at this point that the signs of the crisis were clear. The next step was an attempt to assess the likely consequences of the crisis for operational activity levels. Over the next 20 days a scenario based on a very pessimistic set of assumptions was developed. This pessimistic scenario was presented to the hospital's departmental managers, who were tasked to produce contingency plans over the next month. These were to be based on formal projections of the impact the forthcoming crisis would have on their departments. These contingency plans were prepared in time and then implemented when the crisis struck.

In the case of another hospital which was taken by surprise, divisional heads met on the first day of the crisis event, when they were required to evaluate the cash flow impact of the crisis and to identify cost savings which could be made. The management team met on the following day to approve plans for dealing with the crisis and implementation of the response was begun.

Obviously, advance contingency planning is an attempt to handle the dynamics and complexity of the strategic environment while front-loading all the strategy formulation within a strategic management process. There are alternative approaches, such as strategic issue management where the issue agenda is frequently revised in the light of changing circumstances.

Audits

There is also an argument that suggests that reliance on contingency planning may be overdone. To focus heavily on contingency planning may imply that the source of a crisis is almost entirely the occurrence of an external threat, whereas there may be deficiencies within the design, procedures, culture, skills etc. of the organization which provide fertile ground for even small external developments to trigger crises. So, instead of spending all the time trying to anticipate crises by scanning the environment and drawing up detailed contingency plans, perhaps the 'organization needs to audit how well it would respond to a crisis' (Heath 1997: 302).

Such an audit would be actioned by measures to improve the internal state of the organization in terms of organizational design, procedures, culture, skills etc. Such measures would obviously require budget allocations, and obviously the measures would need to be prioritized so that resources and time were concentrated on improvements to areas where the biggest crisis impacts were anticipated.

Crisis management in unexpected crisis situations

As we have noted already, there is an argument that crises develop when organizations are slow to notice and respond to external trends and events. Moreover, when a crisis has developed it may be difficult to deal with it strategically and effectively. However, Eadie (1997) suggests that even major crises may serve to shock an organization out of its complacency and into action. So, while they may be costly for organizations, crises can spur important strategic learning.

One advantage for the strategic leader in a crisis situation is that it often offers the opportunity to make strategic changes on the basis of direct implementation without having to contend with the problems of opposition that ordinary circumstances might present. In crisis situations people may be more inclined to follow orders. Leaders, in consequence, may find their scope for directing matters increases in proportion to the degree of threat and crisis which is manifest. They may find that followers are more receptive to a leadership's diagnosis of the situation and its remedies.

However, the crisis situation requires skilful handling. People do not automatically respond well to crises. According to Bryson (1995: 83): 'in crisis situations people typically stereotype, withdraw, project, rationalize, oversimplify, and otherwise make errors that are likely to produce unwise decisions'. The leader may need to convince managers and employees to adopt a new pattern of behaviour, and convince them that it is consistent with a shared mission or important values. The leader probably needs to encourage managers and employees to reframe the situation so that they see themselves facing a challenge which they can handle with realistic optimism and creativity.

It should be borne in mind that public services organizations vary in how they approach the handling of a crisis. Some may successfully use unilateral decision making by leaders. Then again, some may use collaborative decision making or delegation to handle a crisis situation (Miles and Snow 1978). The adopted approach will depend in part on how effective the organization is at picking up early warning signals of the impending crisis and thus whether there is time to engage managers, professionals and employees in collaborative decision making and action. It may also depend on how the organization makes decisions in normal times. If the organization is normally run in a centralized way with little wider involvement in decision making, it might be quite risky to attempt to involve others or delegate decisions. Likewise, an organization which usually has a participative management style might find it risky to adopt a centralized approach to decision making in a period of crisis. If there is some continuity between normal decision making practices and those used in a crisis, then some care is needed in applying the view that centralized decision making often becomes more acceptable in a crisis situation. We need to know more about the con-textual factors which influence the choice of decision making practices in a crisis.

The leader may need to offer a vision of how the crisis might be solved, providing a framework for the learning and action needed to rescue the organization from the crisis. Of course, the vision might be unrealistic, and the learning and action might be mistaken. In other words, it is not enough to create optimism and spur action by managers and employees in a crisis situation; the strategic response still has to be suitable for the strategic situation. Finally, the leader needs to find under-utilized or slack resources which can be quickly mobilized to bring about the immediate strategic changes needed.

One other issue is the need for specialist decision making procedures and arrangements to handle crisis situations. Indeed, contingency planning may be seen as having a useful role to play in designing and instigating such procedures. Smith (1993: 150) remarks that 'the contingency plans that the organization has in place prior to the event will be of critical importance in determining its initial response in setting up chains of command, organizational structures and decision making procedures to cope with the high level of demand that is inevitably generated by a crisis event'. The creation of a temporary structure to manage the crisis alongside the usual management structure obviously raises questions about how the two structures will interrelate for the duration of the crisis. Does the crisis decision making procedure override the usual chain of command? Or is there a special unit which project manages the crisis by coordinating and catalysing the usual management decision making? If there is a specialist decision making unit for the duration of the crisis episode, how does that relate to the strategic leadership of the organization? In extreme crisis situations, is such a unit given more executive authority and does this allow very centralized decision making to occur – or does such a unit allow collaboration in decision making to be widened and deepened? There is currently little reported in the literature of strategic management in the public services which addresses these questions, and suggestions about the contingencies which apply would seem to be largely speculative in the light of our current state of knowledge.

Communicating to the public during a crisis

As Heath (1997) says, there are many sources of advice available to organizations on how to communicate during a crisis. The most important advice is that honesty and openness with the public is the best policy in the midst of crisis, although there is a problem that such honesty and openness may produce the intervention of politicians if they do not feel that the leaders of the organization are bringing the crisis under control and are re-establishing public confidence. Communications with the public will need to explain what has happened, why it happened and how it is being managed. Even if the leadership and management of a public services organization has acted reasonably and professionally, the failure to communicate when the public expects answers feeds mistrust and suspicions of irresponsible or incompetent management. If levels of mistrust are already high, public services organizations should consider setting up an independent person or body to ascertain and report on the facts to the public, although this will take time and the organization will still have to engage in open and honest communications with the public.

Poor management information and reporting systems which cause managerial ignorance and prevent the public being informed will underline an image of incompetence or feed ideas of a cover-up. So, it is not just a matter of openness – management must also be well informed and precise in what is communicated to the public. Effective communication in these circumstances will require a good understanding of public expectations about the performance and management of the organization.

Making apologies is a crucial function of the communications to the public about the crisis. Apologies are important for a number of reasons. They diffuse public anger – as is recognized by many customer-care training courses. They also show that the organization is not 'in denial', has been able to identify the cause of the crisis and is thus ready to learn from it and make improvements. Of course, apologies wear thin very quickly if improvements do not take place. The public is looking for signs that the organization is being managed and controlled and that their expectations will be better met in future.

Conclusions

While organizations vary in how they manage crisis events, it appears to be important that crisis responses make use of (re-use) the capabilities they have developed and leveraged through their ongoing strategy.

The problem of handling a crisis may be greatest for an organization that has an unclear organizational strategy and unclear or poorly developed capabilities. If an organization is uncertain about these things it may find it difficult to identify an appropriate approach and the necessary capabilites for surmounting the crisis episode.

Scenario planning is sometimes used for anticipating the emergence of situations which might be disastrous for the organization. Open simulation goes beyond the idea of scenario planning by involving large numbers of people in using their experiences to model a major strategic change. This technique, one of a number of 'soft futures' techniques, enables more ambitious appreciations of multidimensional changes involving the inter-play of the many interests involved.

Monitoring and control systems provide a way of reacting to crises emerging during the implementation of a strategy. Contingency planning can be attempted in more or less sophisticated ways, and can involve more or less complex sets of alternative plans. It can, however, be done on a very simple basis. Planning documents can, for example, include a section that explores answers to 'what if' questions. A risk analysis might be used to enable strategic leaders and managers to sensitize themselves so that they can recognize and react to developments quickly. Audits of the internal state of the organization may be used to complement contingency planning.

Contingency planning may also be done in real time, that is, outside of a regular planning cycle, and as a result of identifying the early warning signs of a specific crisis. Contingency planning may even need to be under-taken in the midst of disruption caused by an unanticipated crisis. If all else fails, good leadership is essential to deal with crises.

Crisis situations, finally, require open and honest communications with the public. The relationship with the public is *the* crucial relationship for public services organizations, and a breakdown in trust is a critical ingre-dient in the development and deepening of a crisis for such organizations. In the next chapter we look more generally at how the public can be engaged in strategic management by public services organizations.

eight

Public-friendly strategic management

Key learning objectives

After reading this chapter you should be able to:

1 Understand the contemporary significance of efforts to use strategic planning within a governance framework for community problem solving.
2 Identify opportunities for involving and consulting citizens and service users.
3 Discuss and assess the value of community planning and specific techniques for involving service users.

Introduction: the public challenge

The public services went through a very difficult time in the 1980s and 1990s, and it is not clear that the danger to them is yet over. There has been an enormous commitment within the public services to making changes and a recognition that a defensive response and resistance would not make the public and political dissatisfaction with the state of public services go away. The public services have introduced large numbers of managers and installed all sorts of management systems. The role of professionals within the public services has been criticized and various attempts made to redefine their input to the services.

A number of individual public services organizations have acquired reputations for successful and innovative management and services. But, as Zegans (1992) implied, the past performance of the public services is not the basis of the public's benchmark; it is the *current* level of public expectations which is the benchmark for how well the public services must perform.

The only major area of reform which has not yet been successfully tackled on a widespread basis is involving the public in setting the strategic agenda for the public services. Doing things right managerially will not be enough if the public judges the public services not to be doing the right things. The public challenge – closing the gap between the public and its services – is a major challenge for the further development of strategic management.

In the models of strategic management reviewed in Chapter 1 there was little evident role for the public in strategic management processes. In this chapter we will discuss some experiments in involving the public, including attempts at community planning. We will be referring to a number of different ways in which public services organizations have sought to make themselves more responsive and the public more involved. The variety of experiments in this area is impressive. Obviously, we look at these matters mostly from the point of view of strategic management and planning.

The first objective of this chapter is to place the issue of public-friendly strategic management in some sort of context. This is done through a discussion of democratic accountability and the emergence of the idea of governance, which aspires to reconstruct the relationship between government organizations and the public. The second objective is to discuss actual methods of involving and consulting the public. We will approach this primarily through the device of different definitions of the public: as citizens, as the community and as service users. We will look specifically at community planning and a service review process. The final objective of this chapter is to look at the use of whole systems development thinking to design an event which includes the public along with managers and other stakeholders in a process of very public learning by (and feedback to) strategic leaders. This is included as a recently used and publicized technique of strategic planning based on inclusiveness, debate and persuasion.

Key issues of democratic accountability

Public services organizations led directly by politicians could be said to already involve the public. The politicians, as elected representatives of the public may even be part-time 'amateurs', as in UK local government. When politicians are ordinary members of the public, elected to act on behalf of the public and to ensure that public services are directed in line with public wishes, it might seem unnecessary to then worry about public involvement. Moreover, a politician elected through the formal electoral process is in some sense certified as representative of the public as a whole, and is not just any old member of the public with their own axe to grind, or with a sectional interest to pursue. Adding an additional mechanism for public involvement, apart from the elected representative system which places politicians in charge, could seem an expensive and time-consuming diversion from implementing the public will.

On the other hand, there are concerns about the 'democratic deficit', meaning that there are problems about assuming that every direction set by politicians, every priority or policy they establish, is completely in line with the genuine wishes of the public. Poor election turnouts, poor communication systems between electorates and politicians and the general weakness of accountability arrangements through which politicians explain what they have achieved or failed to do, all suggest that sometimes gaps open up between the politicians and the public.

There is much talk about accountability in connection with the public services, and it is assumed that the meaning of this term is reasonably clear. However, there are at least two distinct types of accountability which are currently at issue. First, there is the accountability of managers and professionals employed by public services to the politicians who have a political oversight role. The managers in particular are meant to give account of their actions, use of public money, and results to the politicians. Then there is the second type of accountability, which is accountability to the public. This may be assumed to operate via the accountability of managers to politicians and via the accountability of politicians to the public through the electoral process. During an election campaign, politicians have to explain to the electorate what they have done during their period in office, and if the public is not satisfied it can express its dissatisfaction through voting behaviour.

There are trends towards demands for both types of accountability being increased. The 1990s reforms of federal government in the USA exemplify an attempt to make managers more accountable to politicians: the Government and Performance Results Act of 1993 makes managers accountable to the US Congress for results in line with strategic mission statements. The publishing in the UK of schools 'league tables' in terms of their performance results is an example of an attempt to make public services accountable to the public itself. The providers may feel, for example, more exposed to challenges by the media and therefore feel there is more need to explain their results to service users, or potential service users.

The democratic deficit is seen as a problem partly because it creates a breakdown in trust between the public and their politicians and a growing cynicism about politicians' standards of behaviour. Involving the public in strategic planning can be seen, therefore, as a way of compensating for the deficit and rebuilding trust between politicians and the public: 'The closer a government is to its citizens, polls show, the more they trust it' (Osborne and Gaebler 1992: 277).

It can also seem to politicians that they are very dependent on managers, professionals and other employees of the public service organization to implement public policies. This can lead to the idea (and often does these days) that managers, professionals and employees must have some sense of 'ownership' of the decision making process. This leads to the idea that members of the organization need to be empowered and given more discretion. This in turn automatically creates the possibility that members of the organization will use this discretion to do what they think is right or is convenient or easy for them, and this may not coincide with public wishes. One approach to counterbalancing this loosening of control over members of the organization is to engage them in much heavier socialization into values and culture which will support a mission which is approved by politicians, and to tighten up monitoring of the results of the organization. An alternative is to open up the organization at all levels to more public involvement and scrutiny, so that increased discretion for managers, professionals and other employees is placed under increasing, direct pressure to be used solely to serve the public.

There are tensions regarding how the public is involved in strategic planning by public services organizations. Some of this arises from varying ideas about the reasons for public involvement. Is it intended to empower the public (whatever that means) or is it meant to enhance plans by improving the information for planners about what the needs of the public are? There is some disagreement about whether the public at large should be involved or only those with a direct stake as users of a particular service. This disagreement about who to involve may be associated with the distinction between the purposes of empowering and the purposes of listening to the public. There are also ideological tensions about involving the public, which centre on whether public involvement is enhancing the democratic process or attacking it through the force of, say, consumerism. And even within attempts by public services to be more consumer-friendly, there are differences, and tensions, between approaches which aim at user responsiveness and user empowerment.

The governance agenda

It is now often felt that management in the public services needs to be considered in relation to new processes of governance. The reason for this boils down to the idea that public services have been used by governments to solve society's problems and meet public needs, and that this is no longer sufficient. As Kooiman and van Vliet (1993) argue, it is believed that governments have found it increasingly difficult to govern in the 'face of rising complexity, dynamics and diversity'; yet there is not 'a diminished need for collective problem solving'. So, instead of governance by government,

Kooiman and van Vliet are 'searching for alternative modes of governing and governance in which interactions between government and society, between public and private actors are central . . .' (p. 58).

This changes our conception of good government. It now involves government ensuring that society's problems are solved by a variety of means, and only seeking to solve problems through public services provision where this is the most appropriate means. Good government means encouraging and enabling civil society to contribute to the solution of major problems. When applied to local government, this gives rise to what Leach *et al.* (1994) call the 'community-oriented enabler', which is a local authority that exists 'to meet the varied needs of its population, using whatever channel – local authority direct provision, private sector, voluntary sector, or influence – seems most appropriate' (pp. 242–3). Under this new approach to governance, government and civil society are working together, rather than all the problem solving being left to government. Critically, this new governance agenda entails changes in the relationship between government and civil society, so that it is more focused on interactive problem solving, as against in the past where the emphasis was on government controlling civil society through its legislation and succouring it through its provision of welfare services.

Partnerships

To the extent that good government is changing in this way, public services managers have to adapt to the new relationship in two ways. First, there has to be an acceptance that not all new problems that come along will be solved by using tax revenue to provide new public services, and that some old problems may be handled in new ways which will impact on the current nature and extent of public services. Second, there is an increasing expectation that public services managers will work as partners with the community and with the private and voluntary sectors to help them solve the problems and meet the needs which exist: 'Two-thirds of [British] local authority chief executives believe the most important issue facing local government over the next three to five years is partnership-building' (Everitt 1997). The public services managers may be expected to take the initiative in building partnerships and catalysing the problem solving efforts of others.

The partnership agenda is being addressed through strategy processes. Some public services organizations have become publicly committed to developing strategies by involving partners throughout the entire strategy process – from identifying strategic issues through to coordinated action to address them. It may have become more desirable to do this as society has become 'demassified' and there is now greater diversity in culture and needs, multiplying the complexity of society and creating a greater multiplicity of stakeholders in public services. It may have become more obvious as an option as the realization grew that the state lacked the resources to ever realistically hope to meet all the public needs that exist.

Involving community partners can be done by opening up a public service organization's internal strategic planning process to participation by them. Or special forums or steering groups can be set up for discussion, analysis and strategic decision making by the partners. Whatever the format used, strategic planning is no longer just a tool for single organizations.

Community achievement

This partnership-based view of strategic planning and management implies a concern which goes beyond managerial service delivery responsibilities to a concern about the problems and issues concerning the community. These issues are very varied, and include: community safety and crime prevention, environmental concerns, economic development, and poverty and social exclusion. Of course, public service organizations may wish to be successful in relation to both service delivery and community leadership. These are not mutually exclusive. Indeed, service delivery may be integrated into a community leadership role so that a whole range of services can be adjusted to help address major community problems.

Out of this concern for community problems comes, very often, a desire to access or win extra resources to address the issues of the community. Working in partnership may help to secure additional private and public sector resources for local problems, which may then be pooled in order to take more substantial action than had been possible by independent action. Moreover, some public funds are only available on a competitive basis which formally favours partnership bids and bids which are made more plausible by a convincing strategic plan. Thus, in the same way that private businesses construct business plans to secure bank loans for investment purposes, consortiums of local partners may produce strategic plans to draw down public money which they need to invest in the solution of local problems.

Success of such strategic planning becomes a community achievement rather than a narrowly-based organizational achievement because it takes the concerted action of a consortium of organizations with a stake in the community to solve difficult community problems. The rewards of strategic planning by interorganizational networks may be great, especially for the community, but the process may be more difficult to manage than strategic planning by a single organization. Bryson (1995: 6) points out that: 'More time will need to be spent organizing forums for discussion, involving diverse communities, negotiating agreements in existing or new arenas, and coordinating the activities and actions of numerous relatively independent people, groups, organizations, and institutions'.

It may be significant that some organizations which have experimented with this type of partnership-based strategic planning have found it necessary to ensure that elected politicians are involved in the strategic planning process, rather than standing above it in some type of oversight relationship. Instead of the politicians imposing strategic planning as a means of increasing accountability, the elected political leaders need to be involved if a shared agenda is to be developed. This might be in part due to the authority elected leaders have in relation to community problems, but it also appears to be because the politicians are needed for the process of deciding priorities and making trade-offs which may be seen as a political responsibility that managers are unable to handle with the same degree of effectiveness. However, the elected politicians cannot direct and control partners in an arrogant way, even though they have democratic authority, because the partners have power as well.

Some government organizations in the USA, Britain and elsewhere have been keen to take the lead in a more strategic approach to handling community problems, which they see as requiring a catalytic function in relation to partners. If the problems of the community are seen as complex, requiring problem solving as well as a pooling of resources, then strategic planning may be seen as a vital mechanism for achieving the creativity and innovation necessary for problem solving. These ideas might be seen as pointing towards a provisional definition of strategy under a governance regime as being the use by government of multiorganizational strategic planning in order to provide innovative solutions to community problems.

So, strategic planning and management are important for addressing difficult community problems which require more than a straightforward service delivery response. They can be useful in building partnerships to see the strategic action through to completion and for gaining the resources to address the problems. In these senses, strategic planning and management is important as a tool of governance.

Consulting, surveying and involving citizens

Perhaps the least demanding way of involving citizens in strategic planning is to consult them once the organization has formulated a plan. In such circumstances there must be a danger that the public services managers are looking for the citizens' approval rather than for an input in the decision making process. Nevertheless, such consultation may have a beneficial impact on the quality and approach of the strategic plan, even if it only reminds the planners that they are working ultimately for the public.

There are many examples of UK local authorities creating citizens panels to check out public satisfaction levels. In the case of Epsom and Ewell council, however, the citizens panel has been used to test the council's strategic framework. Such panels have the attraction of being based on large and representative samples of the public, although representative here is a statistical rather than a political concept.

Surveys are arm's-length methods of public consultation and involvement. More intensive methods are also available. Bohret (1993) has described how planning cells may be used to crystallize a citizens' opinion. Groups of about 25 citizens are formed to consider a problem which has been clearly outlined and they are paid for their involvement. They may be selected on the basis that they are concerned or representative members of society, and after they have attempted to understand and solve the issue, their opinion is presented to the decision makers in the public service organization. Something similar has been tried in the UK, where planning cells have been referred to as citizens' juries. These are representative groups of citizens reporting to elected politicians on a particular matter. This has been tried recently – for example, in the London boroughs of Lewisham and Islington.

Whereas planning cells and citizens' juries involve citizens with respect to a specific issue (e.g. drug problems, reorganization of library services in a locality), citizens can also be brought into the planning process aimed at producing the overall or organization-wide strategy of a public services organization. This type of approach to citizen involvement has been attempted in the USA through processes in which citizens are invited to analyse trends, develop alternative scenarios and formulate community goals. This type of involvement initiative has been attempted over many years by numerous government organizations. Details of one such attempt, by the Californian city of Placentia, are provided in Box 8.1. There have been many successful attempts at getting large numbers of citizens involved (Osborne and Gaebler 1992: 20–2).

Community planning

Some public services organizations send their completed strategic documents to a range of stakeholders in their local community and ask for comments. This does not appear to have much impact on the content of the plans, but at least it is a way of communicating strategic intentions to stakeholders in the community. Such a minimalist approach to community consultation may be considered more than adequate where the managers are focused on organizational achievements and are not much concerned with the consequences of the organization's activities for the local community. When, however, the managers think in terms of the results

---

Box 8.1 Citizen involvement in the USA

An early attempt at citizen involvement in planning took place in the Californian city of Placentia in the mid-1960s, and involved a small group of citizens in identifying city goals for a ten-year planning period. In 1983, the city's council again called on citizens to be involved in planning for the city. Kemp (1985) has provided a summary description of this 1980s' initiative.

Twenty-five citizens were appointed to the Placentia 2000 Project Committee, and were allocated to one of its five subcommittees, each of which addressed one of the following issue areas: residential; commercial and industrial; cultural and recreational; city services and finances; and communications and new technology. Kemp (1985: 92) reports that: 'The charge of each subcommittee was to assess the present conditions of the city in their respective area, identify desired goals for the year 2000, develop strategies to achieve those goals, and present their findings to the city council at the end of a 6-month period'. The citizens on the committee did not simply meet by themselves in their subcommittees: there were public meetings, as well as a survey of all citizens and discussions with community leaders. The outcome of this process was a set of community goals and a framework within which the city council could plan its own services and activities. This should be seen as an example of 'community planning', which is discussed further in the next section.

---

for the community, rather than just their responsibility for the results of the organization, they may consider developing forms of community planning.

There has been a growth of interest in the USA and the UK in what is referred to as community planning. This actually takes various forms and need not directly involve the community in the planning process. For example, it may be seen as planning done by planners on behalf of the community and thus be merely a process which features an assessment of the costs and benefits to local communities of various strategic options.

So, public services managers may be interested in conducting community impact assessments, looking at how the services or activities of their organization impact on the problems and needs of the local community. Assessments of this kind could feed into the appraisal of alternative strategic options being considered within a strategic planning process. The use of such assessments could be seen as more likely in a culture of technocratic managerialism in which strategic planners have become conscious that there may be significant organizational costs and risks attached to activities or services which produce outputs without regard to the outcomes valued by the local community. The assessment of community impact plugs an important gap in the knowledge of the strategic planners of public services. It is perfectly compatible with the corporate planning model of how services should be managed in the public sector.

Box 8.2 Involving the public in selecting strategic options: Watford Borough Council (UK)

Watford Borough Council was one of 18 local authorities which began piloting community planning in the mid-1990s. Its community planning process was designed to enable local people to contribute to decision making about the priorities the council set and the action it took year to year. The council consulted every household and committed itself to using the results to inform the budget setting process. It has been reported that the managers were not entirely satisfied with the effectiveness of the public consultation process and were determined to persevere with the search for genuine community planning.

Even where community planning is seen as requiring the involvement of the public in the planning process, the nature and quality of the involvement can vary quite significantly. At one end of the spectrum we have community planning which consists of a fairly conventional strategic planning process with a bolted-on element of public consultation. The strategic planners may, for example, carry out or commission research into the perceptions of members of the local community about the priorities which should be used to identify strategic issues, or into their attitudes towards a strategic action which is being contemplated. The quality of the public consultation is likely to be judged by the canons of good market research, and the consultation will use well-known methods of market research including on-street surveys and telephone surveys. The use of public consultation within a conventional planning process would, like community impact assessments, be consistent with the corporate planning model.

At the other end of the spectrum there is community planning which aspires to the empowerment of the community rather than just an improvement to the results of the strategic planning process. The aim is, in this case, to develop a strategic planning process in which managers enable the community to analyse, choose and benefit from the strategy. This is particularly directed towards those groups in the community who are defined as suffering from social exclusion. Such an approach is at odds with the technocratic managerialist model of corporate planning because the emphasis is on participation and devolved power, and implies quite a different idea of public management and societal culture (Bohret 1993).

In the UK in the 1990s there has been an increased commitment to modernizing government organizations in order to address social exclusion. One sign was the decision by 18 local authorities in 1995 to embark on a programme of piloting the concept of community planning which was being sponsored by the Labour Party (see Box 8.2 for an example of community planning in the UK). Southernwood (1997: 11) has described what this came to mean in Cambridge City Council:

Box 8.3 Strategic management and decentralized structures

Burns *et al.* (1994) carried out research in two London boroughs: Islington and Tower Hamlets. One of their conclusions was that a decentralized structure could enable local strategic management to take place. They implied that traditional bureaucratic structures, with their centralized departments, made it difficult for council departments to cooperate with each other – let alone work closely with public, private and non-profit organizations – with the result that strategic management at a local level was not possible.

The researchers described the approach at Islington as being based on the use of Neighbourhood Action Plans: 'These represent a bold attempt to develop a new kind of very local, highly engaged planning' (Burns *et al.* 1994: 130). Islington Council had 24 neighbourhoods in 1991 and all of them prepared plans for the first time in that year. Each of the neighbourhoods had a neighbourhood forum, which included representatives of people living in the local area, and this forum was involved in the preparation and review of the plan. 'The plans, which are to be updated annually, assess local problems and opportunities, examine local needs, review services, and specify performance targets for the coming year' (Burns *et al.* 1994: 131).

We came to see Community Planning at two quite distinct levels. Firstly, city wide, across the authority as a whole. Here the fundamental purpose was to create a dialogue with citizens, customers and stakeholders, both about the services the council provides or purchases on the public's behalf, and the policy choices we make within the powers and resources available to us. Secondly, and more directly, we wanted to focus on problems of social exclusion and develop people's own ideas of the needs and issues that were important to them in their neighbourhoods.

Particularly noteworthy here is the phrase 'develop people's own ideas of the needs and issues that were important to them'. This implies that community planning does not necessarily want to take excluded groups' initial view of their needs and issues at face value, but recognizes that, as a result of being excluded, the aspirations of such groups may have been suppressed.

Community planning may be carried out at the level of the whole organization, but some local authorities in the UK have been experimenting with involving community representatives in planning processes at a neighbourhood level. An early example was the introduction of Neighbourhood Action Plans within the London Borough of Islington in the early 1990s (Burns *et al.* 1994). These plans involved identifying development targets and performance targets (see Box 8.3 which provides more details on this experiment with neighbourhood level planning.) At Cambridge City Council

Box 8.4 Community planning at Ipswich Borough Council

In 1997 Ipswich Borough Council was able to claim the use of a wide variety of methods for involving the public and the local community. It had used, for example, 22 service user panels, four area housing forums, opinion surveys and customer surveys, strategy consultation meetings and voluntary sector and business sector forums. As a result, it seems that changes had been made in policies, service priority, and service delivery.

During 1995 Ipswich had become a pilot authority for community planning. These pilots were instigated by the Labour Party while in opposition. The council set out to integrate its public involvement activities into an annual process which would affect budgetary decisions. The community plan process which emerged incorporated public opinion obtained through surveys, service panels and roadshows. The annual cycle was as shown in Figure 8.1.

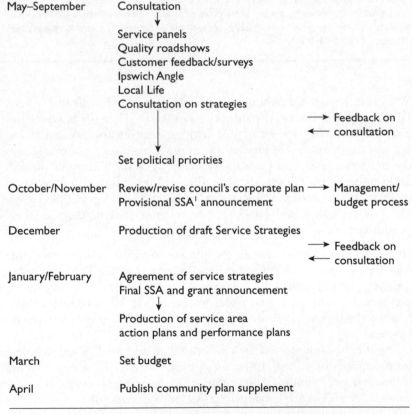

May–September	Consultation
	↓
	Service panels
	Quality roadshows
	Customer feedback/surveys
	Ipswich Angle
	Local Life
	Consultation on strategies
	⟶ Feedback on
	⟵ consultation
	↓
	Set political priorities
October/November	Review/revise council's corporate plan ⟶ Management/
	Provisional SSA¹ announcement budget process
December	Production of draft Service Strategies
	⟶ Feedback on
	⟵ consultation
January/February	Agreement of service strategies
	Final SSA and grant announcement
	↓
	Production of service area
	action plans and performance plans
March	Set budget
April	Publish community plan supplement

¹ SSA = Standard Spending Assessment, made by the central government.

Figure 8.1 The annual planning cycle at Ipswich Borough Council

the pilot community planning work involved neighbourhood community planning in one ward. This neighbourhood pilot involved consultation of local people about what they wanted, partnerships, and a bid for revenue and capital resources from the council.

Community planning is clearly not an easy phenomenon to summarize. It offers, variously, a way of better informing strategic planning, getting closer to local community concerns, and increasing opportunities for local people to participate in planning to improve their community and their public services.

Community planning can end up being just window-dressing for what remains in reality a fairly old-fashioned bureaucratic organization. To avoid this, ways have to be found of making the plan a community plan, rather than a council plan, in the sense that it is the public's plan as much as possible. This means, for example, that community planning must go beyond direct service delivery concerns if it is to generate a plan for the community rather than just a better organizational plan for direct service delivery. Ways have to be found to combine the public's views and needs with the ideas and direction of elected politicians. And, finally, ways have to be found of ensuring that the public's involvement in planning pays off in terms of better services. The community planning process at Ipswich Borough Council, at least on paper, does appear to combine the public's views with political priorities and management planning. It is important to stress that the community plan process was seen by Ipswich Borough Council as having a wider scope than direct services. So, community planning at Ipswich was not just about using public opinions to modify the annual service planning process (see Box 8.4).

User reviews of services

Although service users form a section of the public, they have a distinctive interest in services, which differs from that of the general citizen. It is Bryson's (1995) view that the public is less likely to be involved in the overall strategy of the organization than it is in the strategic planning of particular programme areas. He argues that this involvement is likely to focus on the public's status as 'customers' (that is, service users), and that members of the public may be asked to provide information on their needs and responses to service options. So, the focus of strategic planning – organization-wide or service level – may have an influence on whether or not the public is involved and in what capacity.

Where service users are very well organized, as is sometimes the case with people who use disability services, it is much more likely that voluntary bodies can be involved in identifying strategic issues and taking part in formulating strategies to resolve them.

Enabling service users to participate in this way may be valued from the point of view of a general commitment to the value of consumer empowerment in the public services. It may also be valued as a way of increasing the flow of ideas and information into the strategy process.

One possible consequence of involving service users in planning strategic changes is that innovative service programmes may be designed in which service users take more responsibility within the service delivery process. According to Frost-Kumpf *et al.* (1993) the fundamental changes in the Ohio mental health system in the 1980s were brought about in part by experiments with new types of services for mentally ill people. The consumers, and their families, had been involved in the strategic changes through frequent planning conferences. It should be stressed that genuine involvement through these planning conferences was encouraged by the top managers of the Ohio Department of Mental Health: 'The language used by the director and her top staff at these conferences evoked empowerment, choice, participation, community support, and "independence from dependency" to the maximum possible extent' (Frost-Kumpf *et al.* 1993: 144). Perhaps not totally surprisingly, as a result of this collaborative approach to planning with the consumers and their families, the outcomes of the strategic changes included the design and operation of some services run by the consumers themselves.

Programme planning model

A very specific planning process has been devised by Delbecq and Van de Ven (1976) as a way of involving service users in identifying strategic problems and developing programmes to solve them. Their particular approach could be interesting to organizations wishing to experiment with more interactive ways of developing strategy with the public.

Delbecq and Van de Ven call their approach the programme planning model (PPM). It is essentially a blueprint for a planning sequence which brings together the public, professionals, managers and resource controllers in a process of cooperative decision making. Five main steps make up the complete process of planning:

- Step 1: problem exploration
- Step 2: knowledge exploration
- Step 3: priority development
- Step 4: programme development
- Step 5: programme evaluation

In Step 1 a cross-section of service users is formed into a number of groups, taking care that the different types of user that actually exist are well represented among those involved. (The basis for the grouping will depend on the service in question, but nowadays we would look for the different stakeholder groups within the whole totality of people who use a service.) These groups are invited to explore the problems they have and to prioritize them in order of importance. Delbecq and Van de Ven advise the use of techniques to increase creativity and disclosure (notably, the use of the nominal group technique to generate lists of problems and round-robin sharing of ideas). The specific design of activities within this first step are intended to help with 'interfacing' service users and professional employees. This is done partly by the fact that Step 1 is focused on the problems and needs of service users and on their priorities for solving problems. This is also done by shaping the statements of service users in ways which maximize the likelihood of professionals understanding them. Delbecq and Van de Ven warn that: 'Contemporary literature is replete with instances where social agency professionals have planned client services which do not meet real needs of the clientele' (1976: 286).

Step 2 involves experts drawn from outside the public services organization who possess the expertise needed to address the top priority problems identified in Step 1. They are joined by employees who have relevant knowledge. These two groups work on problem solving, following a presentation describing in qualitative terms the problems identified. The definition of solutions in this process means coming up with ideas about how the problems might be solved and identifying the necessary resources The participants in this phase of the process are encouraged not only to come up with familiar solutions using resources already available, but also to recommend new types of solution. They are required to discuss the various ideas and the resource implications, and then formulate the solutions and resources which should be part of new programme developments. One of the issues during this step is to minimize the defensiveness of internal specialists who might be tempted to justify current services rather than explore creatively new ideas for better services. Delbecq and Van de Ven stress the need for 'cognitive remapping' of problem situations: 'Unless existing problems can be perceived through new types of conceptual lenses, the probability of innovative programs of solutions remains limited' (1976: 290). This is obviously particularly an issue for professionals who have very institutionalized thinking or habits of thought that make it difficult for them to imagine solutions. The inclusion of external experts and the request for new types of solution are designed to counter parochial thinking and to stimulate creativity in the search for solutions.

Step 3 is built around a review of the priorities and solution elements emerging from the planning process and involves representatives of the first two steps as well as key resource controllers and senior managers. (It could involve politicians, who are the ultimate resource controllers.) This review draws out the possible objections of those who control the resources before firm plans have been drawn up. The representatives present the conclusions of the first and second phases of the process, and the resource controllers and senior managers respond by suggesting adjustments to solutions and resourcing requirements which will make them acceptable given the constraints which exist. The representatives of the users and the specialist experts are expected to see the input of the resource controllers and senior managers in a positive way and to respond in a problem solving mode. Constructive negotiations between service user representatives, specialists, resource controllers and senior managers is an important element of interactions between participants in Step 3.

In the next phase, Step 4, internal specialists and line managers develop the results of the previous three steps into a plan with details of a new programme. In Step 5, a meeting is held to consider the plan for the new programme to be implemented. The meeting also reviews the control and evaluation measures which will be used, checking that these are consistent with the work and conclusions of the process. Some detailed changes may be made to the programme or to the control and evaluation measures as a result.

Delbecq and Van de Ven commend their model as follows: 'It both highlights critical issues and provides a guideline for developing innovative solution strategies where clients or consumers, specialists, resource controllers, and administrators must be interfaced' (1976: 295). They reported that the model had been applied in social service planning and health planning organizations, and on the basis of this and other grounds, they were 'convinced of its practicality and power' (p. 295), but warned that it was a process requiring considerable skill.

It can be seen from the specific process designed by Delbecq and Van de Ven that there is a lot more to involving service users in planning than simply asking them what they want. Indeed, it is very significant that the process produces a problem agenda which is prioritized. This kind of information provides a sounder basis for public service responsiveness than simply asking the public to generate a description of their needs. Even so, if service users are to contribute effectively in, say, planning conferences, then time and effort must be expended in facilitating their input. Public services at the very least need to provide information and real access to decision making processes if anything worthwhile is going to come out of consulting service users about strategic change. In the case of the major change process at the Ohio Department of Mental Health, referred to above, this was forthcoming: 'At all points in the process, consumers were actively engaged in decision making about their own treatment and in the planning and development of mental health policy' (Frost-Kumpf *et al.* 1993: 149). This real involvement of service users appears to have been the result of a strategic vision and a set of values which said that they were 'consumers of mental health services' and no longer to be treated as 'patients to be placed in treatment programs' (Frost-Kumpf *et al.* 1993: 139).

The public and whole systems development

Wilkinson and Pedler (1996) have advocated the use of 'whole systems development' as a way of 'involving large numbers of people in live dialogue with one another and with the leaders of the organization' (p. 39). This approach is based on staging an event and does not directly influence the normal relationships inside a public services organization. It was used by Walsall Metropolitan Borough Council to involve 280 employees and service users in developing a new corporate plan for 1995–6. If it can be shown to work effectively, it provides a model for very inclusive forms of strategic planning.

In the case of Walsall Council, the big event was designed by a team comprising 15 representatives of the staff and six service users. The event took place over two days and involved participants working at 30 tables. The two days were divided into a number of sessions. The first session concentrated on a diagnosis of Walsall's service delivery problems, with each table using flip charts and a roving microphone to communicate their ideas. As with other sessions when flip charts were used, the participants toured the flip charts put up by other participants and 'voted' by showing their agreement with items on the flip charts. (This obviously provides some indication to top management about how popular are the various items listed on flip charts.) The second session was a presentation by the chief executive which was then discussed at the tables. As a result of these discussions questions were put to the chief executive by participants. On the first day there were also workshops to provide information on solutions which were already in the pipeline. The final session consisted of the participants at the tables evaluating the day, and drawing up on flip charts what they liked about what they had heard, what they had not liked and what they thought was missing. The chief executive and the rest of the leadership team studied the data produced on the flip charts and evaluation sheets on the evening of the first day and prepared their joint presentation for the second day of the event.

The first main session of the second day was a presentation by the leadership team. This presentation was supported by the circulation of a paper to all participants. This was followed by discussion at the tables and questions were then put to the leadership team. The responses of the leadership team to the questions from participants was the basis for another table discussion, followed by a session in which the participants put their evaluations of the responses on a flip chart (what they had liked, what they had not liked and what was missing in the response). This data was taken and used by the leadership team to prepare another response in the afternoon of the second day.

For the afternoon of the second day, the participants were reorganized into departmental groupings to generate ideas for departmental actions which could be linked into the emerging corporate plan. The event ended with the leadership team presenting a finalized response which was agreed by a show of hands, and with a final evaluation by participants.

The Walsall Council experience shows that a large number of participants can be involved by staging such an event. However, Wilkinson and Pedler (1996) were not able to say whether this process produced a good quality corporate plan or whether implementation was made easier as a consequence of such widespread participation.

It is clear from how the event was organized that a major objective of the process was to get a dialogue going between top management and everybody else. The event was a carefully sequenced set of presentations, discussions, questions, responses and evaluations. It is also clear that the decision making processes of the event made much use of democratic forms of argument, with post-and-vote sessions which indicated levels of support for items on flip charts, and even a show of hands following the presentation of the final response by the leadership team. These represent a quite different experience from that usually found within a centralized and hierarchical public service bureaucracy.

Wilkinson and Pedler place a good deal of emphasis on the public learning which took place within the event. The chief executive and his leadership team 'was seen to move – to learn in public in two of the conference sessions' (1996: 46–7). Perhaps it is very motivating for participants to see their efforts at supplying data and giving feedback and evaluation rewarded by the top managers showing that they are able to learn from the knowledge and experience of employees and service users. Perhaps such a public display of learning might legitimize learning behaviour when everybody has returned to their everyday routines within the public service organization.

It should also be noted that there was a substantial presence of service users in the event, although they were in a minority. It is interesting to compare this process with the PPM of Delbecq and Van de Ven (1976) (see above) where service users alone define their problems and needs, and prioritize them. In their model the service users are also involved in shaping up the strategy through representatives who may negotiate to some extent with resource controllers, specialists and others over the solutions to be enacted through new programmes. It would be interesting to know how service users' experiences of these two very different types of process compare, and which empowers the service users most.

The whole systems development model may be applied to corporate plans and to other types of strategic planning around community problems.

Conclusions

Although we have reviewed a wide variety of initiatives, methods and techniques for consulting and engaging the public in this chapter, it is not easy to offer an assessment of their durability or their achievements. The launch of experiments in public consultation and involvement may easily be rationalized on the basis that there is a crisis in the relationship with the public – a crisis caused by bureaucratic rigidity which has prevented organizations from correcting and adjusting their activities for new social realities (see Chapter 7). As a reaction against old bureaucratic ways of working, any and every way of demonstrating responsiveness to, and engagement with, the public may be tried.

There is evident in all this a real commitment to extending the democratic consensus underpinning public services provision. But our understanding is limited – which of the policies and methods of consulting and involving the public in strategic planning produces real gains?

That there is a need for public services to become not only strategic but also more aligned to the public's needs and desires seems to be clear. The gap between the public services and the public has been seized upon by politicians all around the world, and acted upon in the form of the reform of public services throughout the 1980s. The gap cannot, however, be closed by internal management reforms alone. It needs the development of new public services with a closer relationship to the needs of the public. The development of new services has to be organized, so we cannot just turn our backs on the attempts to create a new public management in the 1980s. The problem with that new public management was that it was so often based on hierarchical reforms (setting objectives, measuring performance, holding managers accountable to higher authority), that it neglected the need to develop a new public management which had a strong relationship to the public.

In reaching out to the public, the leaders and managers of public services need guidance and direction in how to interact with the public. Strategic management and planning provides that guidance and direction. It disciplines the efforts of leaders and managers to interact with the public. The processes of strategic planning provide an experience in which the public services leaders and the public can participate. But this will only be the case if the right kinds of strategic planning process are developed. The PPM reviewed above seems promising in this respect. It brings together and guides the public, professionals, managers, and resource controllers in an organized and focused way. Likewise, the use of whole systems development also has promise as a way of bringing together a wide range of stakeholders so that they can discuss and debate the right strategy for an organization.

However, community planning may be seen as a better umbrella concept for the idea of consulting and mobilizing public opinion. It implies an importance and scale which is required for the growth of a connection between the public and public services. It suffers, or seems at the present time to suffer, from being an overly elastic concept with a excessive diversity of meanings. This seems to allow any procedure which involves any kind of consultation with the public to be labelled 'community planning'. It does not yet seem to have developed sufficiently to embody the purposeful and disciplined interactions which are needed to make it a powerful element in democracy. Perhaps there is a need for community planning to experiment with, absorb and consolidate a range of techniques – techniques which might include PPM and whole systems development.

nine

Transformational strategic management

Key learning objectives

After reading this chapter you should be able to:

1 Formulate your own foresights about the future of strategic management for the public services.
2 Appreciate the importance (and legitimacy) of public and political pressures on strategic management processes.
3 Identify some of the key requirements for a transformational practice of strategic management for the public services.

Introduction

Strategic management in the public services is a complex phenomenon. It is complex in part because it is an unfolding and emerging practice. It is also a very difficult management practice to get right. This is partly because it has to confront the entrenched habits of short-termism which are bundled up with the reliance on budgeting processes for planning purposes. It is also difficult because it faces dilemmas in managing the public services (e.g. short-term operational efficiencies versus developing services which are well-used and popular with the public). It is difficult as well because public services are expected, certainly by today's politicians, to work in partnerships and contribute to effective networks for public service provision. It is not the intention of this book to argue that strategic management is either a simple phenomenon to understand or a simple management tool to apply. It is fully accepted here that strategic management is complex and difficult to use.

Public services have been required to set up strategic management and planning and produce strategic plans by governments and political bodies in many countries. But strategic management and its forerunners in corporate planning and strategic planning have been espoused by managers working in the public services as well. Many organizations have appointed enthusiastic new agency leaders or chief executives, keen to bring about change and improvements, who have championed the launch of strategic planning efforts. We know this from Berry and Wechsler's (1995) survey of state agencies in the USA which found:

> Contrary to other reform efforts (e.g., productivity improvements, program budgeting), which have been initiated by governors on a statewide basis, the initiation of strategic planning seems to have been primarily a decision of individual agencies. Eighty-eight per cent of the survey respondents said their agency's leadership made the decision to adopt strategic planning without other statewide mandates or requirements.
>
> (Berry and Wechsler 1995: 160)

These sponsors for strategic management and planning have varied in their motivation. For example, some leaders have seen strategic planning and management as about establishing a clear strategic direction and installing goals and plans to guide performance improvement and service initiatives. For others it was a matter of unleashing a latent spirit of innovation and entrepreneurial dynamism which was stifled by bureaucractic policies and procedures.

These enthusiasts for strategic management and planning produced a reaction among a wide swathe of managers. There were (and still are) people who labelled strategic plans, missions and vision statements as window-dressing and complained that planning activities were a distraction from the real job of day-by-day service delivery. There were those who saw strategic management ideas and approaches as naive. They said that public services were highly political in nature and that the way politicians ran things meant that decisions could never accord to the simplistic notions of strategic management and planning.

In this last chapter we look at the impact and meaning of strategic management, but hopefully not in a naive or one-sided way. We will take up the idea that strategic management is important because it can change the way the public services are run. This involves a two-stage argument. First, contrary to pessimistic views, strategic management can affect the operational management of public services. Second, there is the potential within strategic management, or at least a certain variant of it, to not only affect public services but even to transform them.

The term 'transformation' may seem overblown and too ambitious for strategic management. However, after two decades of public sector reform the reply might be made that being ambitious has become essential to the future prospects of a successful public services sector. Indeed, the riskiest thing at the current time is probably doing nothing new (Drucker 1985), or trying to do new things in old ways (Hamel and Prahalad 1994).

The objectives of this chapter are to first review the case against strategic management made by pessimists and critics within the public services; second to examine evidence on how strategic management can have real effects on the operational management of public services; and third to explore the idea and practice of using strategic management for bringing about transformation.

The case against strategic management in the public services

There is a view of public services organizations that they are irredeemably short term. This idea was discussed in Chapter 4 when we looked at the way in which strategic planning processes engage – or do not engage – budgetary processes. The view of Eadie (1983) was cited: planning was assumed to be ignored in resource allocation decisions, which were thought to be still made through a traditional style of incremental decision making. The implication of this and other views is that strategic planning documents do not really matter. The organization is really being managed through the budgetary process and this means that everyone is really working only a year ahead at most.

This can lead in some cases to a horizontal split in the public services organization. The chief executive and the top managers are seen as 'playing' at strategic management (writing mission statements, spending ages deciding on core values, drawing up plans for strategic changes and reorganizations, working with external partners, and so on) while harassed middle managers are expected to loyally carry on ensuring services are delivered despite demoralized staff, insufficient resources, old and obsolete premises and equipment, etc.

The other accusation of the pessimists is that strategic planning is formally a rational process whereas the internal decision making environment of public services is very political. A picture of political decision making emerged clearly from the research carried out by Miesing and Andersen (1991) on strategic planning in New York public agencies (see Box 9.1).

It can be argued that strategic planning is not about the effectiveness of public services so much as it is about the transactions between politicians (who allocate budgets and expect compliance with their mandates) and the managers who manage public services. As Miesing and Andersen expressed it: 'The purpose of strategic planning in public agencies seems to be to

---

Box 9.1 Strategic planning in public agencies in New York

Miesing and Andersen (1991) carried out their study of strategic planning in 65 state agencies in New York during 1989. They sent the person responsible for strategic planning in each agency a questionnaire, then held a conference of the strategic planners to discuss the survey results. They also conducted a focus group with seven of the strategic planners who had responded to their questionnaire survey.

They found that most of the state agencies did use strategic planning. It emerged from the survey questionnaire that just under a third of the agencies had established the position of strategic planner ten or more years earlier.

Despite evidence that strategic planning was being widely used by the agencies, the results from the focus group suggested that the agencies were 'preoccupied with either operational planning or political maneuvering' (Miesing and Andersen 1991: 131). The authors also concluded that the agencies were managed through the budget process rather than through a strategy process that steered operations to meet the mission of the organization. They said: 'several respondents stated that strategic planning is not coordinated with agency budget processes' (p. 131). Indeed, the general tenor of their remarks was to doubt the general conception of a strategic planning process as a rational and ordered sequence of decisions. It was unclear that mandates and environmental threats and opportunities were being used to formulate strategic issues. There was no coordination of strategic planning and budget processes, and 'few agencies have assessed the results of their planning' (p. 131).

---

legitimate or justify the agency and its budget requests and meet mandated requirements of authorities' (1991: 131). This is the idea that the language of strategic management and planning appears to be about directing and adapting services, but that this conceals the fact that managers use strategic planning to manage politicians and the politicians' use of budget allocation to control public services.

Can strategic management and planning have an effect?

There are surveys of managers in the public services which elicit positive responses about the effect of strategic planning (Berry and Wechsler 1995; Flynn and Talbot 1996). However, these might be regarded as providing what might be called 'soft' data, and they lack the convincing power that is offered by research which helps us to model the nature, context and consequences of strategic management and planning.

For example, we need more evidence about how strategic management and planning affects middle managers. Of course, the usual presumption is that middle managers are meant to implement the strategic plans. So, are the pessimists and sceptics right – do middle managers ignore the strategy process and simply concentrate on the operational management task? Further, do they, therefore, only pay attention to the budgetary process which directly and immediately impinges on their resources for meeting operational plans? There is case study evidence (see Chapter 4) that suggests strategic planning can affect budgetary and operational processes – providing the integration of planning and budgetary processes is ensured, and time is spent providing managers with strategic communication.

Is strategic management and planning a political game?

There is no doubt that public services operate in a political context. Wechsler and Backoff (1986: 321), for example, suggested that public organizations operated in a governmental authority system: 'Rather than maneuvering in markets, public organizations act within relatively complex, multilateral power, influence, bargaining, voting, and exchange relationships'.

Some pessimists and critics of strategic management and planning in the puiblic services assume that it is incompatible with this type of political environment. The reality of strategic management in the public sector generally certainly seems at odds with the idea of strategic planning as the embodiment of rationality. On the face of it, the accusation that the public services must find strategic management and planning difficult because decision making is political rather than rational does seem to have some plausibility. At least, over many years, many public services managers have complained about the problems of oversight by political bodies. They have inveighed against the corruption of managerial decision making by politicians intent on gaining party political advantages, seeking cheap popularity in the eyes of the electorate and so on. Thus, Zegans (1992: 147) reported the views of nine civil servants who saw politicians as most likely to support innovations which save money, are uncontroversial, and offer 'quick payback and credit-claiming opportunities'.

There are accounts of strategic management and planning which present them as logical and rational in the extreme. They may, for example, place a strong emphasis on starting off with a clear strategic direction expressed in goals, objectives or mission statements. They may stress measurements, either to calculate and forecast for the planning process or to measure performance. Corporate planning was promoted as an approach which tries to shut out extraneous opinions and interests in pursuit of objectivity. More recent views of strategic planning assume that the employee interest can be aligned with the corporate mission through culture management, but with the aim of setting up logically linked mission statements, strategic goals, performance goals, contingency planning and rational coordination with other public services providers.

Politics matter

Of course, the reliance by public services organizations on budget appro-
priations creates the political nature of the public services context. In other
words, whereas strategy in the private sector has to manage competitive
forces, in the public services strategy has to deal with pressures and forces
deriving from the public and politicians. Public services strategy has to pay
attention to a range of political processes including voting, the creation of
legislative mandates, budgeting, pressure-group lobbying, political bargaining and so on. While it may be considered that planning and strategic
management are tools for responding to the turbulence of the environment
(Berry and Wechsler 1995), as they are in the private sector, it should be
remembered that it is political processes which create the public services'
experience of a turbulent environment. Political processes are, in fact,
the way in which change is transmitted from the public to the public
services via the political system and are the causes of strategy changes in
the public services. This is the more accurate view of the antecedents of
strategic decisions. This central idea of the theory of political strategic
management is partly corroborated in the following judgement offered by
Bryson (1995: 203):

> Even when change advocates are successful in challenging existing
> strategies on intellectual grounds, they should not expect new stra-
> tegies to be adopted without a change in the political circumstances
> surrounding the strategy – particularly in public organizations. As
> Kingdon (1995) notes, these changes may arise from public opinion
> swings, election results, administrative changes, ideological or part-
> isan redistribution in legislative bodies, and interest group pressure.
> Before new strategies can be adopted, key decision makers must be
> receptive – and political changes may be necessary before this is likely
> to occur.

The pervasiveness of politics as an explanatory factor can also be seen in
the fact that the adoption of strategic planning in the public services has
been linked to a certain phase of the political cycle (Berry 1994), and the
fact that strategic planning has to work within political time frames (Nutt
and Backoff 1992).

But, so what if public services operate in a political context? The four
case studies in Ohio by Wechsler and Backoff (1986) suggested that sometimes the locus of strategic control lies with external forces – including
organized constituent groups, professional opinion and a national legal
rights movement. In other cases, the locus of control was internal, and
this meant that a strategic agenda was developed which reflected internal
strategic thinking. Both the Ohio case studies and other case study work
show how public services face strong public pressures, and how this creates

---

Box 9.2 Strategic change in the Sydney metropolitan rail network

The New South Wales State Rail Authority was responsible for the Sydney metropolitan rail network which carried 800,000 commuters each day. Changes had not taken place in this network even though there had been significant levels of growth of new suburbs. As a result, it appeared that some commuters, living in established areas, were 'overserviced' by the network, and commuters living in the new suburbs represented a growing demand for the rail services.

The key strategic issue for the New South Wales State Rail Authority consisted of the tension between improving services to customers in the new suburbs and the strength of forces seeking to maintain the high frequency of services in the established areas. It appears that the answer was seen as switching resources to customers in the new suburbs from the commuters in the established areas, which meant that the latter would have to receive lower service levels. This issue was only slowly resolved. Perrot (1996: 344) reports that 'the changes were resisted with the support of state politicians who had the weight of numbers to maintain the status quo'. It took, consequently, seven years to bring about the changes.

---

difficulties for some organizations (see Box 9.2). Thus, the case studied by Perrot (1996) could be seen as an example of the difficulty of a compromise strategy where new public needs are creating an issue for current patterns of services and the politicians do not want to see an existing stakeholder constituency adversely affected by attempts to respond to the new needs.

There is another point which may be made: While public services strategies may seek to deflect public and political pressure, strategies may also aim at changes that lead to public needs being met in a more satisfactory way than hitherto. Consequently, it can be argued that the Ohio study by Wechsler and Backoff (1986) demonstrates the one-sided view of strategic management and planning in a political environment to be found in Miesing and Andersen's (1991) claims. Public services strategies may go beyond legitimizing and justifying budget requests and may be instrumental in efforts at serving the public better.

The transformational strategy

The Ohio study by Wechsler and Backoff (1986) provides some support for the idea that public services can transform themselves in order to address public needs better. However, this study provides very little insight into the actual processes and requirements of transformational strategic management.

A case study, also in Ohio, provides a grounded theory of transformational strategy. This is the analysis by Frost-Kumpf *et al.* (1993) of changes at the Ohio Department of Mental Health. There seem to be three key findings. First, strategic transformation requires a kind of leadership which can use symbolic action to provide an intellectual foresight about the future of a public service. Second, success in realizing the strategic direction conveyed by the leadership depends in part on developing core capabilities in respect of management, participation and planning. This includes capabilities in enabling the consumers of the service to participate in decision making, as well as other stakeholders. Third, effective transformation manifests itself in new services organized and delivered cooperatively with other public services agencies and with community-based agencies.

This adds up to an approach to strategy which places a lot of emphasis on the interaction between the organization and its environment (defined in terms of consumers, the community and other public services agencies). For more details of this research, see Box 9.3.

The significance of these arguments and studies is to underline the difference yet again between public services and the private sector. The issue is that the pressures originating in the public services environment cannot be seen as equivalent to environmental pressures building up for a private sector company. The existence of overwhelming external pressures for change are certainly not equivalent to the private sector concept of a 'threat'. This is because the pressures are demands by the public to meet unmet needs. Environmental turbulence in the public services sector, therefore, means that public services are facing high levels of public need volatility. Since the public services exist to meet public needs, speaking ideally, public services should innovate in the face of such external pressures.

Strategic analysis for transformation

The transformational strategy which emerges from the previous section does not look as though it is compatible with forms of strategic analysis which are geared to results-oriented, goals-led performance planning. Instead, we might suggest a strategic analysis process based on a variation of Nutt and Backoff's (1992) model:

- Step 1: analyse why the strategic planning process is needed, and roughly identify the opportunities and constraints of the situation.
- Step 2: identify who needs to be involved in the strategic planning process (drawing on the need for planning, opportunities and constraints identified in Step 1).
- Step 3: describe and review (a) the strategic direction of the organization, (b) the legislative mandates, (c) the external environment, (d) the internal

Box 9.3 Transformation of the Ohio Department of Mental Health

As a result of the Ohio Mental Health Act of 1988 the state Department of Mental Health ceased to be primarily concerned with service provision and instead became responsible for ensuring that the necessary services were contracted and delivered through community-based boards and local agencies. The change process began in 1983, was given statutory expression by the 1988 Act, and established Ohio's reputation for the quality of its healthcare as among the best in the USA by 1990.

The change was effected through a large number of actions, some of which were purposefully structured and some which had a more emergent character. The leadership of the department developed a new vision of the future of mental healthcare, based on models enshrining new values and a critique of the failings of the existing system of mental healthcare.

Frost-Kumpf et al. (1993) identifed three 'streams' of action:

1 use by the leadership of strategic language to give form to a new strategic direction which was then linked to strategic actions that transformed the agency;
2 the development of management, participatory and planning abilities through collaborative planning efforts and training (and involving consumers along with other constituency groups inside and outside the agency);
3 cooperative ventures with other government agencies.

The analysis identified nine thematic action patterns among the strategic actions, but it is not clear how these patterns and the 'streams' were related. Some of the action patterns (taking symbolic actions, developing new programme thrusts, empowering key constituencies, developing alternative sources of revenue and responding to opposition) look as though they might be important for the leadership stream. Others (building internal capacity, developing technical expertise, and utilizing training) might be important for the second stream, and the action pattern of gaining external support might be associated with the third stream. This is not clear from the report by Frost-Kumpf et al., but it is clear that this grounded analysis of strategic transformation provides a rich set of ideas about making strategic change.

resources (including skills and core competencies), and (e) performance results.

- Step 4: formulate the purpose of the organization as a vision of the ideal future.
- Step 5: summarize strengths, weaknesses, opportunities and threats in a situational assessment.
- Step 6: agree a strategic issue agenda and prioritize issues.
- Step 7: formulate strategic actions (and group into programmes).
- Step 8: agree evaluation criteria and select strategy for implementation.
- Step 9: carry out stakeholder analysis and resource analysis.
- Step 10: plan the implementation of the strategy.

It will be noticed that this planning process refers to formulating a vision of the ideal future rather than agreeing a mission statement or agreeing objectives. There are in fact those who argue that goals are more ambiguous in the public sector (Nutt and Backoff 1992), or that in the public sector there are comparatively large numbers of objectives for strategic planning (Steiner 1979). However, the vision can form a strategic target just as much as does a mission statement or a set of objectives. The real point of interest is that this particular process pivots around the agreement of an issue agenda. By focusing on issues – and issue resolution – rather then mission formulation, perhaps organizations find it easier to create a more construct-ive and pragmatic process. In other words, what matters here is ensuring that strategy is dominated by issue resolution rather than goal setting.

Nutt and Backoff (1992) believe that, in the future, working through the strategic planning process will not occur as a 'one-day-affair' or as 'one concerted effort'. They argue that it will be necessary for organizations to repeatedly work through the process leading to continuous involvement in strategic management. In consequence, strategy may take on the form of emergent streams of strategic action, as in the case described above in Box 9.3.

Issues for transformational strategy processes

This analysis of transformational strategic management places us at the leading edge of developments in public services, which is a place where the unfinished and still evolving nature of strategic management is most pronounced.

We have seen that transformational strategic management draws our attention to three challenges: leadership, empowering users, and cooperative ventures with partners. Inevitably, each of these pose questions for those involved in applying strategic management in public services. These issues have been referred to in earlier chapters, but they need mentioning again now so that the agenda for strategic management can be clarified.

First there is the issue of leadership and how elected politicians are to relate to leadership if this is defined in terms of strategic management. Should the politicians, with their representative responsibilities concentrate on enabling chief executives and top management teams carry out the strategic leadership role, or should politicians reserve the strategic leader-ship role for themselves?

Second, how can community planning and user empowerment be encom-passed most effectively within a strategic management process which is transformational?

Third, what is meant by cooperative ventures with partners, and how is a community leadership role positioned within partnership arrangements?

Political leadership

Elected politicians have a key role to play in responding to public pressures through their role in directing public services. Politicians also obviously have a key responsibility to exercise this direction of the public services in a way which strikes the right balance between different public needs. In other words, politicians have a key role in determining priorities. It is not evident that managers have the legitimacy to do this, and thus politicians have to become more involved in strategic leadership.

Community planning and user empowerment

The problem here, as will have been evident from Chapter 8, is how do we make consultation of the public and service users real? This means, most crucially, how does the public get included in determining the strategic framework, and how do users get involved in reviews designed to achieve service improvements?

The theory of user involvement and consultation is as yet little developed. Some insights can be obtained, however, from those techniques which have been tried and tested. First, as shown by the PPM (see Chapter 8), consulting the public service user is not about asking crudely what service is required by the user. Firmer ground for service innovation can be found by asking not just what users want, but why they want it. An understanding of the needs and problems of the service user provides useful data for public services managers and professionals to figure out how services can be developed with the resources available and within the political mandates which exist.

Second, and again a lesson from the PPM, it is important to involve the public in prioritizing the needs and problems to be addressed. Prioritization is an important tool for managers who lack sufficient resources (including time) to address all the issues and meet all the needs that may be articulated. The involvement of the public service user in prioritization not only provides additional knowledge about users to managers and professionals in public services, it also underlines to the users the inevitable limits on resources – not everything that would be desirable can be done.

A third lesson, this time from whole systems development, is the need for forms of involvement and consultation which give service users some control over how conclusions are being drawn by managers and professionals. The users of public services will experience more control in an interactive process which allows them to input their ideas and see how these ideas have been incorporated by managers and professionals in strategic and operational plans. The process enables them to express their response to the way their ideas have been used and lets them see managers and professionals shift their thinking and learn from the process of interacting

with service users. This may be contrasted with public consultation processes using large-scale surveys, focus groups and other methods to collect
information from the public, where managers and professionals by themselves make sense of the information and decide on actions. This latter
approach does not confer much control on the public in relation to how
their views and ideas are used and actioned.

Working with partners in cooperative ventures

With the advent of theories of strategic management which emphasize
the political context in public services, the focus switches from goals and
missions to the management of issues. As a result, the focus also shifts
from measurement of performance to problem solving. And in place of
liquidating internal dissension through culture management there is an
interest in building and sustaining coalitions for change. In other words,
this approach to the theory of strategic management, with its end point of
transformation of the public services, recognizes the ongoing interactions
of interests and seeks to use them – to exploit them – in order to bring
about radical improvements in the current situation. In this sense, it is
pragmatic in facing up to the existence of rival interests and creative in the
use of conflict to bring about innovation.

Stakeholders, partners and collaboration

One result of accepting this view of the distinctive nature of strategic
management in the public services is that it becomes unconvincing to argue
for the strategic management and planning process to be copied from
private sector ideas (Nutt and Backoff 1992). Instead, the idea of strategic
management in the public services has to be developed as one which
implies a stakeholder-oriented practice. The key stakeholders include
professionals and other employees, the public (service users and citizens),
and other providers (including other public services organizations). This
stakeholder orientation complicates strategic management by requiring
action to ensure intraorganizational and interorganizational coordination,
as well as extensive consultation with the public. Such action is needed to
turn stakeholders into a coalition for change. Nutt and Backoff (1992: 43)
underline the importance of coalitions for change:

> To create strategy one must emulate the secretaries of successful U.S.
> Government departments, who recognize that action depends on a
> coalition of interests that push things along. To overcome inertia, we
> create a coalition of interests to keep the process on track. The coali-
> tion identifies contextual features, carries out situational assessments,

forms issue agendas, and identifies strategy. The discussions and inter-actions in the coalition are carried out to discover ideas and set the priorities needed to deal with context, situational issues, and strategy to help the coalition create a shared interpretation of interests and possibilities.

It is obviously not the case that all public services organizations engage stakeholders in a substantial way or develop coalitions to pursue collab-orative strategies. Those that do engage their stakeholders and develop collaborative strategies seem to be more pressurized by, or aware of, chang-ing public needs and political demands. Politicians are quite forceful in this process. Contradictory pressures or dilemmas are 'used to demand massive changes in public organizations' (Nutt and Backoff 1993: 304). Public service organizations find it more and more difficult to be bureaucratic and self-sufficient in the face of public needs which are changing and increas-ing, and in the face of assertive politicians demanding more from public services. Under conditions of intense volatility in public needs and intense political pressures, the innovations that public services leaders need to make become transformational in scale. This produces not only a stronger concern for stakeholder management, but also provides an impetus to col-laborative strategies (and cooperative ventures). As Nutt and Backoff (1992: 97) put it: 'Transformations are possible when organizations recognize that needs are volatile and choose to respond in a collaborative fashion'. The decision to collaborate may be a matter of choice, but, to repeat, this is in the context of strong political demands for change.

This theory of strategic management emphasizes the need to create a consensus in order to develop strategy formulations; it does not assume that this consensus is either pre-existing or easy. Indeed, public organiza-tions are full of groups and interests that are intent on pursuing their privileges (Crozier 1964). It is no wonder that strategic management in the public services so often produces very little change or improvement. Thus, building a coalition for change, as suggested by Nutt and Backoff, involves disrupting the coalition of vested interests in the status quo. At its most optimistic, this theory suggests that, with skilful and creative stakeholder management, the self-interests of those involved 'are subordinated to the greater interest of serving people's needs' (Nutt and Backoff, 1992: 423). The coalition partners contribute resources and programmes which are combined in a collaborative strategy. Instead of bargaining over resources, we have negotiations to pool resources. Instead of compromise between competing groups, we have creativity and innovation to solve public prob-lems. And instead of the government seeing its role as standing above and balancing sectional interests, we have the government acting to sub-ordinate sectional public service provider interests to the greater interest of serving the public's needs.

Conclusions

To summarize, a grounded theory of strategic management in the public services suggests that strategy is directed towards the management of public and political pressures and takes place in the context of public and political forces (public opinion, elections, pressure groups, changes of government etc.). There are generic strategies for positioning public services organizations in relation to the public and political forces. The strategies may involve an attempt to deflect or stall public pressures, but they may also involve a transformation which rebuilds the relationship with the public and its needs. This requires leadership, empowerment of the public and cooperation with other organizations. The critical intervening condition for the successful implementation of strategy is a consensus among the forces representing a coalition for change and those representing inter-organizational and intraorganizational coordination. The consequences of strategy, in the face of overwhelming external pressures, can be major innovations in the services and activities of public services organizations.

Worksheets for comprehensive strategic planning

Introduction

These worksheets were influenced by the United Nations guide to performance improvement programming (PIP) (Department of Economic and Social Affairs 1977), and the approach of Nutt and Backoff (1992) to strategic issue management. The worksheets support an analysis which commences with a mission statement and ends with the formulation of performance targets. Other matters covered by these worksheets include: strategic issues, management information requirements, and project management. Consequently, the approach is broadly that of the 'classical' planning model outlined in Chapter 1. Such an approach is consistent with the results-oriented strategic planning styles preferred by politicians and political oversight bodies.

Why use worksheets? They may be used in order to quickly capture the perceptions of those involved in strategic planning and management. They have to be backed up by serious research or they become an unwise encouragement for leaders and managers to base strategy on mistaken opinion, ideas and assumptions. They may also encourage superficiality. So, it is important that perceptions and opinions stated in the worksheets are subsequently grounded with factual data. Nevertheless, the worksheets provide a very useful starting point for strategic thinking by generating an overall analysis. They are also useful as a tool for building up an analysis in a deliberate order, in which views crystallized in earlier worksheets structure, or influence, thinking produced for later worksheets. In summary, if used intelligently, the worksheets can be good aids to thinking; but if used wrongly they may delude managers into thinking they have carried out a 'proper' strategic analysis.

Some managers say that they have used the worksheets in order to learn about strategy. The experience of completing the worksheets gave them a better understanding of the idea of strategic analysis than they had achieved by reading about it. So, it is possible that the manager with newly-acquired responsibilities for strategy will find the worksheets more useful than a manager with more experience of strategic management.

How can the worksheets be used? In the public sector, during recent years, workshops have been very popular devices for formulating strategies. The worksheets could be used in such workshops, with managers working in groups, and possibly with a facilitator. It is also possible for individual managers to work through the worksheets by themselves, but many public service managers find this difficult to do – they lack the patience. However, individual managers who are facing pressing problems in relation to strategy may have the motivation needed to work through the worksheets by themselves.

Because the worksheets are mainly designed to capture perceptions and opinions (which must then be corroborated, or, better still, challenged), it is a good idea to work through all the worksheets quickly, and in one day, if possible. This is particularly useful from the point of view of the influence of earlier worksheets on later ones. Ideas developed for the worksheet on a mission statement should, for example, influence the content of the worksheet on strategic goals. This is easier to achieve if the successive worksheets are completed on the same day, when ideas produced for earlier worksheets are still fresh. Worksheets provide very little space to present ideas or opinions at length, so it is important to express ideas in short phrases which provide a good label for them.

One other way in which the worksheets might be used is by a facilitator who wishes to ensure all participants in a workshop have a chance to form their independent views before meeting and discussing ideas. The worksheets can be sent to all participants and completed prior to the workshop, enabling the facilitator to feed back those perceptions and opinions which are held by a significant proportion of the participants. This can also be useful where discussion time in the workshop is limited and it is important to ensure widespread contribution of ideas.

Worksheet 1   Mission statement

What is your organization's mission? Provide a short statement which identifies the intended beneficiaries, the main activities, the geographical boundary of operations, the desired consequences of the activities and any basic assumptions which are fundamental to your organizations's identity.

Worksheet 2 Strategic goals

Based on the mission statement in Worksheet 1, what are the top 6–8 strategic goals of your organization? These goals may relate to the activities of your organization, but it might be useful to also think about: service user satisfaction, the excellence of internal organizational processes, performance on innovation and budgetary and income performance.

1 _____

2 _____

3 _____

4 _____

5 _____

6 _____

7 _____

8 _____

Worksheet 3   Comparison with other organizations

This worksheet is included because it encourages you to be more critical of your organization's current performance, and thus may lead you to revise the strategic goals stated in the previous worksheet.

Please answer the question: how do you rate your organization's level of achievement as against that of other similar organizations? (Circle the appropriate answer first in relation to similar organizations in your region and then in relation to similar organizations elsewhere.)

You may find this difficult to answer initially. It may help to think through what you regard as your organization's most important areas of achievement. Try not to answer the question simply on a reputational basis. If you still find this difficult, make your ratings as best you can and plan to do some proper benchmarking work to check out your provisional judgements.

	Your organization's achievements relative to similar organizations			
(a) Similar organizations in the same region	Higher	Same	Lower	Not sure
(b) Similar organizations elsewhere	Higher	Same	Lower	Not sure

In the light of the comparisons, do the strategic goals need revising? Do you need to set strategic goals which will help you catch up with your comparator organizations? Do you need to be more ambitious? Please amend Worksheet 2 if appropriate.

Worksheet 4 Identification of strategic issues

Now, please list the strategic goals again (taking them from Worksheet 2) but list them in order of importance, starting with the most important and continuing down to the least important. This may be a little difficult to do, but if you rank them in rough order of importance first, you can then think through your reasons for the relative importance you place on them. So, rank them first, and then reflect on your reasons afterwards. You may decide to alter the order (or even revise the strategic goals) after you have done this.

Next you should have a go at rating the difficulty of achieving the strategic goals. This will be largely a matter of judgement at this point. Begin by thinking about which of them you think will be the easiest to achieve. Now think about which of them will be the most difficult to achieve. Finally, please rate as best you can the difficulty of achieving each strategic goal, using a scale of 1 to 10, with 1 being 'very easy' and 10 being 'very difficult'.

Strategic goals listed in order of importance	Difficulty of achieving the strategic goal (rate 1 to 10 with 1 = very easy and 10 = very difficult)
1 _____	_____
2 _____	_____
3 _____	_____
4 _____	_____
5 _____	_____
6 _____	_____
7 _____	_____
8 _____	_____

Worksheet 5   Strategic issues

If you now review the results of Worksheet 4, you can ask yourself what you think are the causes of the difficulties. Begin by taking the single most important strategic goal you have listed. How difficult to achieve have you rated it? Think about what will make it difficult to achieve. Can you think of three or four factors which will cause difficulties? These may be labelled 'strategic issues'. Please list them in the left-hand column below.

Next, concentrate on the strategic goals you have rated as second and third most important, and try to add three or four more factors which you think will cause difficulties. Please add them also to the left-hand column below.

You should now have approximately eight strategic issues. In order to make yourself more aware of them throughout the strategic planning process, please rate each of them in terms of your level of 'concern' regarding them. Again, please use a scale of 1 to 10 to do your rating, using 1 for 'only slightly concerned' through to 10 for 'very concerned'.

Issues	Concern (rate 1 to 10 with 1 = only slightly concerned and 10 = very concerned)
1	
2	
3	
4	
5	
6	
7	
8	

Worksheet 6   Final strategic issues list

Arguably the most difficult strategic issues are those which are difficult to handle because action to tackle them makes matters worse in some other respect. An example might help to make this idea clear. Consider the case that the achievement of a strategic goal of developing a new service may be difficult because of a budgetary deficit. Attempts to cut spending on some existing services may be seen as a possible solution to the budgetary problem. Unfortunately, this may then cause difficulties for another important strategic goal which is affected by the cuts to some existing services. Obviously, there is a need to find a strategic action which will enable the organization to find the investment needed for the new service without damaging the prospects of achieving this other important strategic goal. The strategic issue in this case might be formulated as follows: how can investment be found for the new service without reducing the level of existing services?

The example shows that strategic issues can be stated as tensions. Can you formulate the strategic issues you have listed in Worksheet 5 as tensions (or contradictions)? To repeat, you may be able to recognize the issues in your situation as containing tensions by the fact that action to improve the situation has the effect of making the situation worse in terms of another strategic goal. Write the issues on the worksheet in order of importance giving a brief description of the nature of the issue (preferably written as a tension or contradiction).

Issue (in order of importance)	Brief statement of the issue (express as tension or contradiction)
1 _____	_____
2 _____	_____
3 _____	_____
4 _____	_____
5 _____	_____
6 _____	_____
7 _____	_____
8 _____	_____

Worksheet 7   Situational analysis

Part A

First, please list what you see as the key events, trends and turning points which you think will be occurring over the next five years. These can be inside or outside your organization. Please rate them for importance on a scale of 1 to 10, using 1 for 'only slightly important' and 10 for 'very important'.

Events, trends and turning points	Importance (rate 1 to 10 with 1 = only slightly important and 10 = very important)
1	
2	
3	
4	
5	
6	
7	
8	

Part B

List the main strengths and weaknesses you think the organization has currently or will have during the next five years. Please rate them for importance on a scale of 1 to 10, using 1 for 'only slightly important' and 10 for 'very important'.

Strengths and weaknesses	Importance (rate 1 to 10 with 1 = only slightly important and 10 = very important)
1 _____	_____
2 _____	_____
3 _____	_____
4 _____	_____
5 _____	_____
6 _____	_____
7 _____	_____
8 _____	_____

Worksheet 8 Brainstorming and evaluating

Taking each of the items listed in Worksheet 7, brainstorm actions your organization might take in response to each. For example, what action might be taken to prevent an event, trend or turning point creating unsatisfactory consequences for your organization? What action might be taken to get some benefit or advantage from an event, trend or turning point? What action might be taken to make use of a strength? What action might be taken to remedy a weakness? When brainstorming, generate as many ideas as you can, and list them, leaving evaluation until the end.

When the ideas have been listed, give each idea a brief title and evaluate below.

Idea for action (brief title)	Which issue in Worksheet 6 would be affected by this action?	Would it address both aspects of the tension?	Which strategic goal does it relate to?
1			
2			
3			
4			
5			
6			
7			
8			

Use this worksheet to identify strategic actions which would solve, or help to solve, the most important strategic issues and help to move your organization towards the most important strategic goals. Discard those ideas for action which are ineffective in terms of the tension or contradiction which makes up a strategic issue. Group together into programmes of action those which seem to be related ideas for action. If any ideas for action seem to promise effective action on a strategic issue but cannot be clearly related to a strategic goal, you will need to review both the strategic issues and the strategic goals – and be aware that you may have overlooked an important strategic goal which needs to be included in Worksheet 2.

Worksheet 9   Option appraisal

This worksheet helps you make decisions about what strategic action you should take. Having identified some useful-looking strategic actions or action programmes in the previous worksheet, you may now be in a position to evaluate and select strategic actions. Begin by listing the actions and programmes in Worksheet 8. Rate them from 1 to 10 in terms of feasibility, acceptability to stakeholders, impact on strategic goals and timeliness of the impact of the action or programme.

Action or programme (brief title)	Feasibility: prospects for success in implementing the action or programme (1 = poor, 10 = good)	Acceptability to stakeholders (1= not acceptable, 10 = popular)	Impact on strategic goals (1 = little benefit, 10 = 100% achievement likely)	Timeliness (1 = impact too soon/too late, 10 = timing of impact just right)
1				
2				
3				
4				
5				
6				
7				
8				

Note: It would be useful to carry out a risk analysis to see if there are any events, trends or developments which might affect the feasibility of actions or programmes. A stakeholder analysis would be useful preparation for assessing acceptability to stakeholders.

Worksheet 10 Resourcing plan

This worksheet is intended to help you draw up a resourcing plan for your top-rated strategic action or programme which you intend to implement. Other actions or programmes would need their own resourcing plans.

Strategic action or programme (brief title): _____

Resource required (including amount)	Brief description of resource	Importance (rate 1 to 10)	Obtainable from?	How obtained?
1				
2				
3				
4				
5				
6				
7				
8				

Worksheet 11 Priorities and timing

This worksheet helps you develop a kind of critical path analysis for the strategic actions and programmes that may be developed by identifying the start dates and dates by which they need to be completed. List below the strategic actions and programmes which are to be implemented, and specify start and completion dates.

Action or programme (brief title)	Implementation timing Start date	Finish date
1 _____	_____	_____
2 _____	_____	_____
3 _____	_____	_____
4 _____	_____	_____
5 _____	_____	_____
6 _____	_____	_____
7 _____	_____	_____
8 _____	_____	_____

Worksheet 12   Establishing responsibilities, project teams and reporting arrangements

The strategic actions and programmes which emerge from the preceding worksheets may be implemented by means of a performance plan. Operational managers will be assigned responsibility for delivering the performance plan. Alternatively, the organization will need to establish projects and identify project managers to plan and manage the implementation of the project.

Action or programme (brief title)	Manager responsible for implementation	Progress reporting To whom	How often
1			
2			
3			
4			
5			
6			
7			
8			

Worksheet 13   Performance goals

Strategic goals are used as the basis of performance planning. This involves agreeing one or more annual performance goals and associated performance indicators and setting performance targets for a number of consecutive years such that the targets for, say, Year 5 match the targets set for the strategic goals. In this worksheet only the annual performance targets for Year 1 are set.

To complete this worksheet, first take the strategic goals in Worksheet 2. Then identify a performance goal, a performance indicator and a target performance for each of them. For example, a public services organization might have a performance goal to 'improve the way we deal with the public'; the performance indicator could be 'speed of answering the phone', and the target performance could be 'answering within six rings'. Target performances should be feasible but challenging.

Performance goal	Performance indicator	Target performance (Year 1)
1 _____	_____	_____
2 _____	_____	_____
3 _____	_____	_____
4 _____	_____	_____
5 _____	_____	_____
6 _____	_____	_____
7 _____	_____	_____
8 _____	_____	_____

Worksheet 14   Information requirements and priorities

There has been considerable criticism that managers fail to monitor and evaluate the results of their organizations. One important barrier to monitoring and evaluation is the lack of information. This worksheet helps you to plan how to meet your information requirements.

The main thing here is to think through systematically what information you require in relation to each of the performance goals you have established. The worksheet invites you to assess the availability of information required for evaluating achievement of the target performance, and to rank the performance goals in order of priority. After carrying out this assessment you should be clearer about what actions are needed to set up information systems, and their relative importance based on the importance of the performance goals.

Performance goal	Availability of information required to evaluate achievement (circle the answer which applies)	Priority of performance goal (show rank order of importance)
1 _____	Available/need to collect information	_____
2 _____	Available/need to collect information	_____
3 _____	Available/need to collect information	_____
4 _____	Available/need to collect information	_____
5 _____	Available/need to collect information	_____
6 _____	Available/need to collect information	_____
7 _____	Available/need to collect information	_____
8 _____	Available/need to collect information	_____

Worksheet 15   Performance targets: next five years

In Worksheet 13 you identified a target performance for the first year of this strategic planning period. This worksheet asks you to identify target perform- ances for Years 2, 3, 4 and 5. As before, try to set targets which are feasible but challenging.

Performance goal	Annual performance targets				
	Year 1	2	3	4	5
1 _____	___	___	___	___	___
2 _____	___	___	___	___	___
3 _____	___	___	___	___	___
4 _____	___	___	___	___	___
5 _____	___	___	___	___	___
6 _____	___	___	___	___	___
7 _____	___	___	___	___	___
8 _____	___	___	___	___	___

Bibliography

Abel-Smith, B. (1994) *An Introduction to Health Policy, Planning and Financing*. London: Longman.

Anon (1996a) Financial devolution in local government. *Management Accounting*, March: 67–8.

Anon (1996b) Managing performance in the public sector: an international perspective. *Management Accounting*, December: 46–8.

Ansoff, H.I. (1968) *Corporate Strategy*. Harmondsworth: Penguin.

Ansoff, I. and McDonnell, E. (1990) *Implanting Strategic Management*. London: Prentice Hall.

Ball, I. (1994) Reinventing government: lessons learned from the New Zealand Treasury. *The Government Accountant's Journal*, Fall: 19–28.

Bennis, W. and Nanus, B. (1985) *Leaders: The Strategies for Taking Charge*. London: Harper & Row.

Berry, F.S. (1994) Innovation in public management: the adoption of strategic planning. *Public Administration Review*, 54: 322–30.

Berry, F.S. and Wechsler, B. (1995) State agencies' experience with strategic planning: findings from a national survey. *Public Administration Review*, 55: 159–68.

Bigelow, B. and Mahon, J.F. (1989) Strategic behavior of hospitals: a framework for analysis. *Medical Care Review*, 4: 295–311.

Blair, J. and Whitehead, C. (1988) Generic strategies for hospital stakeholder management. *Hospital and Health Services Administration*, 33: 153–66.

Blair, J.D., Savage, G.T. and Whitehead, C.J. (1989) A strategic approach for negotiating with hospital stakeholders. *Health Care Management Review*, 14: 13–23.

Bohret, C. (1993) The tools of public management, in K.A. Eliassen and J. Kooiman (eds) *Managing Public Organizations*. London: Sage.

Bonner, G. and McConnell, J. (1993) On a quest for quality, in G. Jones (ed.) *Local Government: The Management Agenda*. Hemel Hempstead: ICSA.

Boschken, H.L. (1992) Analyzing performance skewness in public agencies: the case of urban mass transit. *Journal of Public Administration Research and Theory*, 2: 265–88.

Boyle, R. (1995a) *Towards a New Public Service*. Dublin: Institute of Public Administration.

Boyle, R. (1995b) *Developing Management Skills*. Dublin: Institute of Public Administration.

Bozeman, B. (1993) Strategy and public management, in B. Bozeman (ed.) *Public Management*. San Francisco: Jossey-Bass.

Bryman, A. (1992) *Charisma and Leadership in Organizations*. London: Sage.

Bryson, J.M. (1995) *Strategic Planning for Public and Nonprofit Organizations*. San Francisco: Jossey-Bass.

Bryson, J.M. and Roering, W.D. (1987) Applying private-sector strategic planning in the public sector. *Journal of American Planning Association*, 53: 9–22.

Bryson, J.M. and Roering, W.D. (1988) Initiation of strategic planning by governments. *Public Administration Review*, 48: 995–1004.

Bryson, J.M. and Roering, W.D. (1989) Mobilizing innovation efforts: the case of government strategic planning, in A.H. Van de Ven, H.L. Angle and M.S. Poole (eds) *Research on the Management of Innovation*. New York: Ballinger.

Bullock, S. (1993) Revolution at the local seat of power, in G. Jones (ed.) *Local Government: The Management Agenda*. Hemel Hempstead: ICSA.

Burns, D., Hambleton, R. and Hoggett, P. (1994) *The Politics of Decentralization*. London: Macmillan.

Buurma, H. (1997) Public Marketing in Dutch Traffic Policy. Conference Paper, Second International Research Symposium on Public Services Management (IRSPSM), Aston Business School, Aston University (UK), 11–12 September.

Carter, N., Klein, R. and Day, P. (1992) *How Organizations Measure Success*. London: Routledge.

Cartwright, J. (1975) Corporate planning in local government – implications for the elected member. *Long Range Planning*, 8: 46–50.

Caulfield, I. and Schultz, J. (1993) *Planning for Change: Strategic Planning in Local Government*. Harlow: Longman.

Chalmers, A. (1997) *Strategic Management in Eleven National Libraries: A Research Report*. Wellington: National Library of New Zealand.

Chape, A. and Davies, P. (1993) Implementing strategic management in local government: Liverpool City Council as a case study. *Local Government Policy Making*, 20: 3–10.

Clarke, M. and Stewart, J. (1992) *Citizens and local democracy*. Luton: Local Government Management Board.

Corrigan, P. and Joyce, P. (1997) Reconstructing public management. *International Journal of Public Sector Management*, 10: 417–32.

Cox, P. (1996) 'Joint commissioning for community care in the London Borough of Islington', unpublished MBA thesis. University of North London.

Crozier, M. (1964) *The Bureaucratic Phenomenon*. London: Tavistock.

Davies, S. and Griffiths, D. (1995) Kirklees Metropolitan Council: corporate strategy in a local authority, in C. Clarke-Hill and K. Glaister (eds) *Cases in Strategic Management*. London: Pitman Publishing.

de Buitleur, D. (1996) Acting on strategic change, in R. Boyle and T. McNamara (eds) *From Intent to Action: The Management of Strategic Issues in the Public Sector*. Dublin: Institute of Public Administration.

Delbecq, A.L. and Gill, S.L. (1988) Developing strategic direction for governing boards. *Hospital and Health Services Administration*, 33: 25–35.

Delbecq, A.L. and Van de Ven, A.H. (1976) A group process model for problem identification and program planning, in W.G. Bennis, K.D. Benne, R. Chin and K.E. Corey (eds) *The Planning of Change*, 3rd edn. New York: Holt, Rinehart & Winston.

Denis, J., Langley, A. and Lozeau, D. (1991) Formal strategy in public hospitals. *Long Range Planning*, 24: 71–82.

Department of Economic and Social Affairs (1977) *A Practical Guide to Performance Improvement Programming in Public Organizations*. New York: United Nations.

Department of the Environment, Transport and the Regions (1998) *Modernising Local Government: Improving Local Services Through Best Value*. London: DETR.

Department of Health (1989) *Caring for People*. Cm. 849. London: HMSO.

Dewey, J. (1993) *The Political Writings*. Indianapolis, IN: Hackett.

Drodge, S. and Cooper, N. (1997) Strategy and management in the further education sector, in M. Preedy, R. Glatter and R. Levačić (eds) *Educational Management: Strategy, Quality, and Resources*. Buckingham: Open University Press.

Drucker, P. (1985) *Innovation and Entrepreneurship*. Oxford: Butterworth-Heinemann.

Duncan, W.J., Ginter, P.M. and Kreidel, W.K. (1994) A sense of direction in public organizations: an analysis of mission statements in state health departments. *Administration and Society*, 26: 11–27.

Duncan, W.J., Ginter, P.M. and Swayne, L.E. (1995) *Strategic Management of Health Care Organizations*. Oxford: Blackwell.

Dunsire, A. (1993) Modes of governance, in J. Kooiman (ed.) *Modern Governance*. London: Sage.

Eadie, D.C. (1983) Putting a powerful tool to practical use: the application of strategic planning in the public sector. *Public Administration Review*, 43: 447–52.

Eadie, D.C. (1997) *Changing by Design*. San Francisco: Jossey-Bass.

Eadie, D.C. and Steinbacher, R. (1985) Strategic agenda management: a marriage of organizational development and strategic planning. *Public Administration Review*, 45: 424–30.

East, R.J. (1972) Comparisons of strategic planning in large corporations and government. *Long Range Planning*, 15: 2–8.

Eddison, T. (1973) *Local Government: Management and Corporate Planning*. Aylesbury: Leonard Hill.

Eden, C. (1990) Strategic thinking with computers. *Long Range Planning*, 23: 35–43.

Edmonstone, J. (1990) What price the learning organization in the public sector? in M. Pedler, J. Burgoyne, T. Boydell and G. Welshman (eds) *Self-Development in Organizations*. London: McGraw-Hill.

Everitt, V. (1997) Partnership building is a key concern for local authority chief executives, according to a new survey. *Local Government Chronicle*, 13 June.

Fitzgerald, J. (1996) Response (to Acting on strategic change, by Donal de Buitleur), in R. Boyle and T. McNamara (eds) *From Intent to Action: The Management of Strategic Issues in the Public Sector*. Dublin: Institute of Public Administration.

Flynn, N. (1990) *Public Sector Management*. London: Harvester Wheatsheaf.

Flynn, N. and Talbot, C. (1996) Strategy and strategists in UK local government. *Journal of Management Development*, 15: 24–37.

Fox, C.J. (1996) Reinventing government as postmodern symbolic politics. *Public Administration Review*, 56: 256–62.

Frances, J., Levacic, R., Mitchell, J. and Thompson, G. (1991) Introduction, in G. Thompson, J. Frances, R. Levačić and J. Mitchell (eds) *Markets, Hierarchies & Networks*. London: Sage.

Frost-Kumpf, L., Wechsler, B., Ishiyama, H.J. and Backoff, R.W. (1993) Strategic action and transformational change: the Ohio Department of Mental Health, in B. Bozeman (ed.) *Public Management*. San Francisco: Jossey-Bass.

Further Education Unit (1997) Continuous improvement and quality standards, in M. Preedy, R. Glatter and R. Levačić (eds) *Educational Management: Strategy, Quality, and Resources*. Buckingham: Open University Press.

Gatherer, A. (1971) Planning services, in A. Gatherer and M.D. Warren (eds) *Management and the Health Services*. Oxford: Pergamon.

Goodwin, D.R. and Kloot, L. (1996) Strategic communication, budgetary role ambiguity, and budgetary response attitude in local government. *Financial Accountability and Management*, 12: 191–205.

Grewe, T., Marshall, J. and O'Toole, D.E. (1989) Participative planning for a public service. *Long Range Planning*, 22: 110–17.

Gyford, J. (1991) *Citizens, Consumers and Councils*. London: Macmillan.

Hamel, G. and Prahalad, C.K. (1994) *Competing for the Future*. Boston, MA: Harvard Business School Press.

Heath, R.L. (1997) *Strategic Issues Management*. London: Sage.

Hegewisch, A. and Larsen, H.H. (1996) Performance management, decentralization and management development: local government in Europe. *Journal of Management Development*, 15: 6–23.

Heginbotham, C. (1997) Managing boundaries creatively: multi-agency action for health. Conference paper, Second International Research Symposium on Public Services Management (IRSPSM), Aston Business School, Aston University (UK), 11–12 September.

Higher Education Funding Council for England (1996) *Institutions' Strategic Plans: Analysis of 1996 Submissions*. Circular 20/96. Bristol: HEFCE.

Hinton, P. and Wilson, E. (1993) Accountability, in J. Wilson and P. Hinton (eds) *Public Services and the 1990s*. Eastham: Tudor.

Hodgson, K. (1996) Conclusions: contracting in the future, in K. Hodgson with R.W. Hoile (eds) *Managing Health Service Contracts*. London: WB Saunders Company Ltd.

Holzer, M. and Callahan, K. (1998) *Government at Work*. London: Sage.

Hussey, D. (1994) *Strategic Management: Theory and Practice*, 3rd edn. Oxford: Pergamon.

Hussey, D. (1998) *Strategic Management: From Theory to Implementation*, 4th edn. Oxford: Butterworth-Heinemann.

Jenkins, K. (1992) Organizational design and development: the civil service in the 1980s, in C. Pollitt and S. Harrison (eds) *Handbook of Public Services Management*. Oxford: Blackwell.

Jones, R. and Gross, M. (1996) A tale of two councils: strategic change in Australian local government. *Strategic Change*, 5: 123–39.

Jorgensen, T.B. (1993) Modes of governance and administrative change, in J. Kooiman (ed.) *Modern Governance*. London: Sage.

Joyce, P. (1998) Management and innovation in the public services. *Strategic Change*, 7 (1): 19–30.

Joyce, P. and Woods, A. (1996) *Essential Strategic Management: From Modernism to Pragmatism*. Oxford: Butterworth-Heinemann.

Kaplan, R.S. and Norton, D.P. (1996) Using the balanced scorecard as a strategic management system. *Harvard Business Review*, January/February: 75–85.

Kaufman, J.L. and Jacobs, H.M. (1987) A public planning perspective on strategic planning. *The Journal of the American Planning Association*, 53: 23–33.

Kearns, K.P. (1994) The strategic management of accountability in nonprofit organizations: an analytical framework. *Public Administration Review*, 54: 185–92.

Kemp, R.L. (1985) Planning for local government – a grass-roots approach. *Long Range Planning*, 18: 91–3.

Kingdon, J.R. (1995) *Agendas, Alternatives and Public Policies*. Boston: Little, Brown.

Klein, J.A. and Hiscocks, P.G. (1994) Competence-based competition: a practical toolkit, in G. Hamel and A. Heine (eds) *Competence-Based Competition*. Chichester: John Wiley.

Knapp, M. and Lawson, R. (1995) Community care and the health service, in J.J. Glynn and D.A. Perkins (eds) *Managing Health Care*. London: WB Saunders Company Ltd.

Kooiman, J. (1993) Findings, speculations and recommendations, in J. Kooiman (ed.) *Modern Governance*. London: Sage.

Kooiman, J. and van Vliet, M. (1993) Governance and public management, in K.A. Eliassen and J. Kooiman (eds) *Managing Public Organizations*. London: Sage.

Langan, M. and Clarke, A. (1994) Managing in the mixed economy of care, in J. Clarke, A. Cochrane and E. McLaughlin (eds) *Managing Social Policy*. London: Sage.

Leach, S., Stewart, J. and Walsh, K. (1994) *The Changing Organization and Management of Local Government*. London: Macmillan.

Leadbetter, C. and Goss, S. (1998) *Civic Entrepreneurship*. London: Demos/Public Management Foundation.

Levine, C.H. (1978) Organizational decline and cutback management. *Public Administration Review*, 38: 316–25.

Local Authority Associations' Quality Group (1996) *Quality Initiatives, Report of the Findings from the 1966 Survey of Local Authority Activity*. London: ACC Publications.

London Research Centre (1995). *Performance Indicators in London Boroughs*. London: London Research Centre.

Lyotard, J. (1984) *The Postmodern Condition: A Report on Knowledge*. Manchester: Manchester University Press.

Macdonald, V. (1997) Social workers' training council to be axed. *The Sunday Times*, 21 December 1997: 5.

McHugh, M. (1997) Trouble in paradize: disintegrated strategic change within a government agency. *International Journal of Public Sector Management*, 10: 433–43.

McKevitt, D. (1992) Strategic management in public services, in L. Willcocks and J. Harrow (eds) *Rediscovering Public Services Management*. London: McGraw-Hill.

Metcalfe, L. and Richards, S. (1990) *Improving Public Management*. London: Sage.

Metcalfe, L. and Richards, S. (1993) Evolving public management cultures, in K.A. Eliassen and J. Kooiman (eds) *Managing Public Organizations*. London: Sage.

Miesing, P. and Andersen, D.F. (1991) The size and scope of strategic planning in state agencies: the New York experience. *American Review of Public Administration*, 21: 119–37.

Miles, R.E. and Snow, C.C. (1978) *Organizational Strategy, Structure, and Process*. London: McGraw-Hill.

Morley, D. (1993) Strategic direction in the British Public Service. *Long Range Planning*, 26: 77–86.

Nath, D. and Sudharshan, D. (1994) Measuring strategy coherence through patterns of strategic choices. *Strategic Management Journal*, 15: 43–61.

Nevis E.C., DiBella, A.J. and Gould, J.M. (1997) Understanding organizations as learning systems, in A. Campbell and K.S. Luchs (eds) *Core Competency-Based Strategy*. London: International Thomson Business Press.

Newchurch and Company (undated) *Creating the Catalyst: Planning Systems for Primary Health Care*. London: Newchurch and Company Ltd.

Nosowski, G. (1994) Strategic planning for a public service – the British Post Office. *Long Range Planning*, 27: 108–17.

Nutt, P.C. and Backoff, R.W. (1992) *Strategic Management of Public and Third Sector Organizations*. San Francisco: Jossey-Bass.

Nutt, P.C. and Backoff, R.W. (1993) Transforming public organizations with strategic management and strategic leadership. *Journal of Management*, 19: 299–347.

Nutt, P.C. and Backoff, R.W. (1995) Strategy for public and third-sector organizations. *Journal of Public Administration Research and Theory*, 5: 189–211.

O'Donovan, I. (1990) Using consultants to integrate management and organizational development, in M. Pedler, J. Burgoyne, T. Boydell and G. Welshman (eds) *Self-Development in Organizations*. London: McGraw-Hill.

Osborne, D. and Gaebler, T. (1992) *Reinventing Government*. Reading, MA: Addison Wesley.

Perkins, D. (1996) Can strategic management influence value for money? in J.J. Glynn, D.A. Perkins and S. Stewart (eds) *Achieving Value for Money*. London: WB Saunders Company Ltd.

Perrot, B.E. (1996) Managing strategic issues in the public service. *Long Range Planning*, 29: 337–45.

Peters, T. and Waterman, R. (1982) *In Search of Excellence*. New York: Harper Collins.

Piggot, C.S. (1996) *Business Planning for NHS Management*. London: Kogan Page.

Pollitt, C. (1993) *Managerialism and the Public Services*. Oxford: Blackwell.

Porter, M. (1980) *Competitive Strategy: Techniques for Analyzing Industries and Companies*. London: Free Press.

Potter, J. (1994) Consumerism and the public sector, in D. McKevitt and A. Lawton (eds) *Public Sector Management*. London: Sage.

Pratten, B. (1997) 'Community involvement in commissioning health care', unpublished Ph.D. thesis. University of North London.

Provan, K.G. and Milward, H.B. (1995) A preliminary theory of interorganizational network effectiveness: a comparative study of four community mental health systems. *Administrative Science Quarterly*, 40, 1–33.

Quinn, J.B. (1980) *Strategies for Change.* Homewood, IL: Irwin.

Richards, S. (1993) Defenders of their realm, in G. Jones (ed.) *Local Government: The Management Agenda.* Hemel Hempstead: ICSA.

Roberts, N.C. (1993) Limitations of strategic action in bureaus, in B. Bozeman (ed.) *Public Management.* San Francisco: Jossey-Bass.

Rogers, S. (1994) *Performance Management in Local Government.* Harlow: Longman.

Rugman, C.A. (1973) Corporate planning in local government. *Long Range Planning,* 6: 17–21.

Ryan, F. (1996) Response (to Strategic management: choices and imperatives, by Brendan Tuohy), in R. Boyle and T. McNamara (eds) *From Intent to Action: The Management of Strategic Issues in the Public Sector.* Dublin: Institute of Public Administration.

Savoie, D.J. (1992) Public service reforms. *Optimum,* 23, (1): 6–11.

Schacter, H. (1994) Revolution from within. *Canadian Business,* 67: 31–47.

Schick, A. (1969) Systems politics and systems budgeting. *Public Administration Review,* 29: 137–51.

Schwartz, H.M. (1994) Public choice theory and public choices. *Administration and Society,* 26: 48–77.

Smith, D. (1993) Crisis management in the public sector: lessons from the prison service, in J. Wilson and P. Hinton (eds) *Public Services and the 1990s.* Eastham: Tudor.

Smith, L. (1993) Management's new breed, in G. Jones (ed.) *Local Government: The Management Agenda.* Hemel Hempstead: ICSA.

Smith, P. (1995) Performance indicators and outcomes in the public sector. *Public Money & Management,* 15: 13–16.

Southernwood, K. (1997) The benefits of designing and flying your own plane. *Local Government Voice,* 1: 10–11.

Steiner, G.A. (1979) *Strategic Planning: What Every Manager Must Know.* London: Free Press.

Stewart, J.D. (1973) Corporate planning in local government. *Long Range Planning,* 6: 18–26.

Study Group on Local Authority Management Structures (1972) *The New Local Authorities: Management and Structure (The Bains Report).* London: HMSO.

Talbot, C. (1996) Devolving from the centre: the UK experience, in R. Boyle and T. McNamara (eds) *From Intent to Action: The Management of Strategic Issues in the Public Sector.* Dublin: Institute of Public Administration.

Thomas, P. and Palfrey, C. (1996) Evaluation – stakeholder-focused criteria. *Social Policy and Administration,* 30: 125–42.

Timmins, N. (1997) Management: the day the NHS imploded, *Financial Times,* 10 September.

Tuohy, B. (1996) Strategic management: choices and imperatives, in R. Boyle and T. McNamara (eds) *From Intent to Action: The Management of Strategic Issues in the Public Sector.* Dublin: Institute of Public Administration.

Van Vliet, M. (1993) Environmental regulation of business: options and constraints for communicative governance, in J. Kooiman (ed.) *Modern Governance.* London: Sage.

Walsh, K. (1989) *Marketing.* Harlow: Longman.

Wechsler, B. and Backoff, R.W. (1986) Policy making and administration in state agencies: strategic management approaches. *Public Administration Review*, 46: 321–27.

Wechsler, B. and Backoff, R.W. (1987) The dynamics of strategy in public organizations. *The Journal of the American Planning Association*, 53: 34–43.

Wilkinson, D. and Pedler, M. (1996) Whole systems development in public service, *Journal of Management Development*, 15: 38–53.

Wistow, G. and Barnes, M. (1993) User involvement in community care. *Public Administration*, 71: 279–99.

Zegans, M.D. (1992) Innovation in the well-functioning public agency. *Public Productivity and Management Review*, 16: 141–56.

Zybrands, W. (1995) *A Perspective on Local Government in the New South Africa 1995*. (No place of publication stated): ABSA Bank.

Index

PUBLIC SECTOR MANAGERIAL EFFECTIVENESS
THEORY AND PRACTICE IN THE NATIONAL HEALTH SERVICE

Hugh Flanagan and Peter Spurgeon

Public Sector Managerial Effectiveness:

- examines the confusion surrounding the concept of effectiveness
- offers practical guidance to help managers explore their performance expectations
- illustrates how clarity of understanding can promote improved performance.

Public Sector Managerial Effectiveness examines the assumptions behind terms like 'personal accountability', 'clearly identifiable measures of performance' and most notably the belief that 'effectiveness' is absolute and universal. It argues that effectiveness is a largely subjective and localized concept and that performance criteria, and good managerial practice, must be defined within the context of each organization. This is especially relevant for the transfer of ideas and practices from the private to the public sector.

It will be important reading for health service managers, health professionals, and students of business and management.

Contents

144 pp   0 335 15776 9 (Paperback)   0 335 15777 7 (Hardback)

EQUALITY IN MANAGING SERVICE DELIVERY

Rohan Collier

This book gives practical advice on how organizations delivering a service to the public can meet the needs of different groups of people. Using examples from the private, public and voluntary sectors, Rohan Collier explains how to develop and implement equalities policies which effect real change. She argues that to be successful, an organization must know and address the different needs and interests of its customers or clients, and the only way to fully understand the needs of a diverse public is to take account of equalities issues.

This is the first book of its kind. It will enable organizations to improve their image, enhance their services, and widen their customer or client base.

Contents
Introduction – Why equal opportunities in service delivery? – How services can discriminate – What the law requires – Identifying needs: involving the public – Developing and implementing equal opportunities policies in service delivery – Developing performance indicators and monitoring for equalities – Reviewing and changing services – Barriers to achieving equalities in service delivery – Bibliography – Index.

160pp   0 335 19729 9 (Paperback)   0 335 19730 2 (Hardback)